Contents

UNIVERSITY OF
WOLVERHAMPTON
KNOWLEDGE • INNOVATION • ENTERPRISE

Harrison Learning Centre
City Campus
University of Wolverhampton
St. Peter's Square
Wolverhampton
WV1 1RH
Telephone: 0845 408 1631
Online Renewals: www.wlv.ac.uk/lib/myaccount

– 7 APR 2014

– 3 OCT 2016

Telephone Renewals: 01902 321333 or 0845 408 1631
Online Renewals: www.wlv.ac.uk/lib/myaccount
Please return this item on or before the last date shown above.
Fines will be charged if items are returned late.

See tariff of fines displayed at the Counter. (L2)

CO
SK
IN C

EDITED BY

SALLY AL

AND SAL

British Association for
Counselling and Psychotherapy

WITHDRAWN

UNIVERSITY OF WOLVERHAMPTON LEARNING & INFORMATION SERVICES	
ACC. NO. 2427482	CLASS 316 504
CONTROL NO. 034079964	616. 891 4
DATE 2. NOV. 2007	SITE WV COU

Hodder Arnold

A MEMBER OF THE HODDER HEADLINE GROUP

British Association for Counselling and Psychotherapy

The British Association for Counselling and Psychotherapy (BACP) is the UK's largest counselling and psychotherapy organisation; producing journals and publications, maintaining a training film and video library, and publishing directories of counsellors, counselling agencies and counselling training. Check the BACP Web-site at _www.counselling.co.uk_ or e-mail: _bacp@bacp.co.uk_ for further information.

Every effort has been made to trace the copyright holders of material reproduced in this book. Any rights omitted from the acknowledgements here or in the text will be added for subsequent printing following notice to the publisher.

Orders: please contact Bookpoint Ltd, 130 Milton Park, Abingdon, Oxon OX14 4SB. Telephone: (44) 01235 827720, Fax: (44) 01235 400454. Lines are open from 9.00-5.00, Monday to Saturday, with a 24 hour message answering service. You can also order through our website: www.hoddereducation.co.uk

British Library Cataloguing in Publication Data
A catalogue record for this title is available from the British Library

ISBN 978 0 340 79964 2

First published 2001, reprinted 2004, 2005, 2006, 2007

7 8 9 10

Copyright © 2001 Sally Rigby; Sally Aldridge; Anne Stokes; Jan Jeffery; Sheilea Trahar; Peter Kent; Jean Bayliss.

All rights reserved. No part of this publication may be reproduced or transmitted in any form or by any means, electronic or mechanical, including photocopy, recording or any information storage or retrieval system, without permission in writing from the publisher or under licence from the Copyright Licensing Agency Limited. Further details of such licences (for reprographic reproduction) may be obtained from the Copyright Licensing Agency Limited, of Saffron House, 6-10 Kirby Street, London EC1N 8TS.

Typeset by Fakenham Photosetting Ltd, Norfolk.
Printed & Bound in India for Hodder Arnold, an imprint of Hodder Education and a member of the Hodder Headline Group, an Hachette Livre UK Company, 338 Euston Road, London NW1 3BH by Replika Press Pvt. Ltd

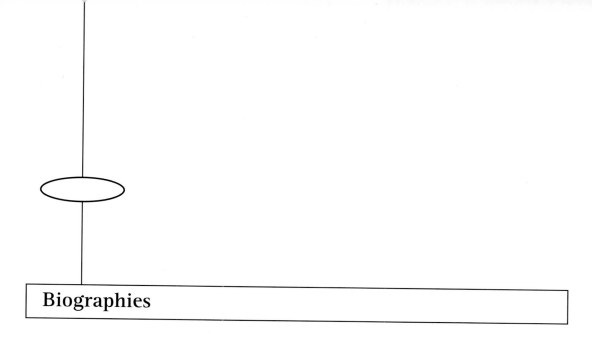

Biographies

Sally Aldridge is now in her fourth career as Head of Accreditation at the British Association for Counselling and Psychotherapy (BACP), a post she took up in 1999. She began work as a teacher of African history in Zambia and returned to the UK to train as a counsellor. Sally then spent a period working as a counsellor and Director of Student Services at Staffordshire University, and taught counselling skills and counsellor training courses at the University of Keele. At Staffordshire she set up the University Harassment and Bullying Network. She is an accredited counsellor and Fellow of BACP

Jean Bayliss is a practising counsellor and trainer, with a special interest in assessment of counsellors and of counsellor training. In this capacity, she works as advisor and consultant to several awarding bodies and institutions. Her original postgraduate diploma grew from a concern about the need for student and staff counselling in further education, where she was a head of department. Since then, she has gained an MA in Counselling and is preparing her doctorate. She has published work on loss and grief and on counselling theory (National Extension College); contributed to the recently published *Why is it so difficult to die?* (Quay Books), and wrote the NVQ/SVQ Level 3 Counselling Workbook, to accompany the NVQ/SVQ Level 3 Counselling.

Jan Jeffery originally qualified in psychology and sociology with a special interest in criminology. She worked with young offenders and adolescents with behavioural difficulties for many years. After bringing up a family, she was employed as a lecturer in sociology and psychology and qualified as a counsellor in the early nineties. Since then, Jan has taught counselling in Bridgend College in South Wales. She has also provided supervision for a number of voluntary organisations and is an NVQ assessor for counselling awards. She represents Wales on the AUCC FE sub-committee and within college is a staff-elected college governor.

Peter Kent is a qualified youth and community worker and has a BA (Hons) in labour studies and sociology. After working in education, social services and chief executives' departments in local government, he moved to the voluntary sector where he developed services for families and adults affected by cystic fibrosis, and chaired the Association for Children with Life-threatening or Terminal Illness and their Families (ACT) and National Transplant Week. Peter established a consultancy, Helix Partners, in 1998 and works primarily with voluntary organisations that provide services to people who are socially disadvantaged or have health and social care needs.

Sally Rigby is head of Research and Development at the British Association for Counselling and Psychotherapy (BACP). She formerly worked in the further education sector, where she taught social sciences and co-ordinated health and social care programmes. In 2000 Sally gained her Doctorate in Educational and mentoring was an integral part of her thesis. She co-edited the NVQ/SVQ Level 3 counselling text and also wrote the chapter on Assessment and Portfolio building. Sally also writes performance management training materials for an online training company.

Anne Stokes has an independent practice as a counsellor, supervisor and trainer, with a major element of her portfolio focusing on issues relating to the workplace. This includes involvement with large and small organisations in the private, public and voluntary sectors throughout the UK. She also works part time within the Graduate School of Education at the University of Bristol, as the co-ordinator for the supervision and training line of study within the MSc in Counselling. For a number of years, Anne led the Diploma in Counselling at Work at the university.

Sheila Trahar works in the Graduate School of Education at the University of Bristol. She is the co-ordinator of and lead tutor on the Diploma in Counselling at Work, Director of the Certificate in Counselling Skills and also teaches on the MSc in Counselling and the MEd programme. Sheila has extensive experience of counselling skills training and has successfully integrated such training into many other courses. A former student counsellor, Sheila continues to be a practising counsellor and supervisor. She is also an associate lecturer at the Open University.

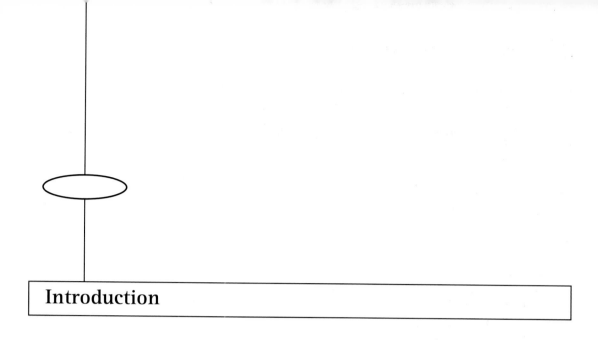

Introduction

This book is for people who want to learn about and use counselling skills. You may be already using these skills and would like to develop them further; or your interest may have been triggered by a desire to learn more about the way people function. Whatever your reason, this book will help you.

Interpersonal communication is at the core of all our relationships, and counselling skills are an integral part of this. Good interpersonal communication can make difficult issues, and life, easier to tackle. Poor interpersonal communication leads to misunderstanding, problems and the breakdown of relationships. Some people believe that because we communicate all the time, we are doing it well. This is not the case. Good communication requires intentional effort to understand other people and yourself, together with the deliberate use of specific counselling skills.

The value and use of counselling skills in some contexts and jobs is very clear, such as nursing, teaching and human resources, but in others it is less overt and recognised; for example the police force, hairdressers and traffic wardens. Some employers, particularly those who recognise the value of effective communication, encourage staff to undertake counselling skills training as part of their development.

Counselling Skills in Context will help you find out how you became the person you are, and how you can communicate better with people. The book is divided into three sections.

SECTION 1

This section defines counselling skills and their distinctiveness from counselling. It also provides underpinning knowledge on human development and theoretical approaches. The chapters comprise:

Ethics and Process: This chapter sets out the difference between counselling skills and counselling. It also considers the limitations in the use of counselling skills and how you might develop your personal way of working effectively and ethically, within your main functional role whilst using those skills.

Life Stages: This chapter looks at major life events and how we cope with them, through the work of Freud, Erikson and Piaget. It also considers issues of attachment, separation and loss, drawing on the work of Bowlby, Harlow and Hodges, and Tizard. Following this, three different theoretical approaches to the self-concept are outlined and linked to the development of self-esteem and self-awareness.

Theoretical Perspectives: This chapter offers an overview of three theoretical approaches, citing those people considered to be influential in developing each approach, together with an indication of the strengths and limitations of each. The three approaches considered are psychodynamic, person-centred and cognitive-behavioural.

Values, Attitudes and Beliefs: This chapter provides an introduction to the generally accepted views about the origin and importance of values, attitudes and beliefs in our lives. It also examines the nature of prejudice, stereotyping and discrimination.

SECTION 2

This section covers a broad range of counselling skills, and encourages the reader to practise them by completing structured activities.

Introduction to Counselling Skills: This chapter introduces basic counselling skills, through an analysis of what makes an effective communicator. This includes attention giving, observing, listening and responding.

Further Counselling Skills: This chapter develops those skills introduced in the previous chapter and introduces the skills of challenging, immediacy, self-disclosure, concreteness, goal setting and barriers to communicating and listening.

SECTION 3

This section begins by looking at where counselling skills are used and the issues that arise in the various contexts. It then focuses on two specific situations, one which causes widespread distress (bullying and harassment) and one which is positive and developmental (mentoring).

Settings: This chapter focuses on the settings in which counselling skills are used and the issues that arise; for example record keeping, roles and responsibilities. The practical impact of legislation and the requirements of professional bodies are also examined.

Bullying and Harassment: This chapter looks at what constitutes bullying, sexual and racial harassment; how and why some of us become bullies and others victims. It also looks at the difference and similarities between bullying and discrimination and the legislation that exists to protect us. Finally, it outlines approaches and strategies that can be used to counter bullying and harassment.

Mentoring: This chapter provides a basic understanding of the concept of mentoring. It describes what mentoring is, how and where it is undertaken, and the benefits that accrue. It also covers the characteristics and range of mentoring relationships. Finally, the qualities of a good mentor and mentee are discussed.

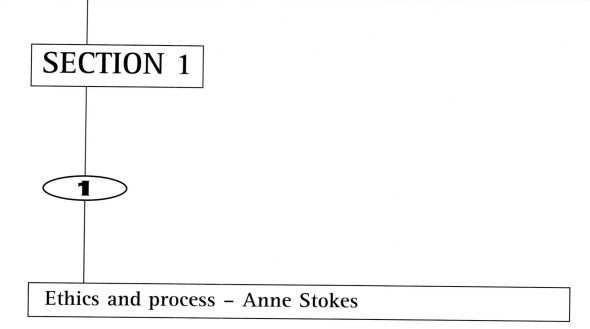

SECTION 1

1

Ethics and process – Anne Stokes

It seems fitting that this book should start with a chapter on the ethics and processes involved in counselling skills since if those are understood and paid attention from the outset, there is a greater likelihood that practitioners will work in a way that is within their capabilities and roles. It is important to be clear from the outset about the different levels of competence and skills training which are needed to meet the demands of those who are counsellors and those who use counselling skills. It is likely that if you are using this book in conjunction with a training course, you are in the latter category, and are probably using counselling skills as part of another role you hold either in paid employment or in a voluntary setting. Chapter seven explores these settings in more detail. This chapter sets out to distinguish between counselling and counselling skills, to consider boundaries and limitations in using counselling skills, and to consider how you might develop your personal way of working effectively and ethically within your main functional role while using those skills.

There has been a dilemma about what names or titles should be used for those involved in the process. 'Client' is a useful shorthand term, but may imply a different relationship, while 'speaker' may not appear to fully value the extent of the process. In the same way, 'counselling skills user' is a mouthful, 'counsellor' is incorrect, 'helper' sounds like jargon, and you will be more than a 'listener'. All except 'counsellor' have been used. Perhaps you will be able to find better terms to apply to your own context.

COUNSELLING AND COUNSELLING SKILLS

There is still much confusion between the terms 'counsellor' and 'counselling skills users', and in lay parlance 'counsellor' tends to be used to cover both, as well as all sorts of other activities. The British Association for Counselling and Psychotherapy (BACP) defines counselling as involving a deliberately undertaken contract with clearly agreed boundaries and a commitment to privacy and confidentiality (BACP, 1998). The client must be in a position to agree to working in this way, and know that they are entering a counselling relationship.

Counselling skills will certainly involve some of the same skills as those a counsellor uses; the difference is in the intention behind their use. If you are using counselling skills, you will be seen primarily in your role of nurse, teacher, manager, Church worker etc, and be using your skills to enhance that role. The BACP offers two useful questions to help to ascertain which activity you are engaged in.

◆ Are you using counselling skills to enhance your communication with someone, but without taking on the role of their counsellor?

◆ Does the recipient see you as acting within your professional/caring role?

If the answer is 'yes' to both questions, then you are using counselling skills. However, if the answer is 'no', then you may well be perceived as a counsellor, and should ensure both that you have sufficient training, and are working to a Code of Ethics and Practice which has been designed for counsellors. If the answer to one question is 'yes' and to the other 'no', there is a conflict between your expectations and those of the recipient and you need to resolve it with them.

Your workplace or the agency in which you are using counselling skills may well have a Code of Practice and, if so, you should make sure that you have read and understood it.

As you read these paragraphs, you may have begun to feel that there is an implied hierarchy between counsellors and those using counselling skills. This is not the case – they are simply different usages of overlapping skills. If I want a house built, I might well go to an architect to design it, but I certainly would not want the architect to actually build it for me – I would go to a builder! They have overlapping skills and knowledge about the construction of my house, but also have different roles and jobs. As a counselling skills user, you will have a different brief from a counsellor and will be using your other roles and specific in depth knowledge as a human resource practitioner, a minister, or a prison visitor, for example, to aid your work. Indeed, you will sometimes be much better placed to help an individual in those roles, as an early move to help an individual may forestall the need for the help of a professional counsellor later.

A definition which I find helpful is given by Sanders (1993).

> Counselling Skills are interpersonal communication skills derived from the study of therapeutic change in human beings, used in a manner consistent with the goals and values of the established ethics of the profession of the practitioner in question. In addition the user of counselling skills will find that their own professional skills are enhanced by the process.
>
> (Sanders, 1993)

One of the overlaps with counselling will be in the area of underlying values. Both processes are concerned with the recipient being responsible for determining their future rather than the helper. There is an emphasis in both on the client's capacity for self-determination.

ACTIVITY

Read through the following scenarios and decide how you would respond to them in order to ensure that the individuals involved knew what your role was in relation to them.

◆ As part of your welfare function in your organisation you are running a series of workshops to prepare people for retirement. Your line manager has sent you a memo to ask you to offer one-to-one counselling sessions in addition to the group workshops.

◆ You are the leader of a local community group and have got to know Janet and Paul quite well. After a talk on effective parenting, given by a visiting speaker, they approach you and ask if they could talk to you about one of their children whose behaviour is worrying them.

If you can work with a partner, try out your responses on them and ask them to give you feedback.

Using counselling skills

So why might you wish to use counselling skills? They are relevant to a wide range of settings – paid and unpaid – in which 'people helping' is involved. As Sanders suggests in the definition, it might be to enhance your professional role. For example, a teacher might be aware that a young child in a primary class is very upset about the death of his/her pet. He or she could set time aside to talk to the child, using active listening skills so that the loss and grief can be acknowledged and worked through. A doctor could find out more about the reasons for the repeated surgery visits of an apparently fairly healthy patient by using counselling skills rather than dismissing the person as a hypochondriac.

The skills can also be used to help the organisation as well as the individual. An employee may be underperforming and instead of simply writing them off or moving into more formal procedures, a line manager might use counselling skills to try to discover any underlying issues. Instead of 'telling', there would be a desire to listen and discover, and to help the individual to find a satisfactory outcome, if possible. The individual gains by feeling valued, and the organisation may well find that they have regained a committed worker.

In a recent initiative BUPA offered a number of employees the opportunity to undertake a certificate in counselling skills so that they could work within 'The Knowledge Net', a centre that was conceived to enable staff to enhance their personal and professional development in a number of ways, including having the opportunity to talk through issues with the trained staff. There were interesting additional benefits. For example, the staff who had been trained felt that they had gained enormous insights into themselves as well as having a better understanding of their colleagues. Their main role, which was mainly as call centre operators, benefited as they found that they were much better able to respond to stressful calls in ways which enhanced the members' perception of the organisation.

Alison Platt, deputy managing director of BUPA, commenting on the scheme said:

> The development of those individuals and the creation of that framework (the Knowledge Net) has been an absolutely fundamental part of growing an ethos that genuinely is beginning to make our people feel that individuals matter.
>
> (Platt, 1999)

Nursing staff who have undergone a counselling skills training often find that they feel better able to respond to ill, and sometimes frightened, patients (and their relatives) as they no longer have to remain locked into a 'medical' role, but can listen empathically without feeling helpless because they are not able to restore the person to immediate health. Although we tend to think of counselling skills being used to help the recipient, it is also important to realise that their use can often make us feel more confident. We have a better sense of how we can help, and what can make for effective interpersonal relationships. Egan (1998) uses the term 'the skilled helper', and if we are skilled, we are usually more effective. If we recognise our effectiveness, our self-esteem increases. So there is an additional spin-off for the counselling skills users!

Conflict resolution is also enhanced by the use of counselling skills. Take the case of Anna, who was a volunteer in a community centre. Her role was to co-ordinate the allocation of blocks of times and rooms to the various user groups. Sometimes she found that she was 'piggy in the middle', for example when there were two groups using different rooms during the same morning of the week and problems arose. On one occasion there was a mother and toddler group there at the same time as a group for young unemployed teenagers. Both groups complained to her about the other, claiming that the facilities were not being used properly. While on the surface it seemed to be all about noise, nappies and naughtiness, by using her counselling skills, Anna discovered that the mothers felt intimidated at times by the sheer exuberance of the teenagers and thought they were laughing at them. They, on the other hand, had the impression that the mothers looked down on them for not being in employment and for 'looking different'. By exploring the situation with the two groups individually, then having a meeting together, not only did they agree to some ways of co-existing, but got to know and like each other (in the main!). Anna said that she had not really done anything, 'only listened, and reflected back what they were saying, then got them to think of ways forward'. Another interpretation might be that she had used the

---

ACTIVITY

Take a sheet of paper and list the main paid and unpaid roles you have had in your adult life.

Which of these roles would or did benefit from the use of counselling skills?

Are there any roles in which it would be inappropriate to use counselling skills?

If you are doing this activity in a group, work with someone else to explain your reasons for having included these roles.

counselling skills she had learned on a course to enable those involved to feel heard and she had empowered them to find their own solutions.

Limitations and boundaries of counselling skills

The role of a boundary sentinel suggests a demanding practitioner stance and it would be disingenuous to imply or imagine otherwise. Being in a position of constantly having to juggle relationships boundaries and be clear about the limits and extent of confidentiality in any given situation is not for the faint – or even the feint – hearted. Such a complex context requires comprehensive containment.

(Gabriel, 2000)

The second part of the activity will have begun to make you think about the limitations of counselling skills. You may have already begun to see that there could well be parts of an occupational role where it would be manipulative or unethical to use them. For example, Andy, a secondary school teacher, had been working over a period of time with Jo, one of the students in her tutor group to help her increase her self-esteem. She was asked by the pastoral head of that particular year group, who knew that Andy had built up a very trusting relationship with the pupil, to talk to Jo to try to get information about a series of incidents which involved others in her class. Andy felt torn. She knew that she probably could get Jo to tell her about this, and that this might well bring the culprits to light. On the other hand, she knew that Jo would feel betrayed if it came to light that Andy had deliberately used their time together in this way. Her dilemma was about whether the possible benefit for the school, or at least a part of it, overrode her relationship with her student.

This particular example has been used because often the reaction has been that Jo is young, is 'only' a schoolchild and will get over it, thereby implying that the choice is obvious – Andy should obtain the information. However, if challenged to transfer the scenario into their own adult working life, the responses are nearly always less clear cut. People would not want to find that they had been 'tricked' into giving away information about their colleagues. In some work environments and voluntary organisations, those in positions of authority can forget this and appear to treat individuals as they might their children. Maybe they also forget what it feels like to be young – the same sense of being manipulated or abused is still there.

Andy decided that she would not do this and explained her position to the pastoral head. However, because she recognised that her primary role was as a teacher, she was able to discuss whether there was any other way in which she could help to resolve the incidents. Between them, they agreed that Andy would talk to a small group of pupils together to try to gather information. She would be using her counselling skills to communicate effectively, and using her relationship with them, but she would be working to a known and overt agenda.

POWER

Power balances and imbalances are present in every relationship, but in one in which someone is offering help and another person is asking for help, there is likely to be an inbuilt power difference, particularly at the beginning of the work. Speedy (1998), writing about women trainers, discusses three aspects of power which would equally apply to the relationship formed when using counselling skills. There is ascribed power which is 'given' to you because of your status, title or something else (real or imagined), by another person. It is easy to see how a client might ascribe power to you as a nurse, teacher, social worker, or line manager. In the same way, you may be ascribed power as you interact with someone using your counselling skills – you are an 'expert', it seems. While this power may in some ways be very seductive, it is vital that it does not become one of the reasons which encourages the use of counselling skills. If it does, then surely the process has become about satisfying the user's needs rather than the client's.

Owned power is an acknowledged power, for example power which originates from your primary function. As a doctor, you have the power to recommend treatment or not; as a social worker, you have the power to enable people to access services; as an employer, you have the power to promote. To deny that this power exists is unrealistic. People seeking your help with personal or work-related issues cannot simply forget that you have another role in their lives. Indeed they would be foolish to do so, as you do have a dual role. If you hear something which may affect medical treatment, work performance, or examination achievement, you are not going to be able to 'unhear' it or forget it completely, however much you may choose to bracket it off. Your owned power may also be useful in helping people to achieve their goals. Those subscribing to counselling values may well see empowerment of others as part of their core philosophy. If you disempower yourself by denying your role power, how are you going to model empowerment? Issues concerned with owned power will be less of a problem if they are seen to be acknowledged by those using counselling skills, and by discussion of how that affects the work, being actively encouraged.

Disguised power is precisely what it says, and is often associated with a misuse or abuse of power. One way in which this might be demonstrated is in the example discussed where Andy was invited to use her counselling skills in a covert way to gain information for another purpose. In Speedy's research, the words used by those she interviewed to describe this type of power, include 'sneaky', 'oppressive' and 'turning on a style' .

As well as demonstrating that counselling skills can be used manipulatively, Andy's dilemma highlights role conflict. The user needs to act responsibly to ensure that they know whose interests are being served. Is it the recipient's? The organisation's? Or even the user's? If you are likely to be in a position where there are conflicting interests (and that probably means most of us), it is helpful to try to consider the main issues involved before situations arise, and maybe to discuss them in principle with those who would be involved. Of course this is often a counsel of perfection, so at the very least, when a conflict has arisen and hopefully been resolved, it is essential to reflect on it, deciding what you have learned from it and what you would do differently in the future. The most unhelpful course of action is to immediately heave a sigh of relief and push the issues back under the carpet in the hope that they will not arise again. Almost inevitably they will!

ACTIVITY

Work in threes to do this exercise. Person A outlines a situation they have experienced in which there has either been a role conflict, or a conflict of interests. The task of Person B is to help them to unpack the issues involved, and what was done, but without offering advice or solutions. Person C, sitting slightly apart, listens to the exchange without speaking, and notices any ethical, boundary or organisational issues which seem to have been missed, jotting them down if necessary. There may not be any at this stage. After the situation has been outlined, Person C enquires about the possible omissions. Then all three people brainstorm other options. These will not necessarily be more appropriate than the original, but allow the group to explore different ways of resolving situations. If there is time, each person has a turn in each role. If you are working on your own, you can do this activity by writing down the dilemma, then going through it as if you were now Person C. Finally, consider other courses of action which were open to you and evaluate them against your original decision.

SUPPORT

Those who work as counsellors in the UK have the support of being in supervision. This is a requirement for counsellors belonging to professional bodies like the BACP, or the United Kingdom Council for Psychotherapists, or those who are on the UK Register of Counsellors. In fact, even if they do not belong to one of these, very few counsellors would practise without supervision. In supervision, counsellors talk about their individual clients, their practice, and any ethical dilemmas, which would include role conflicts.

For people in other roles, where the use of counselling skills is only one part of their work, there is no such requirement and rarely the luxury of such support. There are some exceptions, such as social work and, increasingly, the nursing profession, but even here it may be about managing casework rather that about the limitations and boundaries or the personal impact of using counselling skills. It could be beneficial to consider whether you could set up some support for yourself if you think you might find it valuable, either on a regular basis or on a 'need' basis. This could be with someone who also uses counselling skills in their functional role. If you are in skills training, it might be helpful to talk to someone who has more experience than you. Someone within the same organisation has the advantage of knowing the systems and the culture, but they have the disadvantage of perhaps also being placed in a dilemma as you talk through your work, if they disagree with your action. What would happen in such a case is one of the things that you would need to discuss when you contracted to work together in this way. Supervision involves the regular and structured discussion of the way counselling skills have been employed to ensure that their use is ethical and appropriate.

You might want to consider talking to a counselling supervisor, but if you take that option, there has to be clarity about the fact that you are not working as a counsellor, but a counselling skills user. Not all supervisors have organisational experience, so check this out with them. There is likely to be a charge for this type of supervision, so it may not be a practical choice.

ACTIVITY

What type of support do you need for your skills work?

Consider the sources from which you currently get support. Are there gaps between what you need and what you have? If so, how could you obtain the necessary support?

OTHER LIMITATIONS

People are often fearful of using counselling skills because they do not believe they can cope with emotional or difficult situations. However, even a chance greeting such as 'How are you?' may cause someone to respond emotionally. It is therefore essential to know one's limitations and it is good practice to set boundaries and be clear with the other person involved about what those may be. The counselling skills user is not entering into a therapeutic contract, as that is likely to be in conflict with their main role. That is not to say that the effect of talking with someone will not be therapeutic for them, but it will be an informal arrangement and only forms one part of any other relationship the helper has with that person. Any relationship outside the one involved in the specific implementation of counselling skills will inevitably alter and also be altered by the intervention.

A counsellor would enter into a specific contract with a client, and though they might come across each other on occasion in a workplace setting, for example in coffee rooms or at briefings, their main working relationship would be the counselling relationship. Obviously this is not so in the case of the counselling skills user, who should take responsibility for making the distinction and stating what the limitations of any one-to-one discussions might be. One of those limitations will be about confidentiality and this will be looked at in more detail later in this chapter.

Another limitation in the use of counselling skills is training and working within your level of competence. It is not enough simply to have good intentions and 'warm fuzzy feelings' about people. To engage in helping others is a complex process, which may involve dangers for the helper and the recipient, and therefore should not be entered into lightly or without reflection on whether the helper has the necessary personal and skills resources. To balance this, it is true that most skills users will not be dealing with those who have profound psychological issues and, with good training, a counselling skills approach can be used in ways which enable you to help by means that are neither ineffectual nor over-controlling. Even after an initial training has been completed, there is a place for ongoing professional development as there is always new learning about the helping process, and a truly skilled helper will constantly be refining and improving their work.

A final issue in this section is that of 'the feel-good factor'. In my experience of training individuals in counselling skills to be used as an adjunct to their main role, initially trainees go through a real 'high' in terms of self-esteem as they discover how they can use the skills to enable others to come to grips with a problem, or to make a decision for themselves. After that a period of self-doubt seems to set in. Questions are raised about how ethical it is to feel good about one's self when perhaps talking with someone who is experiencing a number of difficult or even traumatic emotions. Is this exploitation or self-gratification? In my opinion, the satisfaction in knowing that skills have been used well to help another is not only ethical, but also, at least for some of the time, essential. To put it bluntly, unless people do get, or at least feel that they get something out of their involvement, they will not stay committed to that way of working for long. That something may not, indeed cannot, always be the satisfaction of 'a happy ending'; it may be as elusive as the awareness that helping others to help themselves is part of your core values and beliefs.

ACTIVITY

Take a few minutes by yourself to do the first part of this activity. Think about the role(s) in which you use counselling skills. What are your personal and professional reasons for doing this? Explore how you will deal with boundary and limitation issues. With a partner, reflect on what you have been considering.

CODES OF ETHICS AND PRACTICE

At the beginning of this chapter, reference was made to the difference between counselling skills and counselling. The BACP has a code which applies to both and it is desirable that anyone using counselling skills should obtain that code as well as any other Code of Ethics and Practice which pertains to their functional role. Before examining the various sections of the BACP code, some reflection on underlying principles is needed.

Ethical codes have to be able to cover a range of perspectives and practices which will encompass the stances which are 'generally acceptable' to a wide variety of people subscribing to them. If they do not do this, individuals will not agree to be members of that particular professional body, or will simply pay lip service to the codes. Codes therefore are rather general documents and, with certain exceptions, do not comment on specific situations. They offer guidelines and principles, and help to set standards and norms within a profession. Importantly, they are designed to protect clients, and also to protect users from unethical practice.

While this book is addressed to individuals using counselling skills, the six principles set out by Thompson (1990) for ethical practice by psychotherapists might also be useful to consider here. They are:

◆ respect for client autonomy
◆ fidelity (honouring the promises which frame the relationship)

◆ justice (a fair distribution of services within society)
◆ beneficence (a commitment to benefiting the client)
◆ non-maleficence (avoiding harm to the client)
◆ self-interest (the worker's entitlement to numbers 1–5).

ACTIVITY

Consider the six principles. With a partner, discuss whether you think they apply to your counselling skills work. Which ones can you illustrate with real or hypothetical situations quite easily. Are there any which do not seem to have relevance to your work? Explain why not. If there are any you do not understand, discuss them with other people in your training group.

Bond (2000) states that the distinction between counselling and counselling skills is arguably one of the most important role distinctions to have emerged in recent years. He then discusses the idea that counselling skills are a set of activities unique to counselling, and highlights the invalidity of this notion, since so many of those activities which might be labelled as 'counselling skills' are also used in many other spheres, for example social skills, interpersonal skills etc.

One way of distinguishing between counselling skills and other forms of communication might be to look at the balance in the amount of time the recipient is speaking. Bond offers a helpful chart to illustrate this.

DIFFERENCES IN COMMUNICATION		
STYLE	PATTERN OF FLOW	TIME RATIO
Imparting expertise	interactor>recipient	80:20
Conversation	Interactor>recipient	50:50
Counselling skills	Interactor>recipient	20:80
		(Bond, 2000)

ACTIVITY

During the next week, monitor the interactions you have with people. Is the balance of speaking and listening as you expected? Is there anything you want to change as a result of doing this activity? Note your findings in your journal, if you are keeping one.

Counselling skills users have a dual responsibility here – to the recipient and to the organisation within which they operate. Sometimes 'therapy by stealth' (Hoffman, 1990) occurs, whereby a relationship is entered into without perhaps either party being aware of its nature and potential. For example, several young people established good relationships with Bill, a youth and community worker, and he began to meet regularly with individuals during the time the local youth club was taking place. Bill saw this as simply an extension of the role, but two difficulties arose. The first was that the young people expected those sessions to happen, withdrew from other activities within the club to which they had committed themselves, and to a large extent formed a separate community. Secondly, Bill's co-workers found that they were having to cover for him during the evenings while these 'conversations' were taking place and he was increasingly aware that he was neglecting other parts of his role.

Part of the difficulty here was that Bill had not clarified what was on offer to the young people; the situation had crept up on them. In addition, although clearly the sessions were helpful for the individuals, ongoing one-to-one work was not seen as a major part of his brief. It took the skilful intervention of Bill's manager to unravel the situation and to work out ways in which he could use his counselling skills more appropriately in line with his main functional role.

A different situation arises when considering whose interests are being served. Take the example of a saleswoman for a large manufacturing company who until recently has been performing well, easily reaching sales targets. Her manager initiates discussions with her when there is a fairly dramatic reduction in her sales and following two complaints from customers about her aggressive manner with them. The manager uses counselling skills to try to establish what has caused the change, and discovers that her husband has unexpectedly left her and their children.

As someone who knows and likes her, the manager might like to be entirely understanding of the situation and tell her that until she has been able to find a way forward, there will be no problems or pressure from the organisation. He might even suggest that she might find it helpful to come back at another time and talk her personal issues through with him. However, he clearly has a responsibility to his company and to their customers. What he could do instead, would be to spell out his main role plainly. In this case, he could suggest that she might like to contact the company's Employee Assistance Programme providers, or an external counsellor, to talk about the break-up of her marriage, and possibly the effect it is having on the way she relates to other people. In his managerial role, he could look with her at how the company could support her in the meantime, perhaps by a temporary reduction in her sales targets, and possibly a discussion with human resources on any financial problems which she might be experiencing. All the time, he would be drawing on his counselling skills to enable the employee to feel heard and understood, but would be serving the interests of the organisation.

If the limitations of roles are not taken into account, there is a greater potential for harm – both to the individual and to the organisation. It is often impossible to be impartial when working, for example as a manager, doctor, teacher, or trade union officer. People in such roles have a responsibility to others, as well as the person speaking to them, and may also have power, control or authority over them. It is very difficult, if not impossible, for there never to be any ambiguity within roles, but users of counselling skills need to work overtly around the limitations.

Using counselling skills can be seductive and exploitive. For instance, a care worker could be aware that an elderly person with whom s/he is working is increasingly unable to remain in their home. It would be valid to use counselling skills to discuss how that person feels about moving into temporary or permanent sheltered accommodation. However, it would be exploiting the relationship if pressure was brought to bear, through the use of those skills, to engineer such a decision being made without taking into account the real feelings being expressed – i.e. in being selective about what is reflected back or brought out into the open. The seductive element in such an example might be that the care worker would know that s/he would receive praise or gratitude from others involved – doctors, social workers or relatives – for having managed to bring about a result that they believe is in the best interests of the elderly person. It is not being argued here that it might not be better medically, or practically, for that person to leave their home; that is not the issue. What is at stake is whether the care worker has worked in an ethical way. Have the counselling skills used over a period of time, to establish a good relationship, then been put to use to manoeuvre someone into doing something they do not wish to do?

ACTIVITY

Reflect on the situation just described. Are there ways of managing that situation which are non-exploitative? Think about it from the perspective of both the carer and the elderly person. Have you ever been in a position where you felt that you were being pushed into doing or saying something which you did not want to by another person using counselling skills? With the benefit of hindsight, how could the occasion been better handled?

Confidentiality

There are all kinds of assumptions about what the word 'confidentiality' means, and both counsellors and those using counselling skills often agonise about the limits of confidentiality. In ethical terms, the purpose of confidentiality is to provide safety and privacy for the process that is taking place between those involved in the intentional use of counselling skills.

Privacy

For those using counselling skills as part of their primary role, confidentiality has two aspects, one of which is the setting and the other the process they are engaged in. The person to whom counselling skills are being offered may be in a setting which exists for another purpose, and which may militate against confidentiality. Think of open-plan offices; an occupational therapist working in a ward setting; a teacher in a classroom; or a parish worker in a church hall. None of these places is ideal for conducting a conversation which is very personal or where the speaker may be revealing their emotions. It may be possible to take steps to ensure greater confidentiality by moving to another room, by use of a screen, or simply by positioning oneself to shield the speaker. However, moving may interrupt the person's flow and the moment may be lost, and a screen or moving position only provides some privacy – sound still travels. The shared environment may mean that information, and indeed gossip, about one person can quickly be spread around.

With experience, it is possible to pick up signs that you may be about to hear something which will require you to use your counselling skills. If you are able to anticipate this happening, you may be able to forestall the person until you have managed to move to a more private environment. However, even the most experienced people can find themselves listening in the 'wrong' environment, and have to make immediate decisions about whether to encourage the speaker to continue, or whether it would be more appropriate to use their skills to curtail the interaction for the moment.

If you are able to choose the room in which you talk to someone, using obscured or curtained glass doors will help avoid the casual passer-by from seeing who you are talking to – even a poster over an inset window is useful. It is often difficult to prevent other people from walking in unannounced, so it is worth thinking about ways of dealing with interruptions. If you habitually work in one room, you may be able to train colleagues to enter if your door is partly opened, or to respect a sign that states that you are busy. Telephones can also be distracting, so if you are able to turn off the ringing tone, do so. As suggested, it is not always possible to anticipate what someone wants to talk to you about, but get into the habit of watching and listening for signs that you may need privacy. It may be more sensible to break into a conversation and shut the door, even if it feels a little intrusive, than run the risk of the speaker realising later that they have been heard by everyone in the vicinity. While ideally both parties should be aware that the conversation has turned from an everyday interaction to one that involves the use of counselling skills, in reality the speaker is often so involved in what they are saying that they may be blocking out the physical limitations of the setting for confidentiality.

Some organisations where people do not have their own private space, set aside a particular room that can be used for these purposes. One drawback to having such a room can be the label it is given by others. If it is only used when people are 'in trouble', whether that is interpreted as disciplinary or emotional, then its use can mean that those around become curious or speculate about what is going on inside it. It is also worth remembering that enabling interactions do not just take place when two people come together with the deliberate intention of speaking about an issue. A carer may find s/he is using counselling skills while bathing someone, a teacher while walking with a student on a school visit to a field centre, or a police officer while taking a lost child back to the parents. However, privacy can be found in many settings.

Confidentiality of information

The second aspect of confidentiality is concerned with what can or cannot be spoken about outside that particular conversation or interview. This usually centres more around what the counselling skills user will take out of the room, rather than whether the person is free to talk about the issues elsewhere. Obviously, it is only possible to begin even to think about maintaining confidentiality when the conversation is not overheard. Indeed, the very act of ensuring that there is this degree of privacy may be one of the ways by which misunderstanding is created as to the nature or limits to the extent of the confidentiality. If great care is taken to ensure that environmentally the speaker feels free to say whatever they wish, the impression may be given that the listener will not repeat any of the information anywhere.

One limitation on confidentiality is the impact of legislation on the organisation. This will be explored more fully in the chapter on settings, but an example would be of a teacher working with a pupil in relation to the Children Act (1989). There are clear and unalterable circumstances that compel teachers to reveal information. In a workplace, health and safety or employment legislation may affect confidentiality in respect of certain disclosures. The BACP code refers the user to any agreement around confidentiality being consistent with any written code which governs the functional role.

Absolute confidentiality is not possible within most helping situations and it is almost always best to be very clear about this from the outset. A simple statement may cover this situation, such as, 'I'm hoping that by talking together, we will be able to sort out how the issues can be resolved. I have to tell you though that sometimes I hear things from people – perhaps to do with safety or what is happening within the organisation – which mean that I need to ask for advice from others or take the matter elsewhere.' The argument against doing this is that the receiver will automatically think that nothing can be kept confidential, and will choose therefore not to talk about the issue. That may happen, but the underlying values of using counselling skills include those of the autonomy of the person and their right to make informed decisions.

An additional sentence which states that you would discuss how you might take any information out of the room, so that the speaker would always know that you were going to do so, might be helpful – as long as you are sure that this is how you are able to operate. On occasion, something may be said suddenly, before there has been an opportunity to bring up the limits of confidentiality. Again, when talking to people, it is worth trying to keep a 'helicopter view' of the conversation, so that you might be able to anticipate what is likely to be said. This is not an easy skill, but generally, as with most skills, practice and experience does help you to be able to be both present in the conversation and aware of signals that a disclosure may be likely.

If it is necessary to take information elsewhere, it is imperative to do this in the best possible way for the person receiving counselling skills, or at the very worst, in the least harmful manner. Set out in the following list are some ideas for you to consider, but you will need to find your own way in each particular circumstance.

◆ If at all possible, obtain permission to reveal the relevant parts of your conversation, explaining why you feel the need to do so, and to whom you would speak. Be prepared to spend time in this discussion, and be open to considering other ethical and practical possibilities. Are there ways for the person to take the issue to someone else, rather than you?

◆ If the person refuses to agree to this, and you still believe that you must tell someone else, make sure that s/he knows exactly what you are going to do and why. You should also acknowledge that this is not what they wish. Give them time to talk about whatever fears they may have about what will happen next. If possible, say when you are going to take action. It is probably better to do it sooner rather than later, especially if they are upset by your decision. They will then know when their fears might possibly be realised.

◆ On the other hand, do not feel that you do have to rush into premature disclosure. What are the consequences of holding the information for a period of time? If it makes sense to allow more time for discussion and looking at options, without having any major consequences, then consider whether your desire for immediate action is actually your need to do something, rather than in the best interests of the person and/or the organisation.

◆ It may be helpful to also talk with them about anything they may want or need to do in light of your decision, and consider with them how they would take such action. Of course, it is possible that they may be so angry about it that they do not want to continue the conversation, but if you can remain calm, it is often possible to work through this stage with them.

◆ Be clear about your continued availability to be helpful and supportive, even if they feel at this moment that you have let them down. If they do not wish it, or if it is inappropriate for you to continue in this role, then explore with them where else they can get support.

◆ If you have someone with whom you discuss your counselling skills work, talk through it with them first. There may be implications or other ways of proceeding that you have not thought of. It can be difficult to think clearly and widely when you feel as though you have your back against the wall.

◆ If you do not, try to think of someone else within the organisation such as a mentor or a trusted colleague, or even a friend, who has similar experience and background to yours, with whom you could explore what you need to do. In talking with them, at this stage, avoid talking in a way that will identify those involved.

◆ If you change your decision about what you are going to do, let the person know. After all, they may now be anxious and expecting some further event to happen.

◆ When you take the matter forward, think how much has to be revealed. There may well be parts of your conversation that have no relevance to your disclosure, and these are better kept to yourself.

◆ Finally, you may well need support as it can sometimes seem that you have become 'the baddie' and betrayed the person who came to you. This is probably simply your fantasy, but it is useful to identify someone who can listen to you as you reflect on the experience.

Setting out these steps may appear to over-dramatise the issues involved in the area of confidentiality. They are intended to enable you to consider what might happen and how you would work with the need to limit the boundaries. It is an area in which those who use counselling skills within another primary role do have to be mindful. However, in reality, it is usually not as much of a minefield as you might fear, since people often already have some awareness that you will have to take action. Indeed this may be the reason that they have chosen to give you the information. They may have recognised the need for something to be done, but do not know how to do it.

Perhaps another factor to be aware of with regards to confidentiality is what to do if you unintentionally reveal information or have it revealed to you. Caution is therefore needed about using 'real' material, in discussions, even when it is taken from the past. Similarly, in discussions if you hold information about someone which you deem to be confidential, or which that person could reasonably expect you not to share, you will need to ensure that you do not inadvertently reveal it. Your involvement might be picked up, not only through your words, but also through your body language.

There may be circumstances when it is valid to share some part of your knowledge, even if it is not a requirement. For example, if a worker in a rehabilitation centre was discussing the progress of a resident with the manager, it could be acceptable to state that you believe that pressure should not be put on that resident to undertake a particular part of the work programme at this time – as they are dealing with some underlying issues which makes it hard for them to take on anything new. This assumes a degree of trust in the working relationship of the manager and the worker that this general information would not be taken and inappropriately used in another setting.

ACTIVITY

◆ Think of two situations in which confidentiality has been an issue for you, one where it was well handled, and one the opposite. You may have been giving or receiving the information. Make a list of the key differences. What can you learn from this for your current work?

◆ Reflect on your primary function or role. What are the areas where you might need to pass information on to someone else? How might that affect your work when using counselling skills?

◆ Discuss, with other people in your training group, how you will manage situations when you will have to break confidentiality appropriately, and also how you will prevent clients believing that there is total confidentiality in your work.

Complaints procedures

The emphasis in this activity has been on working in ways that do not breach professional codes of ethics, i.e. any codes that govern the primary function and also those relating to the use of counselling skills. It is likely that there will be procedures within those codes which determine what happens if those codes are broken, and workers within any organisation have a duty to ensure that they are familiar with procedures and possible sanctions. It may be reasonable to assume that those around the counselling skills user will be familiar with organisational codes of ethics and practice, but they are less likely to be aware of those that specifically pertain to the counselling skills profession. Thus there is responsibility on your part to ensure that this is made clear. Furthermore, it is important for you to know and understand possible complaints procedures and sanctions.

The BACP has a complaints procedure that may lead to the expulsion of members who breach its Codes of Ethics and Practice and members can obtain information guidelines so that they understand the process. Organisations may also be subject to legislation and it is vital that those using counselling skills do not put themselves or their organisation in jeopardy, since it may be individual employees or volunteers who have to face the implications of breaches.

ACTIVITY

Obtain and read through any complaints processes, and/or mandatory legal codes which apply to your work. Make a note of anything of which you were unaware. Do you think that counselling skills recipients should be made aware of these? Is your answer the same regardless of whether you are the counselling skills user or 'consumer'? When and how do you think information about this process should be made available? Try to think of the ethical implications of your answers.

The philosophy, beliefs and values which underpin the practices and processes of using counselling skills are directly linked to the ethical stances which have been discussed. Nixon (1997) explores the ethical use of counselling skills by managers. The five points which he makes, outlined as follows, would seem to apply to most other counselling skills users. He suggests that the work is likely to be ethical as long as the user:

◆ 'buys into' the basic values of counselling
◆ avoids manipulation by exercising self-discipline in choosing when to use them
◆ adheres to clear boundaries when they do
◆ observes the cross over point into unethical practice
◆ has facilities available and the skill to refer a person for further appropriate help.

In concluding this chapter, which has been concerned with ethics and process, it is worth reminding ourselves who we need to demonstrate responsibility towards. Probably the first person who springs to mind is the one with whom we are using counselling skills. The duty towards them is to ensure that we are working as effectively, appropriately and ethically as is possible. From there, we could move towards our colleagues and their expectations of us in our primary role. Here our responsibility is to work towards the mission of the organisation which we have all bought into by agreeing to be part of it – though some might question whether that is what we do at an individual level, or whether we are selective about the parts of the mission to which we choose to subscribe.

There may be a responsibility to a wider community, for example our profession, our trade union, or the community in which voluntary work takes place, as well as to the intangible professional world of counselling skills users. Last, but certainly not least, there is a responsibility for ourselves. As people involved with helping others, we may find ourselves becoming 'emotionally full up'. If that happens, not only do we become less effective, but we cannot so easily enjoy and gain from other areas of our lives, including our family and friends.

Margaret Hodge, Minister for Employment and Equal Opportunities, announced the Work Life Balance Challenge Fund during 2000. This aims to help businesses achieve the bottom-line benefits of flexible work patterns and help employees to achieve a better balance between work and the rest of their lives. If you are using counselling skills within your role, you may well be enabling others to do just that – the challenge for you is whether you can also do this for yourself.

BIBLIOGRAPHY

Bond, T. (2000) *Standards and ethics for counselling in action*, London: Sage.

Egan, G. (1998) *The skilled helper*, Pacific Grove, CA: Brooks Cole.

Gabriel, L. (2000) 'Dual relationships in organisational contexts' in *Counselling*, vol 11, no 1, 17–19.

Hoffman, L. (1990) 'Constructing realities: an art of lenses' in *Family Processes*, vol 29, no 1, 1–12.

Platt, A. (1999) 'Counselling in a commercial world' in *Counselling at Work*, summer, 3–5.

Sanders, P. (1993) *An incomplete guide to using counselling skills on the telephone*, Manchester: PCCS Books.

Speedy, J. (1998) 'Issues of power for women trainers' in H. Johns (e.d.), *Balancing acts: studies in counselling training*, London: Routledge.

Thompson, A. (1990) *Guide to ethical practice in psychotherapy*, New York: Wiley.

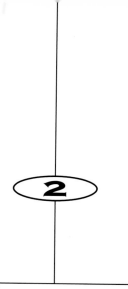

2

Life stages – Jan Jeffery

Why life stages? Shakespeare wrote in *As You Like It* about the seven ages of man, years before counselling and psychology existed as subjects for study. By life stages, we mean those different times of our lives that everyone experiences, like being a baby and becoming a teenager. This chapter starts by looking at three eminent writers on life stages, Freud, Erikson and Piaget and invites you to apply their ideas to your own life and those of people with whom you are working. We shall also look at life events or milestones and how people cope with those, whether or not they are related to the age stage. Then we look at the important issues of attachment, separation and loss and consider the work of Bowlby, Harlow and Hodges and Tizard.

Following this, the self-concept is described including what is meant by it and why it is important to understand it for ourselves and when we are using counselling skills with others. We look at three different approaches to the concept of self: the psychodynamic, person-centred and cognitive behavioral.

Finally, the chapter looks briefly at self-esteem and self-awareness, an important aspect of all counselling skills training.

ACTIVITY

This is an activity that may take some time. Allow yourself plenty of time to work on it. It may be helpful to discuss it with someone else.

◆ Think about your own life up to the present. Take a sheet of paper and write a list of your ideas about the particular stages in your life from birth until the present. There may be five or six stages or more. Leave a space on your paper for three more columns beside your list.

◆ Look again at your list and write in the next two columns what you consider to be the most important needs and experiences for each period of time.

◆ Now think about what might have happened if your needs had not been met at each stage. Write in the fourth column how you think this might have affected you.

Your life stages	The needs of this period	The experiences of this period	What might this period have happened if your needs had not been met

LIFE STAGE THEORISTS

Many writers have written about life stages and how the experiences in early life contribute to the person we become as an adult. We continue this chapter by considering the work of three thinkers and writers who have an influence on how many people work and think today.

SIGMUND FREUD (1856–1939)

Freud described five stages of life and wrote how the early years are crucial in the development of the adult personality. Psychodynamic approaches to counselling and psychotherapy are based on his work. One of his many ideas is that a person may become 'stuck' at an early stage of development instead of progressing through it. He called this fixation. Freud's stages are called psychosexual stages – they are based on what gives pleasure at each stage of life. Freud's stages are as follows.

0–1 years – oral stage

The main source of pleasure at this stage is sucking for food. Freud thought that oral fixations result from deprivation of oral pleasures in infancy. He said that this may cause personality problems later in life, for example an inability to form intimate relationships or a lack of trust in others.

1–3 years – anal stage

After weaning, the child begins to get pleasure from defecating. Freud thought that how toilet training was carried out was vital. Parents were told that failure to do it right could result in lasting personality damage. Too strict training could result in an anal-retentive personality, an adult who seeks to hold on to possessions, a miser or an obsessional collector. Too lenient training could result in a child becoming too generous in adult life. Freud saw close links between defecation and learning independence, handling personal power and aggression.

3–6 years – phallic stage

This is the stage at which children begin to identify with the parent of their own gender. Freud thought that boys at this stage develop an unconscious longing for their mothers and girls for their fathers. He called this the Oedipus complex. Little girls were supposed to be aware (unconsciously) that they had been born without a penis and develop penis envy. The importance in this stage of how parents respond to the child's emerging sexuality, both verbally and non-verbally is thought to have an impact in adult life on sexual attitudes and feelings.

6–12 years – latency stage

This is a period of relative calm in the child's development, and new interests outside the child, in school and the wider society become the focus.

12 years onwards – genital stage

Freud's final stage begins with puberty and the sexual changes that occur then. Adolescents and adults can channel their feelings into intimate relationships, friendships, sport and careers. For Freud, the genital stage continues through adulthood.

ERIK ERIKSON (1902–1994)

Erikson argued that Freud ignored the social influences in life. He called his eight life stages, psychosocial stages. His development covers the entire life and, for each stage, he describes a crisis, or turning point, which needs to be resolved for the individual to move on. If the crises or tasks are not resolved at each stage, it is possible that the person may have personality difficulties of some sort. For example, babies must learn during the first year of their lives, that parents or carers respond to their crying with food, comfort and love. If the baby learns to trust that this will happen, then the child can move to developing some autonomy in the second year. The 'terrible twos' behaviour so often shown at this time demonstrates that the child has developed sufficient trust in the parent to feel safe enough to try out some autonomy, without being anxious that love will be withdrawn if he is naughty. If the child is encouraged to try out some autonomy in the second year, he is able to learn to control his impulses and initiate activities of his own. As a result of self-control and a feeling of pride at his accomplishments, the child feels adequate and is able to become competent at intellectual, physical and social skills. If a parent overprotects or ridicules the child's efforts or is discouraging and blaming, the child is not able to move successfully through the life stages. Erikson's stages are as follows.

APPROX. AGE	STAGE	CRISIS	HOPEFUL RESULT
0–1	infancy	trust versus mistrust	trust
1–3	toddler	autonomy versus shame and doubt	freedom and self-control
3–6	pre-school	initiative versus guilt	purpose and direction
7–12	school age	industry versus inferiority	competence through recognition
12–18	adolescence	identity versus role confusion	integrated self-image
20+	early adulthood	intimacy versus isolation	ability to make relationships and a career
30–50	middle adulthood	generativity versus stagnation	family, social and career developments
50+	late adulthood	ego integrity versus despair	sense of fulfilment and satisfaction

ACTIVITY

Which of the following issues, that concern people, might be the result of early development? Which of Erikson's stages might they relate to?

◆ not being able to trust other people
◆ not being able to make close relationships with others
◆ having low self-esteem
◆ not being able to recognise and express negative feelings such as anger
◆ always worrying about the sort of person one is
◆ being sad about one's life and achievements
◆ not being able to initiate one's own activities
◆ social isolation
◆ excessive guilt over one's attempts in life
◆ discontent.

ACTIVITY

Looking back at your own column of needs and experiences, completed in the first activity of this chapter, how does it compare with the psychosocial stages of Erikson? What was your own experience of dealing with each of Erikson's crises?

JEAN PIAGET (1896–1980)

Another important theory of the life stages in development is one put forward by Piaget, who wrote about intellectual and cognitive development (thinking), rather than the emotional. His theory, which involves four stages, concerns what he called schema (plural 'schemata'). A schema is all the knowledge and experience a person has, which relates to a particular activity, a sort of mental structure. For example, our mental idea of eating involves preparing and serving food, using crockery and cutlery and, possibly, sitting at a table. Many schemata are more complicated than this, such as those involved in playing music.

The first schema a baby develops is the body schema. As s/he lies on her/his back playing in the cot with her/his toes and rattle, s/he learns that when she/he bites her/his toes and fingers it hurts, whereas it does not when s/he bites the rattle. Gradually the baby learns the difference between 'me ' and 'not me' – her/his first schema – and this is the beginning of all her/his learning. The baby starts life as totally egocentric and only gradually becomes aware of the world outside her/himself.

An operation, according to Piaget, is a way of combining schemata, and is not present in a young child. Piaget's stages are as follows.

Sensorimotor stage, or infancy (0–2 years)

In this stage the child is learning thinking skills, like the body schema, ready for the next stage. Piaget believed that young babies do not realise that a rattle, for example, exists separately from themselves. If it cannot be seen, heard or touched, then the child believes that it ceases to exist until the next time that the child experiences it. At around eight months, the child knows that the object is still there, even when it cannot be seen. This Piaget called object permanence.

Pre-operational stage, or early childhood stage (2–7 years)

Piaget thought that children of this age could not think logically as adults and could learn only from direct experience, from objects that are real such as toys and dolls. Children look at everything as they would themselves; for example believing that it is possible to 'smack' the naughty cupboard for hurting the child who bumped into it. This he called animism.

Concrete operational stage, or middle childhood (7–11 years)

The child is now beginning to understand the relationships between things and play in team games. They learn to add up, but need concrete, real objects, such as building blocks, to add and subtract. The egocentricity of early childhood is gone and they learn to see things from other people's point of view.

Formal operations stage (11 years and over)

Now children can understand abstract ideas, like freedom and conscience. Their thinking is rational and logical. Some people, however, never reach this stage of development.

ACTIVITY

By 'abstract' rather than 'concrete' we mean something that it is not possible to hold and touch. List some of the abstract concepts you use in your life in the course of a normal day. You might include telling the time, or a value such as truthfulness.

ACTIVITY

People who use counselling skills must use words that can be understood. If the person receiving counselling skills is still at Piaget's stage three – the concrete operational stage – how might the counselling skills user need to change their usual use of language to best help them? Can you think of some examples?

ACTIVITY

If you have access to a young baby, hide a toy which the baby is looking at under a cloth, and see if the child looks to see where it has gone or if it loses interest.

ACTIVITY

Pour an equal amount of water into two similar glasses and show a young child what you are doing. Then, with the child watching, pour the water from one of the glasses into a long thin glass, so the level of the water is higher. Ask the child which glass contains the most water. At an early stage of development, children are unable to see that both glasses of different shapes contain the same amount of water, although they have watched it being poured from a similar glass. At a later stage of development, the child will recognise that both glasses contain the same amount of water.

LIFE EVENTS

Whatever approach one takes to life stage development, it is not possible to ignore some of life's events which change our development, although they may not happen at the 'right' time. For example, a child may have to become a carer for a disabled parent – an occurrence that hastens the sense of responsibility before other children reach that stage. It can also be said that the birth order has an effect on personality. A firstborn child often assumes responsibility and care for younger siblings, and this may result in a more caring nature throughout life (how many of the people you know who work in the caring profession are firstborn children?). A second or third child may have a more carefree attitude throughout life.

An event which is threatening at any age is the onset of a life-threatening illness. Attitudes, values and habits of behaviour may change as a result of a person coming face to face with what may be an early death.

Transitions

Life events which cause significant change are called transitions. Examples of transitions include the change from being a pre-schooler to starting school; the physical and hormonal changes that happen in adolescence; the start of the first adult job; or retirement from work. With adequate preparation and forethought, these transitions can happen smoothly without anxiety or stress. However, in some cases, this does not happen and the process of adjustment to these periods results in emotional difficulties or physical illness. It is when this occurs that the person using counselling skills needs to use the full range of listening and responding skills, to enable the person to work out how best to make the adjustment more satisfactorily.

Adult life is made up of changes, or transitions, whether as a result of a natural stage of development, such as adolescence, or as a result of a life event, which may not be related to a specific stage. For example, having a first baby may occur at age 17 or 44, but the emotional effect is similar. These changes all require adaptation.

ACTIVITY

Recall some examples of transitions from your own life. To what extent were these related or not related to your 'age' stage?

Schlossberg (1989), described four kinds of transitions that occur:

◆ **Anticipated transitions**
These are events that a person plans and expects, like getting married.

◆ **Unanticipated transitions**
These are things that happen unexpectedly, like being diagnosed with a cancer, or being sacked from a job.

◆ **Non-event transitions**

These are things that are expected to happen, but do not. For example, not being able to have children or failing to get promotion at work.

◆ **Chronic hassle transitions**

These are things which go on unsatisfactorily for a long time, like trouble with a teenage son or chronic illness in the family.

It is important to note that what is an anticipated transition for one person, might be a non-event for another.

Crises

Not all transitions are a crisis for the individual. Some of the factors which turn a transition into a crisis are that:

◆ it is 'off-time' (for example if a child has to care for a parent, instead of vice versa)

◆ it cannot be controlled by the individual

◆ there was little warning of its approach

◆ it involved loss of status

◆ there was no ritual involved in the transition (sometimes called a 'rite of passage'), for example: eighteenth or twenty-first birthday party, or retirement presentation.

It is on these occasions, when a transition is a crisis that the helper using counselling skills is valuable.

ACTIVITY

Think about a time in your own life when a transition became a crisis. Spend a few minutes recalling the time and either writing it down or talking about it with a colleague. Then think about other people who were involved with you at that time. Try to identify what was helpful to you at that time and what was unhelpful.

Stressful life events

ACTIVITY

Most adults in their thirties, or over, will be able to list 20 or 30 transitions that they have experienced. Some of these will relate to the normal age developments we have discussed earlier in this chapter, but some may not. List those events in your own life that had a life-changing result for you. Next, put a star by those events in which a loss occurred for you. We will return to those later. Think about how stressful all the events on your list were for you and rate them in the order of stressfulness using number one as the event which was the most traumatic for you.

Holmes and Rahe in 1967, compiled a list of life events based on the amount of stress each caused and the readjustment required. It is worth keeping this list. If you, or someone you are working with, scores a number of points high on this list, there is a greater likelihood of stress, which can result in physical ill health or emotional disturbances. The worker with counselling skills can have a very useful, even life saving , role to play when this happens.

Life events ordered for stressfulness (Holmes and Rahe, 1967)

Rank	Life event
1.	Death of spouse
2.	Divorce
3.	Marital separation
4.	Jail term
5.	Death of close family member
6.	Personal injury or illness
7.	Marriage
8.	Fired at work
9.	Marital reconciliation
10.	Retirement
11.	Change in health of family member
12.	Pregnancy
13.	Sex difficulties
14.	Gain of new family member
15.	Business readjustment
16.	Change in financial status
17.	Death of close friend
18.	Change to different line of work
19.	Change in number of arguments with spouse
20.	Heavy mortgage repayments
21.	Foreclosure of mortgage or loan
22.	Change in responsibilities in work
23.	Son or daughter leaves home
24.	Trouble with in-laws
25.	Outstanding personal development
26.	Spouse begins or stops work
27.	Begin or end school
28.	Change in living conditions
29.	Revisions of personal habits
30.	Trouble with boss

ACTIVITY

How can someone with counselling skills help someone who is stressed?
It is important not to tell someone what to do or to tell them what you would do if it were you.

ATTACHMENT, SEPARATION AND LOSS

Some of the ideas connected with this part of the chapter, like maternal deprivation and the importance of bonding, may already be familiar to you. In this section the aim is to explain attachment theory and relate it to separation and loss and also to introduce you to the work of Bowlby, who has had a significant impact on the way children are cared for in our society.

JOHN BOWLBY (1907–1990)

John Bowlby trained in medicine and in psychoanalysis. He noticed the impact of loss and deprivation that had been suffered as a child by the adult patients who came to him. He also worked at one time with young delinquents and came to a similar conclusion. He thought that the Freudians, who preceded him, had overlooked the significance of real trauma in people's lives, instead concentrating on the unconscious and fantasy, such as the Oedipal complex. He thought that the environment (particularly mothering) in which a child was brought up, was a significant cause of psychological difficulties.

In 1952, he presented a famous film to the psychoanalytical society, made with James Robertson. This showed the intense distress experienced by a small girl when separated from her mother when she went to hospital.

James Robertson and his wife made two similar films of John and Thomas. John demonstrates clearly how a child reacted to being placed in a nursery and cared for by a number of well-meaning nurses, when his mother was admitted to hospital. He cried at first, but after a few days became very sad, unable to be comforted, withdrawn and apathetic. Thomas, by contrast, was fostered by the Robertsons and was encouraged to talk about the loss of his mother. He had a consistent mother substitute in Mrs Robertson. As a result, his distress was less severe. Bowlby and Robertson thought that the little girl and John would suffer emotional damage and possibly lasting effects as a result of their experience. Bowlby wrote:

> If it became a tradition that small children were never subjected to complete or prolonged separation from their parents in the same way that regular sleep and orange juice have become nursery traditions, I believe that many cases of neurotic character development would be avoided.
>
> (Bowlby, 1940)

Bowlby observed a number of adolescents who were referred to the child guidance clinic where he worked, for stealing, and noted that almost 40% of them had been separated from their mother for at least six months before they were five years old. In his paper, '44 juvenile thieves', he claimed that maternal separation was directly responsible for the delinquency. However, later writers have pointed out that he overlooked other social factors such as poverty.

Maternal deprivation

Bowlby thought that there was a clear link between the child's early bonding relationship with its mother and the ability to make close relationships throughout life. If the mother was unable to make a strong relationship, because she was depressed, absent or ill, this would affect the individual's ability to trust and make a close relationship in later life. Bowlby also linked this bonding, or attachment, with the way people handle loss in their lives. He suggested that people who are separated from their mothers early in life may re-experience those feelings later in life, whenever a loss occurs. He wrote a book on Charles Darwin, in which he explains Darwin's recurrent anxiety attacks as a result of his inability to grieve loss. The first loss Darwin experienced was his mother's death when he was eight.

Bowlby claimed that maternal deprivation caused behavioural, intellectual and emotional damage. Just as we in the UK have been horrified in recent years to see on our television sets the result of institutional care on the orphan children of Romania, so Bowlby was reacting to the institutional care provided for children in the UK in his own period. He felt strongly that absent mothers resulted in disturbed or delinquent children and that mothers should be with their children for the first five years of their lives. He argued that even brief separation had long-lasting effects, and would have been critical of the modern mother who returns to work after her child is born, leaving the child in a day nursery. But his greatest impact has been in the health service, where now, partly as a result of his research, parents are encouraged to stay with their young children in hospital.

Not everyone accepted Bowlby's work as valid. One of the scientists who evaluated his work was Michael Rutter. He found that anti-social behaviour was linked not only to maternal absence, but to family quarrels and the discord that often precedes divorce. Children whose mothers had died were just as likely as children whose mothers were living to be either delinquent or keep out of trouble.

Attachment

Attachment is the term Bowlby used to describe the quality of the relationship between a baby and its mother. Attachment means to feel safe and secure, rather than feeling dependent, fearful of rejection and afraid. If a child is close to an adult with whom s/he has an attachment, s/he feels happy and good, but if s/he is away from her/his parent s/he may feel unhappy and homesick. The mother also feels these feelings. If she leaves her new baby with the childminder for the first time, she will think endlessly about her baby and long to be with her/him.

A baby who is securely attached will be able to explore her/his environment in the knowledge that her/his mother is there, or will return for her/him. On the other hand, a baby who is insecurely attached, will cling to her/his mother in case s/he is abandoned and may hurt her if she shows signs of going away. Bowlby claimed that babies needed to make secure attachments during the first five years of life for emotional, social and intellectual development to take place. We have already looked at examples given by Bowlby of youngsters whose bond with their mothers was broken because of hospitalisation of either the child or the mother.

Bowlby also believed that attachment results in a special type of behaviour. He called this a 'control theory of attachment behaviour'. He believed, for example, that babies learn a way of behaving which keeps their mother close to them. This behaviour would include smiling and cooing. When a baby gurgles and chuckles in his cot, her/his mother is strongly motivated to go to the child and play and talk to her/him.

Separation

Separation is the term used by Bowlby to describe what happens when an attachment is broken. The first attachment for babies is with the mother and when the child is deprived of its mother, separation causes behaviours such as crying and despair, described later in the section on loss. But first we consider the ideas and conclusions of other writers on attachment and separation.

Harlow and Zimmerman

These writers, and later Harlow with his wife, observed baby monkeys who were deprived of their mothers and unable to form an attachment. They demonstrated that the monkeys had a need for cuddling as well as food. The monkeys were raised with two kinds of artificial mothers: a wire mother with a bottle attached and a wire mother covered with terry towelling but which did not provide food. The monkeys showed a clear preference for the terry-towelling mother when they weren't being fed. When they were frightened, they ran to the towelling mother; in fact, they would spend up to 18 hours a day clinging to the furry mother as they would their real mothers, although all their food came from the wire mother. The conclusion was that baby monkeys (and probably also baby children), need contact comfort independently from their need for food.

Another finding was that the monkeys clung more tightly than ever to the 'mothers' when they 'punished' them with blasts of air. A parallel can be seen with abused children who persist in attachment in spite of maltreatment and punishment.

Tizard and Hodges

These researchers studied children who had been placed in a residential nursery before they were a few months old – because their mothers were unmarried, and unable to bring them up. The system of caring was such that children did not become attached to any one member of staff. A child who was in the institution for four years might have up to 50 carers in that time because of the turnover of staff. Later the children were either adopted or returned to their mothers or remained in the nursery.

The children were studied when they were admitted to the institution and when they were four and eight years old. At four, they showed some signs of their experience. Those who were adopted or in foster homes were friendly towards all strangers. Those still in the institution were attention seeking, clung to adults and were quarrelsome with their peers. They showed no preference for individual carers and seemed to care for no-one. At eight, the adopted children were disturbed and difficult, but had made a much better adjustment than the children who remained in the nursery. But the children who returned to their birth mothers showed the most severe behavioural difficulties.

Loss

Loss is a term always used after a person has experienced the death of a loved one, but what is sometimes not appreciated is that life consists of many losses. Most changes in our lives involve a loss of some sort. For example, when we start playgroup, we lose our mother's continuous presence, and when we start work, we lose our freedom to use our time as we please.

ACTIVITY

List some of the losses related to some of the changes in your life up to the present time. To help you, look back to the activity on stressful life events (p. 26). You will be surprised how many there are. Think about the changes that you anticipate will occur in your life in the future (for example retirement). What losses will occur then?

We feel a sense of loss because we are attached to something or someone and the loss causes sadness and a sense of something missing. This is linked with Bowlby's idea that the need to attach, for a baby, is as important as needs such as food and warmth. Attachment is necessary for survival. A baby needs to attach for its security. When the attachment is broken or separation occurs, the sense of safety is also broken and this causes an emotional upheaval. If there is a strong attachment, then the sense of loss is stronger. The distress felt when we are faced with a loss is the price we pay for attachment.

Bowlby described three stages of behaviour which he observed when an attachment was broken. These are :

◆ protest

◆ despair

◆ detachment

Initially the child will be angry, cry and demand her/his mother back. Bowlby says this period may last several days. Later, s/he becomes more quietly sad and yearns for her/his mother, but seems to have given up hope and begins to despair. This despairing phase may alternate with the hope of the protesting phase. Finally, the child detaches. S/he appears to have forgotten her/his mother and if she returns during this stage, s/he may ignore her or even seem not to recognise her. Her/his behaviour during this stage may include temper tantrums and aggression. Throughout these stages the child is extremely upset, which Bowlby calls 'separation anxiety'. He believed that the way we experience and deal with subsequent losses in life are modelled on how we experience separation from our mother.

ACTIVITY

Bowlby believed that all the losses we experience in life and how we respond to them are based upon our first attachment to our mothers. Imagine two adults who both experience the break-up of a relationship. What would you expect to be the difference between the feelings, behaviour and coping ability between an adult who had grown up in a residential nursery with many carers and an adult whose childhood was spent within a secure family?

The death of a loved person is a very painful experience and the fact that we go through other losses in our lives, does not lessen that experience. The reaction to loss is called grief. Everyone reacts differently to loss and although there are some generalised feelings of sadness, other feelings vary according to the individual and the nature of the relationship which existed before the loss. Furthermore, when we are grieving, we often behave in ways which would have been unusual before the death. For example, some people find it comforting to sleep with an item of clothing which belonged to the person who has died. Do you think this might have any connection with Bowlby's control theory?

ACTIVITY

Think of the feelings that you, or someone else you know, felt at the time of the death of someone close to them. Tick any of these that were felt.

unhappiness	pain	anxiety
hopelessness	distress	unloved
hurt	shocked	disbelief
confused	unloved	panic
insecurity	sad	denial
numb	tired	vulnerable
sorry for oneself	guilty	fear
tearful	lonely	unsure
not wanted	worried	useless
helplessness		

Facing up to death

Most of us have experienced a death in our family or among close friends. Counselling skills users need to have considered the way they cope with losses of their own, before attempting to help others. If there is still 'unfinished' or unresolved grief, then it will be difficult for the counselling skills user to help another person with the feelings, thoughts and behaviours associated with their loss. This is because the counselling skills user will be looking for parallels all the time with his/her own loss and it will be difficult to stay in the grieving person's 'frame of reference'. So, with that in mind, complete the following activity. Take some time reflecting on your answers and discuss them with someone else, if possible.

ACTIVITY

Complete the following sentences:

◆ The first death I can remember was ...

◆ At the time I felt ...

◆ The first funeral (or wake or other ceremony) I attended was ...

◆ At the time I felt ...

◆ The most recent death I experienced was ...

◆ The feelings were ...

◆ The most difficult death I experienced was ...

◆ The feelings were ...

◆ I coped with these deaths by ...

◆ If someone close to me were to die, I would cope by ...

Using counselling skills

Initially when people experience a loss, the most important thing to do is to provide warmth, and comfort to help with the shock, and to be there if the person wants us.

After the initial shock, the helpful counselling skills to use are those of attending and listening. The person may need to talk over and over again about their feelings and how and why the death happened.

The counselling skills user can provide the most help at this time by being there to talk whenever it is wanted. Often grieving people feel that they cannot burden their friends and relatives too often, and try to keep their thoughts and feelings to themselves. The counselling skills user can listen and respond, reflecting and paraphrasing and staying with the grief – without distracting the griever from what is clearly the most important issue on his/her mind.

It is important to be accepting of any 'strange' behaviour at this time. Some people need to keep physically busy by, for example, walking, cleaning or digging. Others may feel the need to avoid meeting people and may drive miles to avoid using their regular shops in case they meet people they know.

The grieving person will be experiencing a range of feelings, some of which we have identified earlier. It is important that these feelings are acknowledged and accepted and that the listener is not tempted to talk about his/her own losses (unless asked, and then only briefly).

It is also essential, as in all situations where counselling skills are used, not to give advice. It is particularly important not to encourage or persuade the griever to do anything which may lead to later regret. For example, the possessions of the deceased should not be immediately despatched to the charity shops or given away to others, if the griever is not ready to part with them. Above all a grieving person needs time – time to talk, time to think, to cry and be sad, time to look at photographs and revisit memories and time to just be.

SELF-CONCEPT

How we behave, think and feel, results from the interplay between two factors: the world outside ourselves (our social surroundings) and the world inside ourselves (our sense of self). Imagine a man who would like to become an actor. The possibility of his joining an amateur dramatics group results from first, the existence of such a group and secondly, how confident he feels to make the contact and join. But many of life's issues are more complicated than this simple example and we don't know much of our 'self'. It is essential that people who use counselling skills work on the lifelong process of discovering themselves and begin to become self-aware.

ACTIVITY

Complete the following sentence 20 times: 'I am ...'.

Your answers will begin to define your self-concept. Some of your sentences will probably refer to your role in life – 'I am a mother', 'I am a teacher' etc but other answers will refer to your individual traits – 'I am a patient person', or 'I am afraid to look at myself for fear of what I might uncover'.

If you found this activity hard, be assured that you are in good company. Benjamin Franklin is reported to have said, in 1758, 'There are three things extremely hard, steel, a diamond and to know one's self'.

The self is normally seen as having three parts: self-image, self-esteem and the ideal self. The self-image is the kind of person we think we are, whether or not we like it. You worked out what sort of self-image you have of yourself in the last activity. It will include major social roles, such as our gender and age, together with what sort of person we think we are.

Self-esteem refers to our self-evaluation, or sense of self-worth. It relates to the extent to which we approve of ourselves. Certain characteristics or abilities have greater value in society than others, and our self-esteem reflects that. For example, sporting prowess is valued by most groups in society, whereas academic prowess is not acceptable in some teenage cultures.

Our ideal self is the self we dream of being, a rich self, clever self, thin self etc. The greater the gap between our self-image and our ideal self, the lower our self-esteem will be.

How does our self-concept develop?

What is it in our lives which affects our sense of identity, our image and our self-esteem?

Much of our idea of what we are results from the messages we receive from others. These may be verbal, visual, physical, through observing the body language of others or financial. They are from all significant others – including family, friends, employers, teachers, colleagues, the environment and the media. They may be positive messages or negative. Examples of positive messages range from praise or promotion, to a smile or love. Negative messages can be verbal or physical and can include a frown or verbal rejection.

This sense of who we are and how valued we are, is constantly changing and adapting to new impressions of ourselves that we form from new people we meet.

ACTIVITY

Re-read the last sentence. What important message does it contain for those of us who are using counselling skills?

Some marginalised groups in society, such as people with disabilities and older people, receive more experiences which may make them have a lower self-esteem than, for example, a young able-bodied male will receive. It is particularly difficult for people in some groups to achieve and maintain a positive view of themselves.

As long ago as 1902, Charles H. Cooley wrote about a 'looking-glass self' and said that the self that is most important is a reflection largely from the minds of others.

As well as receiving messages from others, we also compare ourselves with others, through all our interactions and through our experience of how others are portrayed in the media. If we see television advertisements for gleaming, unused houses, we are apt to compare our own slightly worn, and perhaps cluttered surroundings unfavourably. So it is with people.

Our roles in society also play a significant part in our self-concept. If we have a high-status role, such as lawyer or doctor, we may feel differently about ourselves than someone who has a job which is deemed by society to have a lower status, or less value.

ACTIVITY

List some of the roles you play in life, not just in your job, but also in your family, with your interests and in your community. How are these roles valued? If you placed a value on each of these roles, with one given for a highly rated role and ten given for a low-status role, what would you put for the roles on your list?

Another significant factor in our self-concept is our life experiences, which can have a powerful impact on how we see ourselves. Positive experiences, such as academic success or achievement will result in good feelings about ourselves, whereas a different set of experiences, such as abuse or the break up of a relationship may lower our value of ourselves.

Importance of having a healthy self-esteem

Anne Dickson (1989) wrote:

> Self esteem stems from a strong, rooted sense of self worth, which survives both failure and success: it survives mistakes, disappointment and most of all self esteem survives acceptance and rejection from others.
>
> (Dickson, 1989)

This is a definition of healthy self-esteem. Unfortunately this is not held by all of the people with whom we come into contact when we are practising our counselling skills.

ACTIVITY

How is your own self-esteem? What has happened in your life that has made you feel good about yourself? Can you identify some of the factors which made this happen? What has happened which made you feel bad about yourself? Can you see what caused these feelings?

Many of the life events which make us feel good or bad about ourselves are outside our control, such as illness, loss of job, unhappy relationships or getting a good job. However, we can learn to value the self. Perhaps the goal that we should strive towards for ourselves is to have a healthy and realistic self-esteem, not inflated to the extent that we believe we can be all things to all people, but equally not so low that we believe we are useless and incapable of anything worth doing.

Some of the causes of low self-esteem

Some of our earliest good feelings come from being looked after, cuddled, loved and fed. If our needs are not met, we feel bad, and experience a sense of helplessness. Most of us grow up with more good experiences and feelings than bad, and so we can absorb the occasional bad feelings without harm. However, if adults consistently give us the message that we are not wanted, or we are abandoned by the adults with whom we have our attachment, we can become convinced that we are not loved because we are unlovable. A sense of worthlessness results.

Bowlby argues that if we do not get love and approval as a child, and therefore a sense of our own worth, we block or sabotage later attachments, and therefore have difficulties in later life in forming close and meaningful relationships. Outside the family, the wider society gives us messages about our worth. If we are continually receiving negative messages, for example because our skin or hair is the wrong colour, or because we live in the wrong family or the wrong area, we can internalise these attitudes and believe ourselves to have lower value than others.

Improving our own self-esteem

We cannot hope to work with people with low self esteem if we do not value ourselves. Many of us find it easy to be critical of ourselves, but are conditioned not to see the good points. The following activity attempts to change this.

> **ACTIVITY**
>
> Take a clean sheet of paper and write a list of all the things that are good about yourself and the things you are good at. You should be able to reach the bottom of an A4 sheet of file paper! If you find this difficult, get together with a friend or colleague and see if you can help each other to extend your lists.

I often give this activity to new students on counselling skills courses. At the beginning of their course, they sometimes have difficulty with this, but when we repeat the activity at the end of the course, when they have worked on their self-awareness for a year or two, it is much easier.

Working with people who have low self-esteem

If someone you are working with has low self-esteem, it is important to help them feel better about themselves.

> **ACTIVITY**
>
> Think about some of the ways in which you might help someone to value themselves. It may take some time, especially if the person has had a lifetime's experience of believing s/he is of little value, but it can be done! What might you do to help?

Person-centred approach to the self

One of what is known as the core conditions of the person-centred approach is unconditional positive regard or acceptance. Rogers believed that in order to be loved, children have to learn to behave in certain ways. Some of these ways are not what they feel and may be the opposite of how they want to behave. Love is therefore conditional on the children denying their true feelings and conforming to the expectations of others. Children eventually learn to repress 'unacceptable' behaviour and feelings and to behave according to expectations. For example, a child may be praised for being helpful, but criticised for being a 'cry baby'. As s/he grows, a sense of self develops and as positive rewards are received from others, a high sense of self-esteem and a positive self-image grows.

However, if a child receives negative responses from others, the self-image will be negative and self-esteem low. S/he will feel bad about her/himself. Also, if s/he has to behave in ways in which s/he would not naturally behave, in order to gain positive regard from others, a state of incongruence will result, together with bad feelings.

Once the sense of self has been established in childhood, people try to maintain this, and some of the ways of behaving, feeling and thinking which result, get in the way of the person reaching his/her highest potential (which is known as self-actualisation).

ACTIVITY

Think about some of the ways you 'conformed' as a child. Did you, for example, eat your meals at a table and with a knife and fork? Why did you do this? What would have happened if you had picked up your food with your fingers? Would there have been parental disapproval? Can you think of other examples like this?

ACTIVITY

If an adult, perhaps in the place where you work, is always silent in meetings, and seems afraid ever to speak out, what do you think might have happened to that person in early childhood?

Cognitive approach to the self

One cognitive view of the self originated from the work of Aaron T. Beck (1976). This view of the self is based on the idea that as we develop as people, because of our unique personal history and experiences, we develop beliefs and assumptions about ourselves. We also develop them about others and the world we live in. For example, a belief about oneself might be 'I am worthless', about others, 'other people cannot be trusted to meet my needs' and about the world, 'the world is a frightening place to live in'.

These beliefs and assumptions become a 'set of rules', by which we live our lives, although we may not be aware of them in that way. They are formed mainly in our early years and may be revised as a result of later experiences. Included in these beliefs and assumptions are core beliefs, or schemata, such as, 'I am useless' and assumptions, which are an 'if ... then ...' way of coping with the core beliefs. For example, if a person believes 'I am useless' s/he may develop the assumption, 'If I am always helpful and work very, very hard, then other people will not see how useless I am'.

ACTIVITY

If a person holds these core beliefs and assumptions, what might have happened in early life to have led to these? If a person holds these beliefs and assumptions, what type of behaviour or personality might result?

As a result of our beliefs and assumptions, which make up our self, everyone will have a different way of appraising life events. The same event will cause one person to react differently from another person, depending on the core beliefs and assumptions held.

When something unpleasant happens in our lives, these core beliefs can be triggered, although they may have been dormant before. The 'triggering' takes the form of a negative automatic thought, or NAT, a thought which flashes into our minds so fast that we barely perceive it. Examples of NATs are, 'They hate me', 'I'll lose my job', 'Anything I will say will be wrong' and 'I'm stupid'. These NATs can be so much part of ourselves, and such an immediate response, that we are unaware of them. The NAT may result in an unpleasant emotion and perhaps an unhelpful action or behaviour, which in itself feeds back to the NAT. This is described as a vicious circle. An example follows:

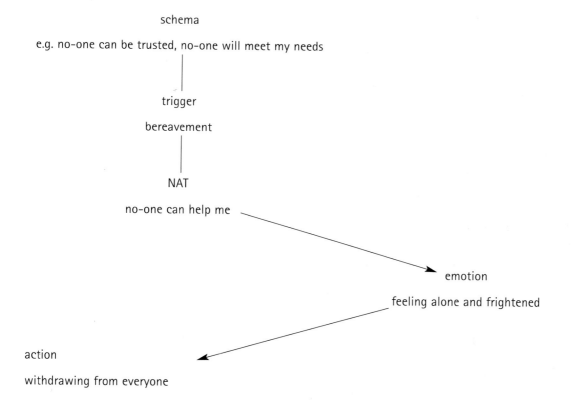

schema

e.g. no-one can be trusted, no-one will meet my needs

trigger

bereavement

NAT

no-one can help me

emotion

feeling alone and frightened

action

withdrawing from everyone

Sometimes a further factor is added to the circle: physical symptoms. Someone who is bereaved may also feel tired and lacking in energy. As a result they feel worse emotionally and even more likely to withdraw from other people.

ACTIVITY

Think of a time recently when you felt something unpleasant (sad, angry, frightened etc). See if you can work out for yourself what thoughts and actions and possibly physical symptoms made up your vicious circle. For example:

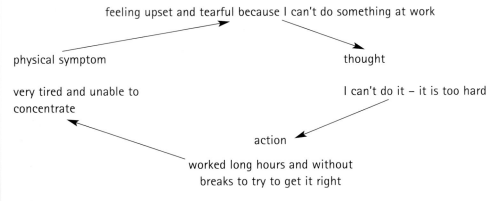

feeling upset and tearful because I can't do something at work

physical symptom

thought

very tired and unable to concentrate

I can't do it – it is too hard

action

worked long hours and without breaks to try to get it right

Can you also identify what triggered this circle? And perhaps the core belief from which it stemmed?

In this example, the trigger event might have been that the boss was angry with the person. The core belief, which stemmed from early childhood, would have been, 'I am no good.'

PSYCHODYNAMIC APPROACH TO THE SELF

According to the psychodynamic view, the sense of self develops soon after birth, when the ego boundaries are established – the 'me' and 'not me'. This is Erikson's second stage, when the baby is still dependent on the mother, but is beginning to separate from her.

There are aspects of the self which may conflict with consciously held ideals. A child might have been taught and believe that it is important to put others first, but this may conflict with deeper needs to be selfish. The result is either that the ideals are denied or that they may become unconscious. The idea of part of ourselves being 'forgotten' is called repression. However, it is not actually forgotten and may return to haunt us, unless we deal, in some way, with these troublesome issues in our unconscious. An example of repression is when a young child has a life-threatening accident, perhaps a near-drowning experience. S/he may repress the memory of this. It is too painful for her/him to recall it in her/his conscious memory, but it does not leave her/him. S/he may wonder why, as an adult, s/he has a great fear of water and swimming.

In psychodynamic terms, the self includes the conscious, the unconscious and what is called the pre-conscious – those thoughts and memories which are not present in the forefront of the mind, but can be recalled with some effort. One way of illustrating the various levels of awareness between the self and others is shown as follows (modified from Luft, 1966).

	KNOWN TO SELF	UNKNOWN TO SELF
KNOWN TO OTHERS	the public self	the blind self
UNKNOWN TO OTHERS	the secret self	the unconscious self

The public self is that part of ourselves which is available for all to see. The secret self, we admit to ourselves but keep from others. The blind self is seen by others but not known by ourselves and the unconscious self is unavailable to both ourselves and others, but may continue to influence our emotions and behaviour, as we have illustrated in the example.

The aim of self-awareness is to increase the open, public self and decrease the other areas. We can reduce the blind self by feedback from others, and reduce the secret self by being more open. There are various ways in which we can work on our unconscious self, including counselling, through hypnosis or by examining our dreams.

Importance of self-awareness in the use of counselling skills

What is the relevance of this knowledge of the self to anybody who practises counselling skills? The answer is – a great deal.

There are three elements of any counselling skills course: knowledge of the skills, an understanding of the theory that underpins the skills, and self-awareness. Self-awareness can be explored in self-development groups and journal writing, but above all it requires the student to be prepared to look at him/herself in a way that they may never have done before.

It is the self-awareness which makes the teaching and learning of counselling skills quite different from that of almost any other subject. It may involve some painful and difficult uncovering of hidden emotions and thoughts. On the other hand, the experience is enriching and challenging and an added, sometimes unexpected bonus for the student, which may change lives! Most students I have taught over the years rate their learning about themselves as something which changes their lives permanently for the better.

Why do we need to be self-aware? We need to be aware of ourselves for several reasons. If we are using our counselling skills with someone who begins to talk about an experience which is similar to an experience of our own, we need to be able to differentiate between our own thoughts and feelings and those of the other person. We also need to have 'worked' on our own issues so that our thoughts and feelings do not get in the way of our empathic listening.

How can we help ourselves to become more self-aware? There are many ways. Hopefully some of the activities in this chapter will have helped. There are ways of reflecting on ourselves, and creative ways of exploring ourselves, but above all we get feedback from our friends and colleagues and, if this is honest, it helps us to see ourselves as we really are, rather than as our ideal self.

ACTIVITY

Complete the following sentences. Your sentences will help you to think about yourself and how you value yourself.

◆ One thing I really like about myself ...
◆ When people ignore me, I ...
◆ When someone praises me, I ...
◆ Those who really know me ...
◆ I am at my very best with people when ...
◆ I feel lonely when ...
◆ I get hurt when ...
◆ Few people know that ...
◆ I dislike people who ...
◆ I hate people to see that I ...

CONCLUSION

This chapter has been about the stages of life, attachment and loss and the self-concept. The work of some of the important theorists in the area is briefly described. But the chapter has also been about you, the reader. The importance of self-awareness for a practitioner of counselling skills has been described. This is a lifelong process and hopefully many of the activities you have completed will have helped you to find out more about yourself, as well as to understand more fully some of the theoretical ideas in this chapter. This will be helpful both to the people with whom you practise your counselling skills and to you, in the relationships you have, in the way you feel about yourself and the thoughts and ideas that you have.

BIBLIOGRAPHY

Beck, A.T. (1976) *Cognitive therapy and the emotional disorders*, International Universities Press.

Bowlby, J. (1971) *Attachment and loss*, Penguin.

Brown, D., and Pedder, J. (1979) *Introduction to psychotherapy: an outline of psychodynamic principles and practice*, Routledge.

Dickson, A. (1989) *A woman in your own right*, Quartet.

Erikson, E.H. (1963) *Childhood and society*, Norton.

Freud, S. (1978) *New introductory lectures*, Penguin.

Freud, S. (1986) *Essential psychoanalysis*, Penguin.

Harlow, H.F. and Zimmerman, R. (1959) 'Affectional responses in the infant monkey', in *Science*, 130, 421–432.

Holmes, J. (1993) *John Bowlby and attachment theory*, Routledge.

Holmes, T.H., and Rahe, R.H. (1967) 'The social readjustment rating scale', in *Journal of Psychosomatic Research*, 11.

Piaget, J. (1969) *The psychology of the child*, Routledge.

Rogers, C. (1980) *A way of being*, Houghton Mifflin.

Tizard, B., and Hodges, J. (1978) 'The effect of early institutional rearing on the development of 8-year-old children', *Journal of Child Psychology and Psychiatry*, 19, 99–118.

Wills, F., and Sanders, D. (1997) *Cognitive therapy – transforming the image*, Sage.

3

Theoretical perspectives – Sheila Trahar

This chapter is written for people undertaking counselling skills courses who wish to use some theoretical framework to underpin their understanding of people and the nature of change. It is also written for the reader who may be considering going on to specific counselling training, and who wants to begin to distinguish between theoretical approaches. Most of the theoretical models of counselling have within them some underpinning relationship that uses communications or counselling skills. These skills are used intentionally within the structures and processes of a particular model.

Counselling is a relatively new activity that developed in the latter part of the twentieth century and continues to flourish in its availability in these early days of the twenty-first. Its development, particularly in western society, needs to be seen in the context of changing social structures such as the decline in the significance of religion and the fragmentation of the family. This continued development has highlighted the need for differentiation between professionally trained counsellors and those who employ counselling skills in order to carry out their role more effectively, whether that role be as teacher, human resources manager or doctor/nurse.

More than 400 different approaches to counselling have been identified, each one of which can be traced back to one of three major theoretical approaches: psychodynamic, person-centred and cognitive-behavioural. This chapter offers an overview of these three theoretical approaches citing those people considered to be influential in developing each approach, together with an indication of the strengths and limitations of each. Activities will enable you to consider how relevant some of the concepts are to your own personal experience, and will help you to examine their strengths and limitations in your professional context.

PSYCHODYNAMIC APPROACH

The psychodynamic approach to counselling is derived from the work of Freud (1856–1939) who developed psychoanalysis, the therapeutic application of the science of the mind, as a method of treatment for emotional problems. Two colleagues, Carl Jung (1875–1961) and Alfred Adler (1870–1937), became disillusioned with many aspects of his theories and broke away from Freud to develop their own psychodynamic theories. In any of the psychodynamic approaches to counselling, exploration of the client's past will play a major part. So too will the aim of enabling the client to gain insight into the reasons for their behaviour.

Freudian theory was closely allied with the mechanistic-deterministic outlook of nineteenth-century science and, as with other theoretical approaches to counselling, it is important to remain aware of the social context from which it emerged. It was regarded by many as painting too bleak a picture of human nature, largely because Freud based many of his conclusions on his study of neurotic, rather than healthy, people. This approach is also criticised because many aspects of it do not have and cannot be made to have scientifically respectable proven procedures. However, all counselling theory is influenced by Freudian ideas, and whilst many of those who followed Freud later rejected some of his key concepts, evidence of his hypotheses is visible in each major theoretical approach. Outside the counselling field, it is almost impossible to ignore the effect Freud has had on twentieth and twenty-first century western thinking. He created a cultural change in how people view themselves.

ACTIVITY

What words and phrases can you identify that we use in everyday life that may have their origins in Freud's thinking?

Freud's early training was medical, and the biological perspective is at the heart of the psychodynamic approach, where the central focus is that of mind and body together. Freud considered the human organism to be a complex energy system that derived energy from food and expended energy for circulation, respiration, muscular exercise, perceiving, thinking and remembering. He saw no reason to assume that the energy providing the power for breathing or digesting was any different, except in form, from the energy needed for thinking and remembering. The point of contact between the energy of the body and that of the mind/personality is the id and its instincts. Instincts create needs that must be satisfied, and behaviour, which is usually a result of the interaction between the three major systems of the personality or psyche – the id, ego and superego – is directed towards a reduction of the resultant tension.

The id is the original system of the personality, and its aim is the avoidance of pain and the securing of pleasure. The second system of the personality to form is the ego. The basic distinction between the id and the ego is that the id knows only the subjective reality of the mind, whereas the ego distinguishes between the mind and the external world. It is that part of the mind that deals with reality. The superego is the third and last system of personality to be developed and its main functions are to inhibit the impulses of the id, particularly those of a sexual or aggressive nature. It might be defined as the conscience. The id and most of the superego were considered by Freud to be largely unconscious and, although behaviour is almost always the product of an interaction between these three systems, it is considered to be under the control of forces, for example childhood fantasies and repressed memories that the individual is unable to consciously acknowledge. Freudian theory claims that we are often unaware of our motives. If we were more aware of these we would be able to make better decisions in life. However, we remain reluctant or 'resistant' to acknowledging these hidden motives, and may often repeat past patterns of behaviour.

Freud's contention was that we are organisms who structure our lives defensively to avoid anxiety. The psychodynamic approach suggests that our central identity, whether we call it ego or self, has to be constantly defended against anxiety, in order to limit disruption and maintain a sense of unity. Psychodynamic theory is concerned with the individual's internal representations of the external world. These internal versions of the world are systematically distorted by unconsciously setting up defence mechanisms such as repression, denial and projection.

One of the other main concepts in Freudian theory is that early childhood experiences are significant in later personality development, and that the effects of these experiences continue to influence the adult without her/his awareness.

Post-Freudians – Jung and Adler

Jung saw human development as a lifelong quest for fulfilment and integration of self, rather than the more biologically based instinct drives espoused by Freud. Much of Jung's work was with schizophrenics and this, together with his interest in religion and eastern philosophy, may have stimulated his writings on symbolism and archetypes. He developed a theory of personality that was very clearly influenced by the Freudian concepts of id, ego and superego. He named his systems the ego, personal unconscious and the collective unconscious. The ego is similar to Freud's ego, the personal unconscious is the domain containing repressed feelings and incidents, and the collective unconscious is that part of the mind common to all humankind. He saw the latter as being constructed through archetypes, which are symbolic representations of universal aspects of human experience. The four major archetypes are.

◆ **persona**: this is the face which we present to the world. This face may be based on what we believe others expect us to be
◆ **animus/anima**: respectively, these are the unconscious masculine side of the female and the unconscious female side of the male
◆ **shadow**: the shadow is similar to the id, in that it is the side of the self which is uncontrolled and therefore often denied
◆ **self** : this is the integration of all parts of the personality into a healthy functioning individual.

Alfred Adler

Adler, in contrast to Freud, believed that all people are born with a need to belong to a social group, whether this is the family or the wider society. This is in contrast to Freudian theory, that was concerned with the individual in relation to her/himself, with very little focus on how the individual relates to others and to the environment. Adler believed that there were three tasks, which he termed life tasks, demanded of individuals. These are work, friendship and love. Adler believed that satisfaction and fulfilment derived from successful completion of these tasks and that psychological problems may occur when people feel inferior to others in their social group. He placed much emphasis on position in one's family of origin, believing that each child, having been born in an inferior position will struggle to become superior. The eldest child will be an only child for some time but when s/he is joined by subsequent siblings, s/he will need to maintain her/his superiority. The youngest child may choose to remain the baby of the family and behave in ways which reinforce this, such as lacking a sense of responsibility and general playfulness. Middle children, who are neither oldest nor youngest, will often feel misplaced, as if they do not fit in anywhere.

ACTIVITY

The following activity is a way of exploring the usefulness of some of Adler's key concepts. If you are part of a group, divide yourselves up according to your place in your family of origin – oldest child, youngest child, middle child, only child (if there is a large gap between you and your nearest sibling, you may feel as if you fit more comfortably with the only children). It is important to position yourself according to your experience in your family. For example, if your parents lost a child/children before you were born, then strictly speaking you were not their firstborn but you would probably still consider yourself to be the oldest child.

In each group, consider the following questions together:

◆ How did you experience this family life position when you were growing up? What words/phrases would you use to describe it?

◆ How did you feel about your siblings? About being an only child?

◆ What would you like to say to your siblings about your experience?

A way of bringing this activity into the whole training group is to then 'speak' to each of the other groups as if they were your siblings and to hear their responses to you. If you are doing this activity on your own, then you might care to write down what you would like to say.

It is then useful and interesting to consider how you behave today and, as Adler believed in the value of work as a significant and fulfilling life task, think especially about how you behave at work. For example, as the eldest child in my family I grew up feeling not only very responsible for my younger brother but also for most things that happened in my family. As an adult I am aware that I still carry this responsibility. I take my work very seriously and often receive feedback on my serious nature. I have come to value this serious side of myself because I can see that it helps people feel they can trust me and have faith in me. However, the other side of this is that my playful side (which I associate with my younger brother who was allowed to get away with anything) often goes unrecognised; people find it difficult to see that I can be both serious and playful.

Key terms

Transference

This refers to the notion that, whilst in counselling, the client 'transfers' onto the counsellor emotions which are connected with a significant figure from the past. This is usually mother, father or siblings. Aspects of these relationships, which the client has repressed, are then enacted in the counselling setting. In the therapeutic encounter, repressed memories can be recovered, repeated and reintegrated. Particular attention is paid to the transference by attempting to show how it influences, both positively and negatively, the relationship between counsellor and client. Psychodynamic counsellor makes deliberate use of the positive and negative transference by bringing it out into the open and sometimes deliberately encouraging it to develop.

Countertransference

Countertransference refers to the feelings which the client evokes in the counsellor and which the counsellor will make use of in order to try and understand the client's own material. In psychodynamic counselling there will be a necessity not only for the counsellor to explore her/his countertransference in supervision, but to have undertaken extensive personal counselling in order to gain insight into the sources of her/his own conflicts.

The unconscious

The unconscious is the part of the mind which is inaccessible to the conscious mind, but which controls much of our behaviour and emotions. Freud believed that this area of the mind is only accessible through dreams and fantasies. In the first activity in this section you were asked to think about the words and phrases we commonly use that may have their origins in Freud's thinking. You will probably have remembered the phrase 'Freudian slip', used when someone says something that is apparently not intentional but which may be an example of what they really think or feel. This may be seen as an example of the unconscious at work.

Free association

The client is encouraged to speak of whatever comes to mind, to 'free associate'. Having encouraged this free association, the psychodynamic counsellor proceeds to link apparently disparate sentences and then to offer an interpretation. The aim of this intervention is to elucidate unconscious feelings or ideas of which the client is unaware. A skilful interpretation will observe those feelings that are close enough to the surface to enter into consciousness. This linking can reunite split-off, or separated, feelings that the client has been unable to acknowledge as belonging together.

Dream interpretation

Both Freud and Jung believed that dreams have much to tell us about the unconscious mind, and so the interpretation of dreams is an important aspect of the psychodynamic approach. The psychodynamic counsellor will encourage clients to record their dreams and to use them as a vehicle to gain greater insight into the underlying motivation for their feelings and behaviour.

Resistances and defences

These terms refer to those childhood experiences which were so painful that they are buried away from conscious awareness; repressed as a way of defence. The individual is then unconsciously resistant to revealing and discussing this material, and sets up defence mechanisms in order to protect her/himself. One of the goals of the psychodynamic counsellor will be to break through these resistances and defences. Any resistance to this within the counselling process will be viewed as a continuation of the client's defence mechanisms.

Projection

The individual is unable to accept her/his more difficult feelings and so unconsciously projects them onto another person. An example of projection is a person who has difficulty in recognising and accepting her/his feelings of anger. This may be for many reasons, including the way s/he was treated when s/he became angry as a child. S/he may project her/his anger onto other people, who are then experienced as being angry with her/him. Energy is directed towards continuing to deny one's own anger and blaming others for their angry behaviour rather than using the energy to accept and integrate it.

ACTIVITY

Work with a partner and draw or depict your partner visually in some way. Now describe and explain your picture to your partner. Notice whether there are any things in your description of your partner that are also a description of you. This can be a useful and visual way of showing that we do often seek to find aspects of ourselves in others, or that we can feel more comfortable depicting someone else as angry or aggressive. We can 'project' parts of ourselves onto others.

This is an interesting activity because it demonstrates how we all tend to fantasise about other people when we don't know very much about them. It can also show how people's fantasies can also be very accurate because you yourself are giving away more about yourself than you think you are.

The really interesting part is when you ask people who you remind them of. I experienced this when I ran a similar exercise with a group of people on a counselling skills course. I was aware that one person in the group had been very warm towards me from the first moment we met. She was very attentive to me, very enthusiastic about the course I was delivering, would seek me out at the end of the evening. During this particular activity, she realised that I reminded her of her best friend from school, who she had not seen for many years. She realised that she was behaving towards me as if I was this person. Although I liked her attention, I did not feel that my behaviour towards her warranted it, and so it was very helpful for both of us when she made this discovery. It can also explain the opposite and help you to understand why someone might be behaving in an unpleasant way, when you know that you have not done anything to deserve it. If your role involves any kind of authority you may well be very familiar with this, as it is not uncommon for people to project/transfer onto the 'teacher', 'manager' all the unpleasant experiences they have had with someone else in the past in that role or, indeed, any authority figure, such as a parent.

ACTIVITY

This activity works well in a small group with a volunteer who is willing to be the 'blank screen' onto which others project their fantasies. It is a way of experiencing what can happen in transference (and projection). The volunteer invites colleagues to write down everything they know about her/him. You need to feel able to allow people to use anything they know about you so if you've shared something very private with someone, then be careful! Then ask them to write down their fantasies about you – what do they imagine about you? Again, you need to give people permission to write down anything. Next ask them to write down who you remind them of. Finally, ask them to write down how they feel about that person. Then ask them to read out what they've written and to be honest!

Techniques

The classical image of psychoanalysis is of the analyst presenting her/himself as a blank screen upon which the client can project her/his feelings. This is probably less true of the psychodynamic counsellor today, who will aim to establish a warm relationship with her/his clients whilst remaining detached, in order to allow the transference and to interpret the resistances occurring in the therapeutic process. The counsellor working with this approach is unlikely to reveal aspects of her/his own life or to share feelings with the client.

Strengths

Psychodynamic concepts and ideas have not only influenced all models of counselling, but have also created a cultural shift in how we view ourselves. They also have wider application to the understanding of groups and organisations. Freud developed the first comprehensive personality theory and identified the significance of early childhood experiences in later development. These approaches work well if you see a connection between your thoughts and your actions, and already have some capacity to reflect on your actions.

Limitations

The focus of the psychodynamic approach remains on internalised versions of the self, with very little emphasis on the social context of the external world. Psychodynamic counselling can be very long and expensive and has, therefore, been criticised as being elitist. It has also been criticised for being based on far-fetched and implausible ideas, which since they rest on the concept of the unconscious can never be tested.

ACTIVITY

Which aspects of the psychodynamic approach do you find useful? Less useful?

What do you consider to be its strengths and limitations? How helpful is an understanding of psychodynamic concepts in your context?

PERSON-CENTRED APPROACH

Experience for me is the highest authority. The touchstone of validity is my own experience ... it is to experience that I must return again and again, to discover a clear approximation to truth as it is in process of becoming in me.

(Rogers, 1967)

Person-centred counselling was originally developed in the 1940s as a reaction against psychoanalytic therapy. Largely credited to Carl Rogers, a US psychologist, originally trained in the Freudian tradition, it has its roots in humanistic psychology and the primarily European concepts of existentialism and phenomenology.

Phenomenology is a method of philosophical enquiry evolved by the German philosopher Husserl in the mid-1930s. It is based on the view that valid knowledge and understanding can be gained by exploring the way events are experienced by individuals. It is an extension of the term 'intentionality', the notion that all consciousness is directed towards interpreting the real world in a meaningful manner. Intentionality was a term originally coined by the philosopher Franz Brentano, whose lectures Freud attended.

Existentialism is associated with the work of writers such as the twentieth-century French philosopher Sartre and the nineteenth-century philosopher Kierkegaard and focuses on the human awareness of the finiteness of life, conceiving people as always being in process of 'becoming'. Phenomenological and existential thinking has significantly influenced the humanistic approach to psychology, which offers potential for understanding and locating the power of one's feelings and experience. Humanistic psychology sees the person as acting to fulfil two primary needs, which are independent of biological survival needs. The first need is self-actualisation, or the need to fulfil one's potential. The second is the need to be loved and valued, and to experience oneself as having an effect upon the lives of others. Humanistic philosophy places the emphasis on relationships with other people, believing that these will provide the acceptance and valuing which aid growth and self-actualisation. Abraham Maslow (1908–1970) was a US psychologist who formulated a theory of human motivation based on a set of innate needs, which he believed gave satisfaction and meaning to life. This 'hierarchy of needs' suggests that once the basic, biological needs for survival, such as food and warmth, are met then the individual will be motivated by higher-order needs, such as relationship and esteem needs, culminating in what he defined as self-actualisation needs; the need to fulfil personal potential.

The person-centred approach to counselling, originally developed by Rogers in the late 1940s after the Second World War, is grounded in this positive view of humanity, which sees the person as innately striving towards becoming fully functioning. Rogers was a psychologist who originally worked from classical psychoanalytic beliefs, regarding his role as being one of helping his clients to gain insight into their behaviour and motivation. However, during a period of work at the Society for the Prevention of Cruelty to Children in Rochester, New York, he met a client who convinced him that she was capable of directing her own therapy. He noticed that if he really listened to what she was telling him, setting aside any need to offer an expert interpretation based on his perception of her situation, then she was able to find her own solutions. Based on the subjective view of human experience, the person-centred approach emphasises the individual's resources for becoming aware and for resolving blocks to personal growth.

In the counselling relationship, it is the client, not the counsellor who is at the centre of the counselling. The basic assumption is that in the context of a personal relationship with a caring counsellor, the client experiences previously denied or distorted feelings and increases self-awareness. Clients are empowered by their participation in a therapeutic relationship and actualise their potential for growth, wholeness, spontaneity and inner-directedness. The client has the capacity for resolving life problems effectively, without interpretation and direction from an expert counsellor. This approach focuses on fully experiencing the present moment, learning to accept oneself and deciding on ways to change. It establishes the individual's potential for directing their own lives and views mental health as a congruence between what one wants to become and what one actually is.

Therapeutic relationship

Rogers emphasised the attitudes and personal characteristics of the counsellor, and the quality of the client/counsellor relationship as the prime determinants of the outcomes of counselling. The qualities of the counsellor that determine the relationship include genuineness, warmth, accurate empathy, unconditional acceptance of and respect for the client, permissiveness, caring and the ability to communicate these attitudes to the client. Given the right conditions, the client is able to transfer her/his learning from the counselling relationship to relationships with others.

This approach, in its pure form, is totally dependent upon the ability of the counsellor to be authentic with her/himself, to be aware of her/his own emotional responses and to share these with the client when appropriate. It relies upon the here and now, the immediate experience of the relationship, based upon the belief that if the client is made aware of the counsellor's reactions to her/him, s/he will be able to use this experience to positively influence her/his life outside the counselling sessions. Rogers believed that the creation of such a relationship was all that was necessary to effect growth in the client, and that it was not necessary to help the client identify action for change, as this would develop organically as a result of the authenticity of the counselling relationship experience.

Key terms

Actualising tendency

Person-centred counselling sees the individual as a whole, as an organism that is motivated towards achieving its potential. This is called the 'actualising tendency'. All human beings want to and are capable of realising their potential. We are all in the process of development and continuously changing, shedding our skin in order to establish regrowth.

Self-concept and the organismic self

Person-centred counselling sees the individual as a whole, and one aspect central to development is the self-concept. The self-concept is our conscious awareness of ourselves. The self-concept develops from the time a baby begins to separate self from others, and the idea of an 'I' or 'me' emerges. If an individual is lucky the self-concept and actualising tendency will develop together, rather than in conflict. Often there is conflict between the growth of the self and the needs of significant others around the person. This gives rise to a distorted image of the self, which develops as a result of messages introjected during childhood. These messages are at odds with the actual experience of the person, often demonstrated by such statements as, 'I found that I was behaving in a way most unlike myself'.

The organismic, or real, self lies within each person and, though it may become buried beneath the self-concept, Rogers believed that it could always be accessed, given appro-. priate conditions. It is based upon the premise that we are experts on ourselves and that our real self becomes distorted by our early experiences of life, when we may receive messages from significant adults which appear to conflict with how we are feeling. An example of this would be the child who falls down, hurts her/his knee and begins to cry. The message s/he hears from her/his parent/carer is, 'Don't cry. It doesn't hurt that much. Big boys/girls don't cry'.

Rogers believed that we have a need for positive regard from others, which is a learned need, developed in early infancy. Positive regard refers to the perception of experiencing oneself as making a positive difference in the field of another. In the example given above, if the child's need for positive regard from significant others is unmet, s/he develops a self-concept that is a distortion of the real or organismic self which responds naturally and authentically to pain. The child introjects the message that its instinctive response to hurt is wrong and as s/he grows up, carries this message into adulthood, 'If I'm hurt, I must not show how I really feel or my feelings will be denied and I will be ridiculed'.

Rogers contended that within a relationship which is warm, genuine and fully accepting, the person could once again find their real self and begin to grow and to move towards their potential.

Conditions of worth

Conditions of worth are the conditions and judgements put on us by other people and ourselves, which in effect say 'you will only be worthwhile if you do this', or 'you will only be loveable if you are like this'. If these judgements are made by important and powerful people, we tend to absorb them and they become part of our consciousness. Conditions of worth are usually established by our parents/significant adults. This leads us to believe that we must fulfil these expectations or be unacceptable. Thus we will only feel valued by others if we behave in ways which fulfil their expectations of us. 'I will only love you if you do well at school.' This phrase may never have actually been used, but we have introjected it from other messages which we were given which linked being loved and valued together with success.

Core conditions

These are usually cited as empathy, congruence (genuineness) and unconditional positive regard (acceptance). Rogers believed that if every relationship was based on these fundamental factors, then each person involved would grow and develop. Any one of the three core conditions may be predominant at one time or another in the counselling relationship, but all three are interdependent, and without all three the therapeutic process will not be effective.

Empathy

Empathy is the ability to see another person's world through their eyes, 'to walk in their shoes.' It involves deep listening to another person in all aspects: emotions, thoughts, body movements. The skill lies in matching the empathic response to the correct level for the clients, thus building a sense of safety and sometimes in working at the intuitive 'leading edge' of awareness.

Unconditional positive regard

This is the ability to accept each human being as a unique individual, whose experience of the world is valid because it is unique. It demands that one does not make judgements about another person, rather accepts. This does not mean wholeheartedly accepting each and every human being regardless of what they may do; one may reject another's behaviour but this does not mean rejecting the person. It involves being aware of one's own values and beliefs, recognising that they will differ from those of others, but that this is not a reason for rejection. It is a celebration of human difference. A counsellor must have some degree of liking or respect for a client to be able to work successfully with them.

Congruence

There are two aspects to congruence, which is also referred to as genuineness. Firstly, the counsellor must be genuinely themselves in the counselling relationship, aware of their feelings, thoughts and perceptions, whatever these are – for example anxiety, warmth, anger, boredom. Secondly, the counsellor should be genuine in the relationship, without a professional façade, and not only be aware of their own feelings towards others, but also share them where appropriate. This raises a dilemma of how much a counsellor should disclose of his/her feelings and thoughts. There is no rule, and what may be right with one client on one day will not be right with another client on another day.

ACTIVITY

Rogers considered that in order for a person to function healthily they need to feel accepted and understood by others and to be aware of their own feelings. Consider your own relationships with other people. Can you recall those within which you experienced feeling accepted, understood and that the other person was always very genuine with you? What effect did this have on you? Conversely, can you recall those relationships where you did not experience those qualities? Were you aware of 'conditions of worth' being imposed on you? What effect did this have on you?

It is probably true to say that when we are in relationships where we know that people care about us, we know that our behaviour, which may sometimes be hurtful to the other person, does not cause that person to reject us. Similarly, if we are angry or hurt, we can freely express those emotions, knowing that we are not going to be rejected or judged. It is this kind of relationship that the person-centred counsellor will aim to establish and develop – one within which the other person feels and experiences the real and genuine contact with another human being.

Techniques and procedures

Person-centred theory stresses the client/counsellor relationship and so there are few techniques. Techniques are secondary to the counsellor's attitude. The approach minimises directive behaviour, such as interpretation, questioning, probing, diagnosis and collecting history. It maximises active listening, reflection of feelings and clarification. Rogers' original approach did not employ techniques and skills, rather it is 'who' the counsellor is, and how s/he shows her/himself to the client, which is significant. However, as the approach developed certain skills were identified which were considered essential for conveying the core conditions to the client. These were the skills of active listening such as reflecting, paraphrasing, summarising and open questions. These skills demonstrate to the client that s/he is being heard and that the counsellor is striving to understand her/his world from her/his point of view (empathy); that s/he is accepted and valued for her/himself (paraphrasing). The key messages are, 'I'm trying to hear how it is for you. I'm not putting my own interpretation on your story. I am accepting that this is your experience of the situation. I will be noticing (internally) how I am responding to your story, the feelings, which are evoked in me. These may be my own responses to your story and/or they may be my own responses to a similar experience of my own. I will hold on to them for now, only sharing them with you if it appears helpful to you'.

Strengths

Because the person-centred approach emphasises the uniqueness of human beings, and focuses on the real relationships which occur between people, including the authentic, here and now relationship, which is created between counsellor and client, it can be applied within any social or cultural context. Its core philosophy and beliefs have had influence beyond the parameters of the counselling field into areas such as education, management and organisational culture.

Limitations

Although the client is at the centre of the therapeutic relationship, and is encouraged to take responsibility for her/himself, this approach demands much of the counsellor, who is expected to be as self-aware as possible and to be able to live life as it happens. The person-centred approach acknowledges that people are influenced by their past, but suggests that individuals can exercise some considerable influence in shaping their own future lives. The past is only significant when the client chooses to focus upon it as having some meaning for them. The counsellor does not probe into aspects of the client's past unless s/he raises them and so it may be viewed as somewhat limiting for those clients who respond more favourably to more directed interventions. It is sometimes also criticised for offering too optimistic a view of human nature and of being anti-intellectual, although this latter criticism may be due more to a poor understanding of the theory which is grounded in significant amounts of empirical research.

ACTIVITY

Read the following extract from a counselling session and then answer the questions.

Speaker: He can't tell me how he feels. He's exactly like his mother. She can't talk about her feelings either. I don't remember her ever showing affection towards the children, even though I know she loves them dearly.

Listener: So he doesn't show affection towards you and his mother appears to also find it difficult to show affection towards him, even towards her grandchildren. I also remember that you told me you had never experienced affection from your mother. I can't help but wonder how you must feel being in the middle of all these people who find it difficult to show affection?

Speaker: Well, it's no wonder he tells me I'm cold. Neither of us really knows how to give and receive affection.

◆ What evidence can you see here of the listener being influenced by the person-centred approach?

◆ What do you consider to be the strengths of these interventions? What might be the limitations for the speaker?

The listener is reflecting back to the client that she has grown up in a family that found difficulty in showing emotion, and has married a man from a similar family background. She shares her own feelings about this. A strength of this may be that the counsellor is staying alongside the client. She is striving to understand how it must feel to be surrounded by people who cannot show affection and not to have received affection herself. It is this self-disclosure together with the sharing of her immediate emotional response to the client's story that allows the client to recognise and understand why she herself struggles to receive and to give affection. A limitation may be that the speaker would like the listener to be more directive, to tell her how she can encourage her husband to be more affectionate towards her.

COGNITIVE/BEHAVIOURAL APPROACH

People are not disturbed by things, but by the view they take of them

(Epictetus, first century AD)

By now it will have become clear that both the psychodynamic and the person-centred approaches to counselling are focused on the exploration of the client's problems with the aim of the client gaining understanding. One of the ways in which the cognitive-behavioural approach immediately differs is that the solution is more to the fore than the problem. One of the underlying tenets of the cognitive-behavioural approach is that all behaviour is learned behaviour, therefore it can be unlearned. This underpins much of the training which is so familiar to many of us today, such as assertiveness and stress management. People are helped to recognise how they behave, and helped to learn different and more useful ways of behaving. This theoretical approach to counselling is probably the most 'scientific' in UK and US terms. This contrasts with psychoanalysis which was regarded as 'unscientific' because it focused on the subjective human experience and on the unconscious aspects of the mind.

Behaviourists believe that an individual's internal world is unimportant as actions are determined by external events. Experimental methods enable the systematic investigation of which variable is causing what effect, by controlling and manipulating variables in order to examine their effects upon each other. The behavioural aspects of this approach rely on such experimentation to provide scientific evidence that psychological problems can be explained and therefore therapeutically treated using behavioural principles. Behaviourists, such as Skinner (1904–1990) and Seligman, carried out research into how humans learn to behave by conducting experiments on animals. This type of research may seem today to be at best naive and, at worst, unethical, because conclusions about human behaviour were drawn from animal experiments. However, it is important to remember that the behaviourists were employing familiar and recognisable research methods, those of scientific experimentation, which were considered to be respectable, and so exerted considerable influence. Some of the most famous experiments, such as those of Seligman (1975) and Skinner (1953), have contributed to the hypothesis that learned helplessness may be a cause of depression. Seligman gave electric shocks to dogs that were restrained in cages and unable to escape or control their situation. After some time, even when they were given shocks in a situation from which they were able to escape the dogs continued to accept the electric shocks. They had learned helplessness. The helpless dogs showed many of the signs common to depressed humans, and so Seligman and his colleagues speculated that learned helplessness might be a cause of depression in people. Albert Ellis and Aaron Beck are the key influences on the cognitive aspects of the cognitive-behavioural approach. They were both trained as psychoanalysts but became disillusioned with the classical Freudian tradition where the individual's thought processes were largely ignored. Beck (1975) also carried out research into depression and this led him to believe that this condition was associated with a form of 'thought disorder', where the depressed person distorted information in a negative way. His therapeutic approach focused on teaching people to identify and modify their dysfunctional thought processes and it continues to be widely used both in the UK and the USA in the treatment of depression. Both Ellis and Beck believed that individuals are born with the potential for rational thinking, but tend to fall victim to the uncritical acceptance of irrational beliefs that are perpetuated through self-indoctrination. Ellis is the founder of rational-emotive therapy (RET), now referred to as rational emotive behaviour therapy (REBT), which stresses the role of action and practice in combating irrational, self-indoctrinated ideas. It focuses on the role of thinking and belief systems as the roots of personal problems. It is an active, time-limited, structured approach often used to treat depression as well as anxiety and phobias.

Ellis (1962) developed what he called the A–B–C of personality functioning where A = the activating event, B = beliefs (rational/irrational/self-defeating) and C = consequences. Ellis contends that A does not cause C; the consequences of an event are always affected by beliefs. A simple example of this is of the person who is unsuccessful in securing a new job and as a consequence of this does not apply for any more jobs, believing that s/he is worthless and unemployable. Ellis would claim that this is an irrational belief, which cannot possibly be the outcome of not getting the job. It is the person's beliefs about her/himself, which cause her/him to behave in the way s/he does, not the event itself. The assumption is that thinking, evaluating, analysing, questioning, doing, practising and re-deciding are at the basis of behaviour change.

ACTIVITY

Bill works as a personnel manager in a large organisation. Sophia has come to see him to talk to him following a recent promotion. Read the following dialogue and then discuss the questions with a partner.

Sophia: The problem is that I'm finding this new role difficult. I can't understand why they promoted me in the first place. After the interview, when they offered me the new job, they told me they had reservations about me. I'm sure I only got the job because I was the only internal candidate.

Bob: What were their reservations?

Sophia: I don't know. I expect they don't think I'm up to the job. My IT skills aren't as good as Asif's.

Bob: But this job is a promotion. Why would they promote you if they felt that you weren't up to the job? There will be parts of it that you have to learn, but isn't that why you applied for the job? Because you wanted to become familiar with the new software in that department?

◆ What is the irrational thinking that Bob is challenging?

◆ How helpful might this be for Sophia?

◆ What might be a disadvantage of Bob's approach?

Therapeutic relationship

The therapeutic relationship within the cognitive-behavioural approach is very different from those of the person-centred and psychodynamic approaches. The counsellor aims to create a good relationship with her/his client, but this may be described as educative rather than therapeutic. The aim of the counselling will be to challenge what is identified as faulty thinking and then to change learned behaviour. In the dialogue, Bob asks Sophia to be more specific about the 'reservations'. The belief behind his question is that it is not useful for her to hypothesise about the reservations. It is irrational of her to expect to be able to address them if she does not know what they are. He also attempts to reassure Sophia that she would not have been promoted if the manager had not thought that she was capable of doing the job. He also points out that in a promotion one is expected to develop into the job not to be able to do it immediately.

Skills and techniques

Identifying client actions provides the focus of the relationship and this will invariably involve the setting of homework tasks and role playing the newly acquired set of skills. There is scant attention paid to the effect the client has upon the counsellor and personal counselling is rarely considered to be essential, or even particularly useful, for the cognitive-behavioural counsellor.

Strengths

One of the strengths of this approach is that the results are easily observable and so it retains the credibility of its earlier, positivist roots. It lends itself to short-term working because it is proven to be very effective in helping people who are not seriously disturbed to find quick solutions to their problems. It has wide application. Beck's cognitive therapy is still used in the treatment of depression and this approach is effective in dealing with phobias, stress and anxiety management, poor interpersonal skills, and training people to behave more assertively. The emphasis is on the client's ability to control her/his own situation and, because there is a focus on experimentation with new behaviour and thinking patterns, there is a continuous reinforcement of the ability to manage a new way of being.

Limitations

There is little focus in this approach on the exploration of emotional issues, or of understanding why the client thinks and behaves in a particular way. It is not an approach for someone who wants to understand about their past in detail. People undertaking cognitive behavioural counselling need to be motivated to succeed and to carry out the homework assignments. In the example of Bob and Sophia given earlier, Bob makes no attempt to explore Sophia's underlying feelings of anxiety; he focuses straightaway on her 'faulty thinking'. This approach also demands a reasonable intelligence on the part of the client. There is a danger that, although dependency on the counsellor is discouraged, the counsellor may come to be seen as a powerful expert who holds all the answers.

MULTICULTURAL ISSUES

The three major theoretical approaches to counselling that have been described in this chapter have all been developed in the western world, mostly in Europe and the USA. Although undoubtedly they have all been very significant in the influence they have had on the way counselling is practised in the UK and the USA and, indeed, much of the rest of the world where counselling is beginning to develop, it is imperative that we consider the tenets of these approaches within a multicultural context. The word 'multicultural' is used to denote differences between people based on their social and cultural backgrounds. Each approach focuses mainly on the individual human being and, whether the aim of the approach is to gain insight (psychodynamic), self-actualisation (person-centred) or a change in behaviour (cognitive-behavioural), the underlying assumptions are that, in order to live a more satisfying and healthy life, it is important to develop oneself as an individual. This philosophy is not congruent with those cultures where the individual sees themselves as lacking in importance, and that what is important is their place in the wider community. You do, therefore, need to remember the philosophical roots of these approaches and to consider their relevance to your own cultural background and to the backgrounds of those with whom you are working. This does not mean that you will not be able to work with a broad range of people, rather that there will be other elements that need to be factored in, such as gender, religion and ethnicity. For example, some women would find it very difficult to talk to a man about certain topics and vice versa. In some Caribbean cultures, people would find it hard to talk to a stranger about their problems, believing that the family is the place to deal with them. In some of the Far Eastern cultures, admitting to a problem can be seen as a failure and carries with it the stigma of shame. Similarly, attitudes to common life experiences will differ. In the UK, for example, grieving is usually very private whereas in many cultures it is much more public.

ACTIVITY

Jackie is from Taiwan and a postgraduate student in the UK. She has emailed Sarah, her tutor, to tell her that she is very unhappy in her accommodation and she would like to talk about it. Sarah is extremely busy but replies offering her an appointment some three days later. Read the following brief extract from their meeting.

Sarah: So, tell me what the problem is Jackie. I'm not sure how I can help you but I'll do my best to listen.

Jackie: I'm very unhappy. I'm sharing a house with a lot of other people who are much younger than I am and they are all very noisy. I'm having difficulty sleeping and working. I've come here to study and all they seem to want to do is have parties and talk to their friends on the phone.

Sarah: I'm really sorry to hear that. Have you spoken to them about the effect their behaviour is having on you?

Jackie: Then, when I got your email I burst into tears.

Sarah: (very concerned) I'm really sorry that I upset you. Can you tell me what I said in the email to upset you? *(Sarah is beginning to worry about the email. Was it the wrong tone? Was it that she said she was busy? Was it that she said that she wasn't sure how she could help?)*

Jackie: I cried because I feel so alone and then you asked me to come and see you. I thought 'At last! Maybe someone wants to listen to me'. I feel that I should be stronger. I am very weak. This is really depressing me. I just don't know what to do. I think that we are too tolerant.

Sarah: I can see how upset you are about this and I know how frustrating it is if you can't sleep or work when you want to. When you say that you are being too tolerant, can you tell me what you mean by that?

Jackie: Chinese people are very tolerant. Even if we have a problem, we feel that we cannot point it out to the person, as this would be being intolerant.

Sarah: I think I'm beginning to understand. The way you've been brought up is to be very tolerant of others and now that's causing you a real problem with your friends.

By listening actively to Jackie's problem, the tutor has fairly quickly realised that there is a significant cultural issue coming to the fore. How do you think that she could continue with this discussion so that Jackie's problem is solved?

Of course there is no easy answer but it also emerges that Jackie finds the accommodation people 'frightening' and is 'embarrassed' to talk to them about her accommodation problems. Sarah offers to mediate on her behalf. She is more familiar with the university system so she will contact the accommodation people and find out the procedure for moving. This is a good example of cultural sensitivity. Sarah does not understand Jackie's Chinese culture, but by listening to her story and asking appropriate and open questions the cultural differences emerge. Had Jackie been one of her home students, Sarah probably would have encouraged the student to approach the accommodation office herself, seeking to encourage the student to take responsibility for alleviating the situation. However, Sarah realises that this would be just too difficult for Jackie at the moment. Although she has logged that she would like to be 'stronger' (and she might want some help with this later) she has recognised that her tolerant culture will not allow her to confront this difficulty any further.

CONCLUSION

This chapter has provided an overview of some of the main concepts of the three major theoretical approaches to counselling and shown how you might usefully consider some of the concepts, where they accord with your own beliefs and values, in your use of counselling skills. Each approach makes certain assumptions about the nature of human beings and you need to remember to question these assumptions, using your own social and cultural background and experience, and to remain wary of making assumptions about others. Theories can offer you a set of maps to assist in the journey of helping, but, like any map, they need regular updating.

BIBLIOGRAPHY

Beck, A.T. (1976) *Cognitive therapy and the emotional disorders*, New York: Meridian.

Clarkson, P. (1995) *The therapeutic relationship*, London: Whurr.

Culley, S. (1991) *Integrative counselling skills in action*, London: Sage.

D'Ardenne, P., and Mahtani, A. (1999) *Transcultural counselling in action* 2nd ed., London: Sage.

Dryden, W. (1999) *Four approaches to counselling and psychotherapy*, London: Routledge.

Dryden, W. (1994) *Progress in rational emotive behaviour therapy*, London: Whurr.

Egan, G. (1998) *The skilled helper: a problem-management approach to helping* 6th ed., Pacific Grove, CA: Brooks/Cole.

Freud, S. (1969) *An outline of psycho-analysis* translated and newly edited by James Strachey (rev. ed.), London: Hogarth Press/Institute of Psycho-analysis.

Hough, M. (1998) *Counselling skills and theory*, London: Hodder & Stoughton.

Jacobs, M. (1999) *Psychodynamic counselling in action* 2nd ed., London: Sage.

McLeod, J. (1998) *An introduction to counselling* 2nd ed., Buckingham: Open University.

Nelson-Jones, R. (1997) *Practical counselling and helping skills* 4th ed., London: Cassell.

Palmer, S., and Laungani, P. (eds.) (1999) *Counselling in a multicultural society*, London: Sage.

Rogers, C. (1967) *On becoming a person: a therapist's view of psychotherapy*, London: Constable.

Rogers, C. (1980) *A way of being*, Boston: Houghton Mifflin.

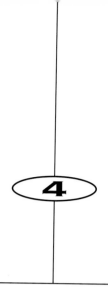

4

Values, beliefs and attitudes – Peter Kent

INTRODUCTION

Values, beliefs and attitudes are such fundamental characteristics of human behaviour that we tend, by and large, to take their existence for granted. Yet, perhaps surprisingly, it was only in the twentieth century that substantial research was carried out in an effort to conceptualise what we mean by the terms, their importance to individuals and societies, how they are passed on, influenced and changed.

However, despite a great deal of thought and attention, by academics and practitioners alike, it is still debatable in which order we should address the concepts. For example, do values underpin beliefs and attitudes making it unlikely, even impossible, one could hold a strong attitude without having a value base? Or are attitudes instinctive and intrinsic characteristics of human nature, which we attempt to conceptualise because we need to explain scientifically what can otherwise seem irrational and inexplicable behaviour? And what of our beliefs? Can we believe that something is right or wrong, good or bad, unless that belief is located in a system of values?

This section does not necessarily provide answers to these questions, but then providing answers is not its purpose. What it seeks to do is provide a basic and reasonably comprehensive introduction to the generally accepted views about the origin and importance of values, attitudes and beliefs in our lives – how they are acquired and the part played by the socialisation process, significant others and groups, and how they are a dynamic force in the world at large for both good and bad. The purpose of doing so is to enable practitioners to locate, express and account for their own sense of values, beliefs and attitudes and to identify, understand and value those of the people with whom they come into contact. For it is important to recognise that values, attitudes and beliefs are dynamic. Whilst we are not held captive by our personal value system, we are rarely free to influence, much less change the dominant values of our group or community or those of the people around us. It is equally important to recognise that other people's values are largely the product of their life experience to date and their knowledge of the world. They may wish to make decisions in the context of these values or may wish to reconsider their values and attitudes in the light of recent experience or new knowledge.

In order to use counselling skills effectively we must first have the knowledge and understanding of ourselves and the way in which we view things, people and events in the world. Without that understanding, not only will it be difficult to account for our feelings and attitudes towards others and their views, but our potential for doing harm is that much greater. We need to understand, too, how it is that people can hold what appear to be contradictory beliefs and how their attitudes and behaviour may not always be consistent with their values and beliefs. We need to manage our responses to people's apparent confusion, to what, at times, may appear perverse behaviour, and their challenging even, perhaps, personally offensive attitudes.

In order to do this we need to open our minds and senses to what others are actually saying and why it is relevant and important to them. We also need to acknowledge and celebrate the diversity of human life and life experiences and remain on guard so that our personal values, beliefs, attitudes and prejudices do not form barriers between ourselves and those on whose behalf we work. We need to understand that we too are products of a socialisation process and that our feelings, thoughts and reactions are influenced, even if only initially, by our psychological and social make-up. We begin with values because they appear, to this writer at least, to provide the basic building blocks for how human beings express themselves, behave and ultimately lead their lives.

VALUES

When considering values it is important to bear in mind that at any given time there may be more than one set of values influencing our behaviour. We have all developed values over the course of our lives that inform and guide our daily behaviour in our personal and professional lives and this section explores how this has happened. There are some values that underpin the effective use of counselling skills. These include respecting and valuing the diversity of values, beliefs, attitudes and behaviour of human beings and each person's right to make decisions that are freely chosen and for which the individual takes ownership.

When using counselling skills we enter a relationship with particular characteristics that need to be acknowledged and understood. There are sound reasons for ensuring the rights, responsibilities and obligations of each party are made explicit. Our personal values may, for example, make it difficult to work with people who have values that are abhorrent, conflict profoundly with our own values, or those of an employer, or may condone unlawful behaviour. Our acceptance of diversity need not be unconditional but must take account of a number of obligations. These can include the laws relating to sex, race and disability discrimination, and the agreement that has been reached between the person using coun-selling skills and the recipient. The nature of that agreement needs to be understood because it may constitute a form of contract, in which case the recipient of our skills has the right to expect we behave in a way defined by that agreement. We may have a duty of care or belong to a professional body with a code of ethics. There are, therefore, not just good practical reasons but laws that require a level of tolerance, acceptance of diversity and non-discriminatory behaviour.

A value is a belief that something is good and desirable. It defines what individuals, com-munities and societies consider to be important, worthwhile and worth striving for. Like norms, values vary from society to society but unlike norms, which provide specific rules for conduct, values provide more general guidelines. A good example is that individual achievement and materialism are major values in western industrialised society. Individuals believe it is important to come top of the class, to win a race or reach the top of a chosen profession. Individual achievement, therefore, is often symbolised and measured by the quality and quantity of material possessions that a person can accumulate. In the west, the value of materialism motivates individuals to invest time and energy producing and acquir-ing material possessions – the trappings of success. We tend to admire people who have done well and have the possessions and lifestyle that signify success in our culture. However, a culture that placed a high value on generosity, for example, would be likely to consider the acquisitive individual of western society as peculiar, or quite probably as grasping, self-seeking and antisocial. Values are, therefore, deeply influenced, and on occasion prescribed, by culture and play a significant part in determining our cultural identity.

Consequently, many norms can be seen as reflections or symptoms of a culture's values. If we consider again western industrial society, the value placed on human life is expressed in terms of a number of norms. The norms associated with hygiene in the home and in public places; those that define acceptable ways of settling an argument or dispute (which usually exclude physical violence and manslaughter); the range of rules and regulations dealing with transport and behaviour on the roads, along with the rules that apply to safety regulations in the workplace, are all concerned with protecting life and limb. The norms concerned with the general health and safety of members of society, therefore, can be seen as expressions of the value placed on human life. Without this and other shared values, it may be argued, members of society would be unlikely to co-operate and work together. With differing or conflicting values they would often be pulling in different directions and be pursuing incompatible goals. In such a society the result would most likely be disorder and disruption.

To have an ordered and stable society requires shared norms and values and when those values are institutionalised and behaviour is structured in terms of them, the result is a stable system. A state of 'social equilibrium' is achieved, with the various parts of the system in a state of balance. There are two main ways in which social equilibrium is maintained. The first involves socialisation, which is the way society's values are passed on from one gen-eration to the next and are internalised to form an integral part of people's personalities. In western society the family and the education system are the main institutions concerned with teaching and passing on values. Secondly, social equilibrium is also maintained by the various mechanisms of social control, which discourage deviance and so maintain order in the system. The processes of socialisation and social control are fundamental to maintaining the equilibrium of the social system and, therefore, to order in society.

Since common values produce common goals, value consensus provides the foundation for co-operation. Since individuals will tend to identify, and feel kinship, with those who share the same values as themselves, consensus forms the basis of social unity or social solidarity, and members of a society will tend to co-operate in order to pursue the goals they share.

The term 'value' is often used by social psychologists to refer to anything that serves as a common goal in a group or society. Consequently, achieving and holding power and wealth would have been values for the 'robber barons' in the late nineteenth and early twentieth centuries. The welfare of a child is usually a value to a parent, and a parent's attitude towards such diverse things as neighbours, the use of money, and public health legislation are likely to reflect the importance attached to the welfare of children. Because values are so powerful and important the term 'value' is not usually used to refer to specific and temporary goals.

Cleanliness in general, for example, or personal comfort in general may be values for some people and the attitudes towards them are widely shared, but the cleanliness and comfort resulting from taking a bath are not. Entire systems of thought and philosophies of life are, for many people, organised around values, which become, for them, more and more inclusive, taking in their social, economic and political lives. In other words, values will affect attitudes and behaviour in many, if not most, aspects of people's lives.

Yet values are difficult to study, because no two people organise their attitudes in exactly the same way. However, we must not forget that within societies, and within groups in any society, most values are widely shared and social life is currently constituted through people's attitudes and their actions.

Values which are culturally prescribed within a society often serve as dominant frames of reference for the members of that society. It is these central values, functioning as common frames of reference in many institutions, which bring together and cement the various attitudes into an integrated system. People will also share the attitudes of other members of a group because of the ways in which they interact with the other members. In this way the 'rightness' of an individual's attitudes is confirmed, reinforced and 'proven' by the fact that 'everyone' agrees with them.

ACTIVITY

Describe your own central values and those of your family and immediate community. What are the most important values you have that are widely shared within your family and community and which groups in society have values that are fundamentally different from your own? Which of your values could lead to tension or conflict with other people?

If shared values provide the general guidelines for behaviours they must then be translated into more specific directives in terms of roles and norms. Institutions such as the family, the economy and the educational and political system can be seen as structures made up of interconnected roles. For example, the family is made up of the interconnected roles of husband, father, wife, mother, son and daughter. Social relationships within the family are structured in terms of a set of related norms, which provide the framework for behaviour. This does not mean, however, that everyone automatically takes on the attitudes of their reference group. There are many reasons why this does not necessarily happen. After all each person has a unique history of experience, from which s/he acquires motives that may or may not be satisfied by membership of this or that group. A person may, for example, consider her/himself to be a non-conformist, but may belong to a number of different groups, some of which may have rules governing behaviour that conflict with the desire to be a non-conformist. Each person is different and perceives her/himself to be different from all other people. Consequently, people can come to perceive the group's norms in unique ways.

Personal values and behaviour

A system of values can provide a framework for personal functioning and behaviour but where or how do these values originate? One answer can be found in cognitive dissonance theory (Festinger, 1957) and self-perception theory (Bem, 1965; 1972), both of which claim that values grow out of freely chosen behaviours. In other words, values originate in our behaviour and, as a result of behaving in particular ways on a number of occasions, we develop a value system that is consistent with these freely chosen actions. A person, therefore, when forming values, tries to make the values consistent with previous behaviour. Self-aware people's behaviour should be reasonably consistent with their value system, so if a man says that he is in favour of sexual equality, we should then expect his behaviour to reflect it. He should not open doors for women rather than for men, or use the expressions 'girl', 'chick' or 'bird'. To do so would create a discrepancy because on the one hand there is the self-description, which provides a standard for behaviour, and, on the other hand, there is the actual behaviour.

By way of contrast, Rokeach saw values as conceptions of what we hope to achieve by our actions and devised what has become a widely recognised measure of western values known as the Rokeach Value Survey. The Rokeach Value Survey distinguishes between what are called terminal values (or the ultimate end goals of our existence) and instrumental values (or the behavioural means of achieving such end goals). In 1981, for example, the six most highly ranked values in the USA were a world at peace, family security, freedom, happiness, self-esteem and wisdom. Instrumental values (surveyed in 1971) produced the six most highly ranked as: honest, ambitious, responsible, forgiving, broad-minded and courageous.

Schwartz, another prominent researcher in the field of values, classified values into ten types: power, achievement, hedonism, stimulation, self-direction, universalism, benevolence, tradition, conformity and security. Based on information, from twenty countries in six continents, Schwartz confirmed each of the ten values was found in at least 90% of the countries surveyed, suggesting that his values are near universal.

ACTIVITY

Imagine you are briefing a visitor from a non-European country and describe to her/him the dominant values of the UK and those of two major minority ethnic communities. Produce a briefing that explains what makes the values important to people, how they have shaped and influenced behaviour and the tensions that can exist.

Nevertheless, despite the universality described by Schwartz, each individual can be considered to possess a personal profile of values, or guiding principles, for his/her life. This profile comprises a set of values ranked in order of the importance the person attaches to each. Listed as follows are some values that Nelson-Jones (1996) argues people consciously or otherwise bring to their relationships.

◆ **Survival**: biological survival is the primary instinctive value, though other values sometimes override it, for example patriotism or religious belief.

◆ **Love**: loving and being loved, appreciating others for what they are and not just for what they do.

◆ **Friendship**: being joined to others outside your family by mutual intimacy and interests.

◆ **Family life**: having, and being part of a family, valuing parenthood.

◆ **Religion**: acknowledging the need for 'connectedness' to some ultimate and superhuman power.

◆ **Achievement**: being ambitious, valuing success, status and influence.

◆ **Materialism**: valuing the accumulation and control of money.

◆ **Security**: valuing financial security and social order.

◆ **Aesthetics**: approving beauty and good taste, and in particular the arts, such as music, literature and painting.

◆ **Intellect**: valuing analytical and rational pursuits.

◆ **Social** interest: helping others, being benevolent and showing social concern.

◆ **Hedonism**: valuing fun, pleasure and having a good time.

◆ **Excitement**: valuing being daring and a varied and stimulating life.

◆ **Conformity**: being obedient, respecting and honouring parents and authority figures.

◆ **Tradition**: appreciating the status quo, accepting your position in life.

◆ **Career**: valuing having a career and the work entailed.

◆ **Practical**: valuing practical pursuits and, where practical matters are concerned, self-reliance.

◆ **Nature**: appreciating and valuing being outdoors and in communion with nature.

- ◆ **Health**: valuing being healthy and engaging in pursuits conducive to good health.
- ◆ **Self-direction**: valuing autonomy, choosing your goals and personal freedom.
- ◆ **Personal growth**: being committed to personal development.

ACTIVITY

Use the Nelson-Jones list of values to audit your values and produce a personal profile (including the relative importance to you of each).

BELIEFS

It would be a mistake to consider beliefs as more flexible or more open to change than values. Nevertheless, beliefs do tend to be more specific, and beliefs about new objects, or phenomena, will form over the course of a lifetime – unlike values, that are more general and less likely to undergo fundamental change. Beliefs are also more likely to occupy varying degrees of importance, and even permanence. People will be more conscious of some beliefs than others, which may exist at a more subconscious level.

Beliefs are also qualitatively different, and people are often more willing to question some beliefs they hold than others. Indeed in some cases they need to review, and perhaps change, what they believe about certain things or events in order to make progress. They may, for example, have recent experience or knowledge that leads them to question a belief, or a strongly held belief may be an obstacle to progress. If a person's behaviour, owing to a strongly held belief, is causing problems in his/her personal life, then gaining an understanding of why the belief is so strong, and how it came to be held, is important, in order to establish how to enable progress.

Similarly, if our own beliefs intrude and influence our behaviour, we must be on guard to ensure our judgement is not undermined and we do not discriminate against people whose beliefs are different from our own. Beliefs are rarely, if ever, isolated characteristics of an individual's personality. They need to be considered as interrelated components of a belief-system. It is important to understand why a belief is held, how it relates to other beliefs and how it is sustained. People will generally be aware of their beliefs, because they are important definitions of their position on everyday matters that can be readily articulated or come under challenge. People with similar values can hold quite different beliefs, a good example being that parents value the safety and well-being of their children, yet some will believe it right to smack a child (it is 'good' for them and teaches discipline) and others will believe it is wrong (it is harmful and causes unnecessary pain).

When using counselling skills it is helpful to anticipate when our own beliefs may be challenged or threatened by someone else's beliefs; and to be able to manage our own feelings when that happens. Equally importantly, we must know what courses of action are available when someone expresses a belief that is contrary to acceptance of diversity and ethical or legal considerations, for example a person who believes it is legitimate to use violence as a means of expressing hostility.

The assumption that people think and act in more or less logical ways is put forward by Fishbein and Ajzen (1975). They believe that our attitudes flow reasonably and spontaneously from the beliefs we have about the object of the attitude and our intentions and actions come directly from our attitudes. They point out that, as a general rule, we tend to behave in favourable ways with respect to things and people we like, and to display unfavourable behaviours towards things and people we dislike.

Let us consider, for example, how the formation of beliefs may lead reasonably to the development of attitudes that are consistent with those beliefs. Generally speaking, we form beliefs about an object by associating it with certain attributes. So, perhaps as a result of watching a television programme, we may come to believe that genetically modified vegetables are harmful. Since the attributes that come to be linked to the object (such as modification is 'unnatural') are already valued positively or negatively, we automatically and simultaneously acquire an attitude towards the object itself. In this way we learn to have favourable attitudes towards objects we believe have largely desirable characteristics, and to form unfavourable attitudes towards objects we associate with mostly undesirable characteristics. The importance to us of each attitude is in direct proportion to the strength of the belief.

Naturally, in the course of our lives we acquire many different beliefs about a variety of objects, actions and events. These beliefs may be formed as a result of direct observation or they may be self-generated by way of inference processes, or they may be formed indirectly by way of accepting information from outside sources, such as friends, television, newspapers, books and so on. Some beliefs may persist over time, others may weaken or disappear and new beliefs may be formed. Although we can hold a great many beliefs about any given object we can deal with only a relatively small number at any given moment. And it is these salient beliefs that are the immediate determinants of our attitude (Fishbein, 1963; Fishbein and Ajzen, 1975). In short, there is a causal sequence of events in which our actions, with respect to an object, come directly from our behavioural intentions; the intentions are evaluatively consistent with the attitude towards the object, and this attitude derives reasonably from our salient or prominent beliefs about the object.

Belief-systems

Most of us live out our lives in a fairly stable pattern of daily encounters with others, whether at home, at the shops, school or work. In these settings our actions can appear automatic and unthinking, and much of the time exchanges between people do not convey new information but serve more as devices for sustaining 'normal' patterns of social interaction. Nevertheless, despite its superficiality, everyday culture and interaction bears the imprint of more sophisticated and critical characteristics such as social myths and ideologies, knowledge and beliefs.

All people are more or less committed to a range of beliefs, attitudes and opinions, and strongly held ideas are usually those that have been institutionalised among a body of like-minded people. The stronger and more persuasive a set of ideas becomes, the more it is likely to become an all-embracing system of beliefs and ideology governing members' actions and interpretations of the world. Some of the strongest belief-systems are those that have been formally instituted with specific ends in mind, such as the major religions or political philosophies of the world. Belief-systems work because the people involved take account of others' ideas, intentions and behaviour.

At the same time, however, it would be wrong to assume that conformity and comprehension necessarily implies social consensus. Given that, in any society, there are different groups with different social, economic and political interests, it is likely that specific belief-systems will be associated with each group. Specific ideas and beliefs may also contradict other sets of beliefs, so that controversy and conflict develop between groups, for example between religion and science in Europe in the eighteenth and nineteenth centuries, and even today in the USA between science education (evolution) and religion (God the creator).

Nevertheless, to speak in terms of a belief-system is not to imply that the beliefs making it up are fully articulated, clearly worked-out ideas, ordered and arranged in a systematic and consistent fashion. People may, for example, hold beliefs without any clear reason for doing so (they may be simply ideas that have been passed on by custom and tradition). Similarly, people may unwittingly hold contradictory beliefs simultaneously without this being in any way difficult or worrying for them.

To summarise, belief-systems refer to those ideas that people hold to be right and true, which provide not only guides and rules for action but also justifications for actions by which we explain our behaviour to ourselves and to others.

ACTIVITY

We generally value human life. However, attitudes may be changing as some families seek to have babies with particular characteristics (so-called designer babies), in order to reduce the likelihood of them being born with a disease or developing one in later life, or even to be a source of treatment for a sibling. How do you feel about this and how do your values, beliefs and attitudes influence your feelings?

Religion may be described as a system of belief about the individual's place in the world, providing an order to that world and a reason for existence within it. It has been institutionalised over the centuries, so that powerful religious organisations and ideas have arisen, like those of the Catholic, Islamic and Hindu faiths. Consequently, religion is a major influence in societies, and affects non-religious institutions, like the family, as well as bringing about general social change through education and major events such as the great religious wars, the contemporary Islamic revolutions and so on.

Generally, however, it may be argued, the predominance of religious institutions has given way to new social institutions, in the realms of politics, education, social policy and morality, and the pulpit has lost out in relation to the power of the mass media. Religions no longer hold the political or economic power that they once enjoyed and have modified their doctrines in the face of pressure from secular society.

ATTITUDES

In some ways attitudes are the most dynamic and immediate of the issues addressed in this chapter. They are close to the surface of everyday life and can be predictors of behaviour. Attitudes are also potentially amenable to change, in a way that values and even beliefs may not be. For many people information, knowledge and understanding may lead to review and change of an attitude that in no way undermines their basic values or beliefs. And although strongly held beliefs may not necessarily lead to intolerance or unfair discrimination a hostile attitude may find expression unconsciously through body language.

It is the relationship with behaviour that is perhaps of greatest importance. If a person's attitude to an individual or group appears to lead directly to prejudice and unfair, perhaps unlawful, discrimination we need strategies for dealing with that. What it is legitimate and appropriate to do depends on a number of considerations. It remains debatable whether prejudice and intolerant attitudes can be changed by knowledge and understanding alone. In the case of some people, and some attitudes, this may be successful but with many deeply entrenched attitudes, that are supported by a powerful belief-system, success may be limited. This, for example, led many organisations, when introducing equal opportunity policies and practices, to concentrate on changing behaviour rather than attitudes. Before embarking on a response, whether it be to challenge or attempt to raise awareness, it is necessary to diagnose the origins of the attitude and the reasons it is so powerful and important to the person concerned.

Socialisation involves learning more than just how to behave. It involves, more importantly, learning a society's rules and socially approved values and attitudes. In western society today, a child learns quite early that monogamy, private ownership and achievement are approved. These are significant social values but, in addition, a host of attitudes are learned about other people: what and how to eat, money and social symbols, to name but a few.

The concept of attitude, describing the cognitive, affective and behavioural orientation of an individual towards a specific object, or class of objects, in the natural or social environments, is a product of twentieth-century North American social psychology. Although an attitude may involve a belief, it does not in general imply the degree of logical organisation required of a belief. And although conceptually attitudes and behaviour have an intimate relationship, and attitudes are to be inferred primarily from overt behaviour, attitudes should not be seen as behaviour.

Allport (1937) produced a definition that has probably had the most enduring influence. Namely, that an attitude is 'a mental and neural state of readiness, organised through experience, exerting a directing or dynamic influence upon the individual's response to all objects and situations with which it is related'. As early as 1918 Thomas and Znaniecki viewed attitudes as the individual counterparts of social values and a large body of social research has tried since then to measure these social attitudes in order to predict or explain social behaviour. Since the 1950s research has been concerned primarily with the relationship between attitudes and behaviour because any stable society relies upon predictable conduct from its members. This is a basic expectancy in all the individual and situational variations that exist in a human community. There is, for example, appropriate behaviour at home, at school, at the office, in the attitudes expressed among friends, in those displayed towards strangers and so on. A major part of socialisation, therefore, is to enable us to learn to make the necessary decisions about the appropriate behaviour in varying situations and with different individuals. Such discriminations are essential for 'proper' role behaviour, which depends upon the setting, the activity and the other people with whom we are interacting. The values of a society, and the goals they imply, also support social norms, by approving some kinds of conduct and not others. Notions of privacy, honour and equity are examples of values that help guide various social relationships.

Perhaps the most highly organised phase of socialisation is the matter of educating children and young people. However, there are many less organised patterns, such as those seen in family relationships, contact with other people, the mass media (especially television) and peer groups. Much socialisation occurs, therefore, as the child hears attitudes expressed by parents and siblings. It is quite informal and not a pattern of conscious learning. This is called implicit learning, where characteristics are acquired without a deliberate design to learn them or, for that matter, teach them. This contrasts with explicit learning, where either or both of these conditions of deliberateness are present. Even more important, however, is that what is learned in this implicit way is readily found congenial or attractive. Society generally shapes experiences in such a way that people want to act, as they have to act and find gratification in acting according to the requirements of their culture.

ACTIVITY

Consider your own attitudes within the context of your personal socialisation. Which attitudes were learned in childhood and remain true for you and which have changed over time? Contrast your attitudes with another person you know well but who has different attitudes and account for the difference.

Insofar as attitudes predict behaviour, they can be said to do so in relation to the immediate situation. Nevertheless, roles are major situational factors and can produce inconsistencies among attitudes and between attitudes and behaviour. The demands of a particular role may, for instance, require that an individual express attitudes that fit the expectations of others. For example, to be accepted within one group may necessitate showing militancy on a particular social issue. But for acceptance within another, it may be that such displays have to be moderated. When negotiations occur privately between representatives of adversarial groups, say between trade unions and employers, there may be a good deal of common ground for settlement. However, in meeting with their own constituents, unions and business leaders may be outspokenly critical of the unreasonableness of the other side. That may also be the case in a political context where cross-party committees can often produce consensus despite normal party hostilities being resumed in the chamber of the House of Commons.

It is also obviously true that an individual may believe one thing but do or say another. This inconsistency between attitudes and actions often results from the demands of roles in social situations. For example, two people leaving a dinner party may both compliment the host on the meal and company that evening. But one actually believes what she says, while the other has a negative attitude and is only being polite. Such apparent inconsistency demonstrates the importance of distinguishing between private attitudes and public behaviour. It is certainly no surprise that the relationship between what is private and what is public is not entirely consistent, considering the social pressures operating on individuals. Not surprisingly, it is occasionally difficult to get people to tell us what their true attitudes are on any given question. They may find it difficult to express negative attitudes towards a colleague or express unpopular political views or admit to bigoted or socially unaccept-able attitudes.

Yet individuals may not be fully aware of their attitudes and this accounts in part for the inconsistency of one attitude with another. Many attitudes are also at a low level of con-sciousness, and both unconscious and conscious processes are involved in human action. Unless circumstances force the individual to face conflicts between attitudes, and perhaps resolve the conflicts, they may remain unnoticed. Many inconsistent relationships are poss-ible: between attitudes and values, attitudes and attitudes, values and values and either or both with behaviour.

ACTIVITY

Many people apparently believe one thing yet do another. Consider examples of such behaviour and offer explanations for it. What are the occasions and circumstances when you have behaved in a manner that the situation seemed to demand rather than accord-ing to your beliefs and attitudes?

People have attitudes towards a variety of things and people: AIDS victims, eating meat, practising safe sex, politics, friends, teachers and so on. Some view attitudes exclusively as sentiments, statements of feelings of affect: 'I like Tony Blair', 'I feel terrible about Third World debt'. Others include beliefs in their definition: 'Abortion is immoral', 'Global warm-ing is responsible for the current bad weather'. And yet others include behaviours as part of their definition. McGuire (1985), after an extensive search of the literature on attitude change reported that more than 500 definitions of attitude had been used by social psy-chologists in their research on the subject. But Petty and Cacioppo (1986) proposed what is perhaps the most economical definition of an attitude, that of 'a general and enduring positive or negative feeling about some person, object or issue'.

How can we account, therefore, for the development of different attitudes? The specific roles played by heredity and environment are unclear. Heredity may play a part, perhaps through physiological characteristics and genetic predisposition, but heredity may also interact with environment to affect attitudes. It is, however, reasonable to consider that parents are extremely important influences in development of our attitudes and values.

In our early years our parents (or the other parental figures that raise us) have control over two important aspects of our lives. Firstly, they control most of our rewards and punishments. They can allow us to do things that we like, and they can oblige us to do things that we do not want to do. Their smiles of approval and their frowns of disapproval can be of disproportionate importance to us. Secondly, they control a sizeable proportion of the information that reaches us. Although as we grow older we realise that our parents do not always, and perhaps do not very often, have the correct answers, they do, nevertheless, begin the information flow that results in the formation of our beliefs and attitudes. Thus categories are formed in our minds on the basis of this early information and most theorists agree that new information undergoes assimilation to the existing category. That is, it will be distorted to some degree to fit into the established category. At the same time, however, the category will also undergo some accommodation to the new information. The child's category will, therefore, show some expansion to incorporate the new information as s/he grows and is subject to new influences.

Nevertheless, because the special influence of parents in forming early attitudes, beliefs and values arises from the fact that they establish the initial categories, these categories are resistant to change. In other words, the result of the clash between existing category and new information is usually resolved in favour of assimilation, rather than accommodation. The explanation for this may be that parents are particularly credible sources of information for a child and that information acquired later, if provided by a different source, may not weigh so heavily because the source may not seem as credible as a parent. It may also be that the pre-existing categories simply exert more influence on new information than information does on the category.

Attitude change

Perhaps no other area of social psychology has generated quite so much interest as that of attitude change. Aristotle was one of the first to construct the basic skeleton of attitude change inquiries and in his work *Rhetoric* he wrote, 'Of the modes of persuasion furnished by the spoken word, there are three kinds. The first depends on the personal character of the speaker; the second on putting the audience into a certain frame of mind; the third on the proof ... provided by the words of the speech itself'. For Aristotle, therefore, the analysis of communication involved an analysis of the speaker, the message and the audience. In the 1930s social psychologists made attitude change their major area of interest; and their concentration was on measurement. Interest declined in the 1940s only to peak again at the end of the 1950s and early 1960s. Although the 1970s saw another dip in the progression of research on attitude change, by the 1980s attitude change had regained its pre-eminence as a focus of study.

Contemporary theoretical models trying to explain the way in which persuasion occurs include the elaboration likelihood model, which attempts to account for attitude change by focusing on the distinction between what are referred to as the central and the peripheral routes. People who take the central route scrutinise the content of the message, whereas the peripheral route leads to persuasion by other means, such as the attractiveness of the communicator.

Although early research on attitude change focused on those aspects of the communicator, the communication and the audience that influence attitudes, currently more attention is being focused on the factors involved in central versus peripheral processing. In terms of the peripheral route, researchers have, for example, demonstrated that highly credible communicators are much more effective in changing attitudes than communicators with low credibility. They have also found, however, that over time the effectiveness of the highly credible communicator decreases, whereas the effectiveness of the communication delivered by a low-credibility communicator increases. This has been termed the sleeper effect and is explained by dissociation between the message and its source. Recent research shows that the cause of the dissociation is that memory for the source and memory for the communication decay at different rates.

Perhaps, not surprisingly, expert and trustworthy communicators are more effective in producing opinion change than communicators whose expertise and trustworthiness are suspect. A person who argues against her/his best interests, or whose communication is unintentionally overheard, is considered to be especially trustworthy. Communicators who are similar to the target of a persuasive message are more effective in producing changes in value-oriented attitudes, whereas experts are more effective in changing beliefs about facts.

ACTIVITY

A father has just learned his teenage son is gay. He is profoundly hostile towards gay men and believes his son has been corrupted and can change with therapy. How would you go about enabling the father to explore his attitude and consider changing it?

Prejudice

Prejudice, stereotyping, discrimination, racism and sexism, are terms that often overlap. Each involves a negative evaluation of an individual or group. That is the essence of prejudice: an unjustifiable, negative attitude towards a group and its individual members. Prejudice is pre-judgement; it biases us against a person based solely on our identifying the person with a particular group.

Prejudice is, therefore, an attitude characterised by a distinct combination of feelings, inclination to act and beliefs. This combination can be said to represent the ABC of attitudes: affects (feelings), behaviour tendency (inclination to act) and cognition (beliefs).

Negative evaluations that mark prejudice can stem from emotional associations, from the need to justify behaviour or from negative beliefs (stereotypes). To stereotype is to generalise and, of course, generalisations can have a germ of truth. But problems with stereotypes arise when they are over-generalised or just plain wrong.

If prejudice is a negative attitude then discrimination is a negative behaviour and discriminatory behaviour often, but not always, has its source in prejudicial attitudes. Prejudiced attitudes need not breed hostile acts nor does all oppression spring from prejudice. If we consider racism and sexism, they are institutional practices that discriminate, even when there is no prejudicial intent. For example, if word-of-mouth recruitment in an all-white business has the effect of maintaining an all-white workforce then the practice may very well be considered racist, even if the employer had no intention of discriminating unfairly. Much investigation and research has suggested that prejudice, like other attitudes, is learned. Children may see their parents discriminating against black people and hear their hostile remarks. As children grow older their peers may tell them that black people are bad and they will be excluded from peer groups if seen associating with them. Parents may point to stories in newspapers of how so much crime appears to be carried out by black youths. Each of these actions contributes towards a child's growing prejudice against black people. This model of prejudice closely parallels what is called social learning theory. The children have models in their parents, who teach them to dislike black people. Parents and peers discriminating against black people positively reinforce their attitudes and they are punished by parents and peers alike for associating with black people. It may be argued that in this way children learn to hate.

If prejudice is indeed learned, it would explain why there are such wide variations in the objects of prejudice. Children in different countries, or different regions of the same country, can learn to hate different ethnic groups. Interestingly enough, the learning approach allows for the formation of prejudice in children even if they have never seen a member of the group against which they become prejudiced.

But where do the attitudes come from in the first place? According to one theory (realistic-conflict theory) competition for scarce resources is the key to understanding discrimination. At various times in history minority groups, such as Jews and black people, have been perceived as a threat. This threat usually takes the form of competition for scarce economic or natural resources, such as jobs, housing, land or money.

Although complex factors underlie prejudices that can be traced back hundreds, even thousands, of years, one simple factor does appear to underlie a great deal of hostility and conflict between groups. That factor is people's basic tendency to divide into groups and to prefer their own group, the in-group, to a different group, the out-group. The theory that perhaps most fully explains this phenomenon is known as social identity theory, which says that, in addition to forming a personal identity (which depends on one's achievements and how they compare with other people's), we form a social identity based on our membership of a set of groups.

So what are the implications of social identity theory for understanding prejudice? People have a need to achieve and maintain a high level of self-esteem and one way they can do this is by raising what they consider to be the value of their social identity. They can enhance their social identity by perceiving the in-group as better and by actually treating it better. That is, people will disparage and mistreat individual members of an out-group, and the group as a whole, in order to maintain a high level of self-esteem, especially when their self-esteem is threatened.

The idea that out-groups, especially minorities, are the targets of displaced aggression is also the central hypothesis of the scapegoat theory. This theory suggests that a variety of frustrations in everyday life – at work, in the home, with friends – can lead to displaced aggression and that ethnic out-groups are convenient targets for such hostility. In an effort to explain how minorities can become the unfortunate victims of aggression Berkowitz (1962) argued that the out-groups are convenient targets because they typically have the following characteristics.

◆ Safeness – the target group is so weak it can be attacked without fear of strong retaliation.
◆ Visibility – the group must have qualities that make it visible and make it stand out from other groups.
◆ Strangeness – humans have an instinctive hatred for what is strange to them.
◆ Prior dislike for the group – aggression may be displaced from one disliked person or group to a previously disliked group.

Prejudice is, of course, complex and springs from several sources. Prejudice may express our sense of who we are and gain us social acceptance. It may defend our sense of self against anxiety that arises from insecurity or inner conflict. It may also promote our self-interest, by supporting what brings us pleasure and opposing what doesn't. Unequal status also breeds prejudice. Once inequalities exist, prejudice helps justify the economic and social superiority of those who have wealth and power. Nineteenth-century politicians, for example, justified imperialism by describing exploited colonised people as 'inferior', requiring protection, and a 'burden' to be borne. Black people were 'inferior' and women were 'weak'. Black people were all right in their place and a woman's place was in the home.

Attitudes are likely to conform with the social order not only as a rationalisation for it but also because discrimination affects its victims. Allport (1954) catalogued 15 possible effects of victimisation, but he believed these reactions were reducible to two basic types: those that involve blaming oneself (withdrawal, self-hate, aggression against one's own group) and those that involve blaming external causes (fighting back, suspiciousness, increased group pride). If the net results are negative (say higher rates of crime) then people use them to justify the discrimination that helps maintain them.

Then, once established, prejudice is maintained largely by inertia. If prejudice is socially accepted, many people will follow the line of least resistance and conform to the norm. They will act not so much out of a need to hate, as out of a need to be liked and accepted. An example is the dilemma faced by many gay men and lesbian women about whether to acknowledge their sexuality publicly and 'come out'.

ACTIVITY

You are a teacher in an inner city school that has increasing numbers of pupils who are refugees. Identify the likely prejudices that other pupils may have and devise a strategy for combating those prejudices.

In a society with complex social, cultural and economic relationships one way we simplify our environment is to categorise – to organise our world by clustering objects into groups. Once we organise people into categories we can think about them more easily, and there is also a tendency to see objects in a group as being more uniform than they really are. Ethnicity and sex are two powerful ways of categorising people. Once we assign people to groups we are likely to exaggerate the similarities within groups and the differences between them. Because we tend to like people we generally think are similar to us and dis-like those we perceive as different, the natural result is in-group bias. When a group is our own we are, by contrast, more likely to recognise and value diversity.

Many of us, for example, may consider the Swiss to be a fairly homogeneous people. But to the people of Switzerland, the Swiss are diverse, encompassing French, German and Italian-speaking people. Also many Anglo-Americans lump 'Latinos' together. Mexican-Americans, Cuban-Americans and Puerto Ricans, however, see important differences, especially between their own sub-group and others. Closer to home, society tends to homogenise individuals so that people will refer, for example, to 'the disabled', thus imply-ing that all people with a disability have similar or identical views and needs.

This willingness to categorise people can be seen in the media, which will often refer to 'black leaders' who supposedly can speak for the 'black community', and white reporters sometimes find it newsworthy that the 'black community' is divided on an issue such as immigration policy. The same reporters, however, apparently presume their own racial group is naturally more diverse. They do not assume there are 'white leaders' who can speak for the white community, or that it is newsworthy when not all white people agree on an issue. No newspapers would headline 'white leaders divided over immigration policy' (Myers, 1996).

It is important to recognise that stereotypes (beliefs) are not prejudices (attitudes). Stereotypes may support prejudice; but then again one might believe, without prejudice, that men and women are different yet equal. Furthermore, the impact of both stereotypes and prejudices is complex.

ACTIVITY

What are your prejudices and how may they inhibit your ability to work effectively in a helping relationship? Using one of the theoretical models, describe and account for the most common prejudices in society today.

Most women know sexual discrimination exists and they believe that sex discrimination affects most working women, as shown by the lower salaries for women and the jobs they predominantly occupy, such as childcare. However, many women do not feel personally discriminated against. Discrimination is something other women face (Crosby, 1989). Similar denials of personal disadvantage, while perceiving discrimination against one's group, occur among unemployed people, lesbians, African Americans and minorities (Taylor).

The process of categorising people and things as masculine or feminine is called gender typing and, most of the time, cues about gender are readily available from physical characteristics such as facial hair or breasts, and from style of dress. People usually display their gender as a prominent part of their self-presentation. The tendency to divide the world into masculine and feminine categories is not, however, limited to perceptions of people. Many objects, activities and behaviours are defined as masculine and feminine. At an early stage children learn that dolls and cooking utensils are for girls and that toy trucks and guns are for boys. Blue is for boys and pink for girls. Little girls are made of sugar and spice and all things nice and little boys of slugs and snails and puppy dog tails.

Gender stereotypes help rationalise a role. If, for example, women provide most of the care for young children, it is reassuring to think women are naturally nurturing. If men run businesses, hunt and fight it is comforting to believe that men are naturally aggressive, independent and adventurous.

The distinction between male and female is a universal organising principle in social life. As children, boys and girls are expected to learn different skills and to develop different personalities. As adults men and women typically assume gender-prescribed roles as husband or wife, mother or father. Cultures vary in exactly what is defined as masculine or feminine and to the degree to which they emphasise gender differences or similarities. But the use of gender to structure social life is universal. In the world beyond western industrialised countries, gender stereotyping and sex discrimination can take harsh and overt forms.

Two-thirds of the world's unschooled children are girls. The world's 600 million illiterate women exceed its 350 million illiterate men by 70%. In Saudi Arabia, women are forbidden to drive. In the Sudan, they may not leave the country without the permission of their husband, father or brother. In South Korea, male births exceed female births by 14% and in China by 18%. Sex-selective abortions and infanticides have led to 76,000,000 'missing women' (Myers, 1996).

Research by Stoller (1968) offers evidence that gender identity (I am a boy, I am a girl) is the primary identity any human being holds; the first as well as the most permanent and far-reaching. Stoller (1968) makes the case for the distinction to be made between sex, which is biological, and gender, which is psychological, and, therefore, cultural.

> Gender is a term that has psychological or cultural rather than biological connotations. If the proper terms for sex are male and female, the corresponding terms for gender are masculine and feminine; these latter might be quite independent of (biological) sex.
>
> (Stoller, 1968)

From research on stereotypes two conclusions would appear to emerge: strong gender stereotypes (people's ideas of how men and women ought to behave) exist and members of the stereotyped group may very often accept the stereotypes. Analysing responses from a University of Michigan survey, Jackman and Senter (1981) found that gender stereotypes were much stronger than racial stereotypes. For example, only 22% of men thought the two sexes equally emotional. Of the remaining 78%, those who believed females more emotional outnumbered those who thought males were by fifteen to one. What did women believe? To within one percentage point their responses were identical.

A useful distinction can be made between cultural and personal stereotypes. Cultural stereotypes are beliefs about the sexes communicated by the mass media, religious teachings, art and literature. As individuals we are familiar with cultural stereotypes but we may or may not agree with them. Personal stereotypes, however, are our own unique beliefs about the attributes of groups of people such as women and men.

ACTIVITY

Begum (not her real name) has been living in the UK for eight months, having moved over here to join her husband and his family. She had had an arranged marriage two years ago, while in her late teens and still living in Bangladesh. Her husband was in the UK and she did not met him until she arrived in this country.

One evening her husband and his brother took her to hospital because, they said, she was constantly drinking water and was agitated and screamed all the time, especially at night. They were not only worried about her but also feared for the safety of members of the extended family living in the same house, including a number of children.

She was found to be physically fit and was discharged but was referred to the family's GP. The GP visited the family and was instantly aware of how frightened the family was. All of them were sleeping together in a downstairs room while Begum was in an upstairs room. The family told the GP that they believed Begum was having a religious crisis and was possessed by at least one demon. They had arranged for a mullah to exorcise the demon but, because he couldn't come for a few days, they wanted her to be safe in hospital until then.

You are the GP. What are the aspects of this case that you will need to take particular account of in the context of your values, beliefs and attitudes? What are the potential values, beliefs and attitudes of the family that you must also consider? What are the prejudices (your own and others) of which you must be aware?

(Based on a case study in *Community Care*, 1346 2–8 November 2000.)

So what determines whether we relate to a person on the basis of stereotypes or as a unique individual? Two important factors are the amount of information we have about the person and the prominence of the person's group membership. The less information available about the person the more likely we are to perceive and react to her/him on the basis of stereotypes. In a recent study, children (aged 5, 9, and 15), students and mothers watched videotapes of infants labelled as male or female. Both the children and students rated the 'female' infants as smaller, nicer, softer and more beautiful than the 'male' infants. The labels did not affect mothers' evaluations of the infants, however, perhaps because their personal experience with babies made them less likely to rely on gender stereotypes (Vogel et al., 1991).

> Because of our social circumstances, male and female are really two cultures and their life experiences are entirely different – and this is crucial. Implicit in all the gender identity development which take place through childhood is the sum total of the parents', the peers', and the culture's notions of what is appropriate to each gender by way of temperament, character, interests, status, worth, gesture and expression. Every moment of a child's life is a clue to how he or she must think and behave to attain or satisfy the demands which gender places upon one.
>
> (Millet, 1971)

Not surprisingly, knowledge that we are male or female, our sense of sexual identity, is acquired early in life. By the age of two or three, children are aware of their own sex and can tell us whether they are a boy or girl. By the age of four or five, children can correctly label other people by sex. However, this understanding of sex differs from that of adults. Research has documented the surprising fact that young children think they can change sex if they want to. In cases of genital malformation and mistaken gender assignment at birth, studied at the California Gender Identity Centre, it was discovered that it is easier to change the sex of an adolescent male, whose biological sex is contrary to his assigned gender, through surgery than to reverse the years of conditioning that have made the subject temperamentally feminine in gesture, sense of self, personality and interests (Millett, 1971).

CONCLUSION

In order to be effective practitioners we need to be self-aware and have a reasonable understanding of others' values, beliefs and attitudes. Along with this insight we need to have some appreciation of how we and others have developed personal and collective values, beliefs and attitudes: the socialisation that has taken place that has shaped our life experiences, helped make us who we are and that influences what we think and do. We also need to take into account the possibility, some would say inevitability, that our personal values, beliefs and attitudes may affect our ability to interact in a non-judgemental fashion with users of our services.

It is important to try, as far as possible, to avoid judging other cultures by comparison with your own. Since cultures vary so widely it is not surprising that people vary widely too; and people coming from one culture frequently find it difficult to empathise with the values, beliefs and attitudes of those from a different culture.

The good counselling skills practitioner is one who can understand and describe his/her own values, beliefs and attitudes and is able to accept and value diversity. They will also recognise that behaviour is a manifestation of values, beliefs and attitudes that are important to people for personal, cultural, political or economic reasons and will develop strategies for managing not just her/his own behaviour but that of those they are seeking to help.

BIBLIOGRAPHY

Allport, G.W. (1937) *Personality: a psychological interpretation*, New York: Holt.

Allport, G.W. (1954) *The nature of prejudice*, Cambridge, MA: Addison-Wesley.

Bem, D. (1965) 'An experimental analysis of self-persuasion' in *Journal of Experimental Social Psychology*, 1, 199–218.

Bem, D. (1972) 'Self-perception theory' in L. Berkowitz (ed.), *Advances in experimental social psychology*, vol 6, New York: Academic Press.

Berkowitz, L. (1962) *Aggression: a social psychological analysis*, New York: McGraw-Hill.

Crosby, F., Pufall, A., Snyder, R.C., O'Connell, M., and Whalen, P. (1989) 'The denial of personal disadvantage among you, me, and all the other ostriches' in Crawford, M., and Gentry, M. (eds.), *Gender and thought*, New York: Springer-Verlag (p. 400).

Festinger, L.A. (1957) *Theory of cognitive dissonance*, Stanford, CA: Stanford University Press.

Fishbein, M., and Ajzen, I. (1975) *Belief, attitude, intention, and behaviour: an introduction to theory and research*, Reading, MA: Addison-Wesley.

Jackman, M.R., and Senter, M.S. (1981) 'Beliefs about race, gender and social class' in Treiman, D.J., and Robinson, R.V. (eds.), *Research in stratification and mobility*, vol 2, Greenwich, CTn: JAI Press (pp. 392, 396).

Kelman, H.C. (1958) 'Compliance, identification, and internalisation: the processes of opinion change' in *Journal of Conflict Resolution*, 2, 51–60.

Lord, C.G., Ross, L., and Lepper, M.R. (1979) 'Biased assimilation and attitude polarisation: the effects of prior theories on subsequently discovered evidence' in *Journal of Personality and Social Psychology*, 37, 2098–2109.

McGuire, W.J. (1985) 'Attitudes and attitude change' in Lindzey, G., and Aronson, E. (eds.), *The handbook of social psychology*, vol 2, New York: Random House.

Millett, K. (1971) *Sexual politics*, London: Sphere Books.

Myers, D.G. (1996) *Social psychology* 5th ed., New York: McGraw-Hill.

Nelson-Jones, R. (1996) *Relating skills: a practical guide to effective personal relationships*, London: Cassell.

Petty, R.E., and Cacioppo, J.T. (1986) 'The elaboration likelihood model of persuasion' in

Berkowitz, L. (ed.) *Advances in experimental social psychology*, 19, 123–205., New York: Academic Press.

Piaget, J. (1932) *The moral judgement of the child*, New York: Harcourt Brace Jovanovich.

Rokeach, M. (1967) *Value survey*, Palo Alto, CA: Consulting Psychologists Press.

Schwartz, S.H. (1992) 'Universals in the content and structure of values: theoretical advances and empirical tests in 20 countries' in Zanna, M. (ed.), *Advances in experimental social psychology*, vol 25, New York: Academic Press (pp. 1–65).

Stoller, J. (1968) *Sex and gender*, New York: Science House.

Taylor, S.E., Peplau, L. A., and Sears, D.O. (1997) *Social psychology*, 9th ed., London: Prentice Hall International.

Vogel, D.A., Lake, M.A., Evans, S., and Karraker, K.H. (1991) 'Children's and adults' sex-stereotyped perceptions of infants' in *Sex Roles*, 24, 605–616.

Wilson, B. (1966) *Religion in a secular society*, London: C.A. Watts & Co.

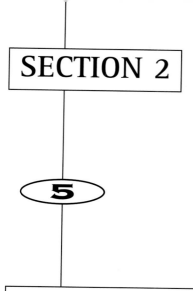

SECTION 2

5

Introduction to counselling skills – Jean Bayliss

This section focuses on skills. Skills are certainly the tools all of us engaged in interpersonal activity, whether personally or professionally, use. But skills that are not underpinned by the core values of empathy, respect and genuineness are in danger of becoming little more than applied techniques.

So, your self-awareness tells you that you are brimming over with empathy; you are full of respect for others' beliefs and values, you're certainly non-judgemental and you genuinely and sincerely want to help people. How would I know? How would someone looking for help with a problem or difficulty know? How can we communicate to others that we are working hard to develop these qualities in ourselves?

Try to think of an interview that you have had; it may have been with your doctor, or perhaps for a job or promotion, or maybe a discussion to help resolve a problem or issue. Now try to list what the person did which made that interview good or bad. If I had been a fly on the wall during the interview what would I have seen or heard to demonstrate to me that the interviewer was helpful (or otherwise)? It is the skills we use that demonstrate to others that we are genuinely concerned to help, that we respect how they feel and that we are trying to get alongside them and are trying to appreciate things from their perspective, rather than from our own. The skills you listed could perhaps be clustered into the following groups:

◆ **Attention giving** – there was a range of skills which clearly indicated to you that the person was giving you their full attention.

◆ **Observing** – the person was able to pick up 'clues' about how you were feeling.

◆ **Listening** – you really felt that both what you said, and how you felt about it, had been heard.

◆ **Responding** – the other person made a comment or responded in some way, indicating that they were 'alongside' you.

These skills – and we'll look at each cluster in greater detail – are usually thought of as the skills of **active listening**. We might wonder whether there is any difference between just listening and active listening – or, indeed, between active and passive listening. The phrase 'a good listener' is used very frequently, but rarely is it clearly or accurately defined. The difference between a listener and a good listener is that the latter really lets the talker know that they are listening. If we are at a lecture, or in the theatre or cinema, we may be listening avidly to what we are hearing, but on the whole the talker has very few clues as to whether we are, or are not. In small groups and, especially, in one-to-one interactions, speakers need to know that they are being heard and if we develop and enhance the skills appropriate to active listening this will happen. Our interactions will be that much more meaningful, because if we are actively listening we are fully engaged with the other person and with the process.

It is interesting that of the four 'clusters' of skills already mentioned, only *one* requires speech. That old saying that if humans had been meant to speak more and listen less, they'd have evolved with two mouths and one ear, instead of the other way round, may be very pertinent for active listening! It has been calculated that in communication, the content of what we say accounts for only 7% of what is heard. The remaining 93% is made up of non-verbal communication 55%, and tone (the way in which the content is said) 38%. Whether this is always accurate may be open to debate, but it certainly lends weight to the saying, 'actions speak louder than words'!

ATTENDING

Be prepared! Before we engage in any sort of listening to another person we can convey that we are attending by being ready. We can prepare both the *setting* and *ourselves*. When you were thinking about the good (or bad) interview you had earlier, did the setting affect your perception? It is not always possible to create the ideal setting for listening to some-one, but we can demonstrate attention giving by making the best of the environment, even when this involves a compromise between what we need and what is available.

Firstly we can eliminate as many distractions as possible. We can, for example, ask people not to interrupt us for an agreed amount of time. In some circumstances, we can make sure that there are no telephone calls; we can certainly ensure that mobile phones are switched off. If we are lucky enough to have a choice, we can arrange to be in a room that is quiet and private, but this is often a luxury.

ACTIVITY

List the ways in which you could make the best of the 'listening environment' – at home, work or elsewhere.

It is also worth noting that for some hesitant talkers, what might be seen as an ideal environment could seem very intimidating. Youth workers have been known to say that their most successful interactions have taken place in litter-strewn, 'urine-stinking' bus shelters!

Arrangement of seating is another way of demonstrating that we are ready to listen. The character or nature of an interview is partly determined by seating.

ACTIVITY

If the listener is beind a desk or table what sort of interview do you think it is? If one chair is much lower than another, what hints might this be giving? If chairs are placed directly facing each other/close together/far part how might this affect the speaker? If both parties sit side by side on a bench, or sofa, will this affect their communication? How?

Carefully organising the seating, so that chairs are at a slight angle, or perhaps inviting the talker to place the chair where they find the distance and angle comfortable not only demonstrates a readiness to listen, but also shows that core value of respect.

Being ready in ourselves is equally important. If we know that really we should be somewhere else, or if we have pressing concerns (anything from needing a lavatory, to having to make an urgent phone call, to being unable to put our own worries aside) it is unlikely that we can really listen. Whilst acknowledging that we're 'only human', we can work hard to be ready to hear what is offered to us. For instance, if we know that we will be 'on pins' if we stop to listen to someone *now*, it might show more respect to explain that we want to give *full* attention and that this will be possible at ... time. No-one is convinced by a 'listener' who is furtively glancing at a watch every other minute. We can make sure that notes or papers which might distract us are out of our sight line. We can also try to suspend our value judgements. This doesn't mean that we have to agree with or condone what is eventually said to us, but that for the duration of the interview we accept that our judgements may not be relevant. This is especially important if what is said is surprising or even shocking: if we have prepared ourselves by setting aside *our* concerns we shall be better able to listen to those of others.

Being prepared may seem almost too obvious to need stating as an active listening skill, but it is astonishing how much difference it can make to a talker.

ACTIVITY

Recall the interview you thought of earlier. Describe the preparedness of the

◆ setting
◆ listener(s).

A powerful silent listening skill, is what is generally termed **non-verbal communication** (NVC) – communication using gestures, posture or facial expression, plus a whole range of behaviours of which we are often unaware. There is a great deal of research evidence that non-verbal communication makes a much greater impact on those we come into contact with than any verbal communication we make. There is also some interesting evidence that when verbal and non-verbal messages conflict, we tend to 'hear' and believe the non-verbal. Non-verbals are especially powerful in first encounters and have been shown to affect the quality of any subsequent relationship in a whole range of ways. It is, therefore, worth becoming aware of our own non-verbal communication and being alert to that of others. It is, however, rather a two-edged sword.

The art of active listening depends, to some extent, on being able to be oneself, and so being over-aware of whether we are using our hands, or frowning or leaning too far forward can make us more aware of ourselves than of the other person and can actually interfere with, rather than enhance, listening. Even so, the power of non-verbal communication is such that to be good active listeners means that we need to practise walking the tightrope between being **self-aware** and being **self-conscious** about the silent messages we convey.

ACTIVITY

Stand in front of a mirror – a full-length one if possible – and imagine what a person meeting you for the first time sees. Make a list of what you think would be seen by a

◆ much younger person

◆ contemporary

◆ much older person.

Some of the points you might have noticed could be hairstyles; make-up and jewellery (or the lack of these); type of dress and shoes; stance. All these (and more) are taken in by someone meeting us and from these will come an expectation of how we are likely to behave. Even in a very simple exercise it is possible to see how difficult it is to suspend value judgements from how we see people.

ACTIVITY

Turn the sound off whilst watching an interchange between two actors on television. What did you think was going on? How did you know?

Much of what you picked up would have been based on assumption – for example that the woman in a twin set and pearls, who waved her hands about a lot and seemed to look away from the other actor was portraying a whole set of values. Similarly that the other actor –

dirty tee-shirt, close-cropped hair, constantly clenching threatening fists – was portraying an opposing set of values. The sound might confirm or totally contradict our assumptions, but there is no doubt that our active listening is profoundly affected by how we interpret non-verbal communication and that we are fooling ourselves if we imagine that others are not affected by ours.

ACTIVITY

(This exercise is especially useful if done with a partner.) Watch a videotape of an interview or of a small group discussion, without the sound, and focus on the non-verbal communucation of one person. Write down:

◆ what feeling(s) that person was experiencing

◆ what attitudes they seemed to convey

◆ your reactions to them.

If another person has done the exercise with you, compare notes. Replay the tape with sound and reflect on the accuracy of assumptions and on your own reactions.

Non-verbal communication is often listed under the acronym S – O – L – E – R:

S – Seating (which we've looked at under 'be prepared')
O – Open posture
L – Trunk lean
E – Eye contact
R – Relax

The way in which we sit can convey a great deal about whether or not we are actively listening. If we have our arms tightly folded across our bodies, it may indicate to the other person that we are 'closed' to what they are saying, or that we feel defensive or even – more prosaically – that we are cold and would therefore like them to hurry up so that we can get to somewhere warm! Either way, we are not conveying that we want to hear what is being offered to us. The **open posture** – sitting with arms resting on chair arms or in the lap – is usually comfortable and can be maintained, without fidgeting, for a reasonable length of time. Fidgeting is a very indicative non-verbal signal! There has been a great deal of debate as to whether the open posture means that legs (or ankles) should or should not be crossed. Cultural aspects play a part here, but in general the consensus seems to be that the listener needs to feel comfortable and this should determine whether or not legs (or ankles) are crossed.

ACTIVITY

In front of a mirror, practise various ways of achieving an open posture and reflect on how long you would feel comfortable in it. Also, evaluate how another person sees you in that posture.

The degree of **trunk or body lean** is also thought to have a strong influence on whether we are, or are not, perceived as listening. Think again about that core quality of respect. If we lean very closely to someone, we may think that this will communicate an absorbed interest in what we are being told, and that we are sincere and genuine about this. Would it necessarily be seen so positively by the other person?

ACTIVITY

How might leaning forward be experienced by:

◆ a pupil from a teacher?

◆ a patient from a doctor? Or a nurse?

◆ an employee from a supervisor?

◆ an elderly person from a social worker?

◆ a passenger from a fellow traveller?

Respect should make us sensitive as to whether leaning forward would be seen as threatening, or 'smothering' or uncomfortably inappropriate. Commenting on this, a friend said, 'someone leaning towards me as if I've shared a profound truth when I've only commented on the weather is bound to be a phoney'. So not only may we not be respecting how others feel, we may also be seen as insincere! Leaning too far back can also be seen as disrespectful in that it can be perceived as a lack of interest. Someone leaning (or lolling) back in a chair may appear very relaxed, but whether they seem really interested in what they are being told is, perhaps, less certain.

ACTIVITY

Ask a friend or colleague to tell you about something in which they are really interested. Alter the way in which you lean as they talk and ask them to give you their impressions.

Trying to find the right balance perhaps seems like a daunting task, but if we remind ourselves that non-verbal communication is more than half of how we are perceived as listeners, it will help us to persevere until 'getting it right' seems natural rather than self-conscious and artificial.

Eye contact can seem a similarly daunting skill to acquire, so that the right amount of it feels natural. Eye contact is especially influenced by culture. In the UK (and to some extent in the west generally) looking people 'straight between the eyes' tends to be seen as a virtue. It is viewed as a mark of honesty, and people who find it difficult to make eye contact are often labelled as 'shifty'. The reasoning behind this seems to be that they must have something to hide, and that that 'something' is probably shameful. This assumption could, in itself, be seen as judgemental – even if the person does have something to hide, it need not necessarily be shameful. Perhaps it says more about whether the listener is to be trusted than it does about what is being concealed. We need also to be clear about whether direct eye contact is culturally acceptable, or comfortable, for everyone. Once again the issue of 'respect' is raised, by a skill as apparently straightforward as looking at someone when they speak to us. Even if making eye contact is acceptable for both partners, the intensity needs considering. Never moving the gaze from the other person, in an attempt to convey attention, can seem like a rather threatening stare. Similarly looking away too often can make the speaker wonder whether we are just planning what to say next!

ACTIVITY

Ask a friend or colleague to listen whilst you describe something important to you. Ask them to keep their gaze firmly fixed on you for as long as possible. Pause, and reflect on how this made you feel. Repeat the exercise, with your partner looking away frequently. Change over as listener and talker.

The final item in the SOLER acronym is *RELAX* – with so much going on in the non-verbal skill area, this may seem almost impossible! Yet if we are to be good active listeners, being able to convey that we are relaxed really does matter. Nervousness and tension seem to be contagious and if we are feeling them, then we are likely to pass them on to the speaker, who may be experiencing them already. Making sure that we drop our shoulders and that our breathing is even will certainly help.

ACTIVITY

From time to time, every day, check whether you are relaxed or can relax yourself. For example

◆ is your jaw relaxed?
◆ are you frowning?
◆ are your shoulders up round your ears?
◆ what are you doing with your hands?
◆ are you tapping your feet?
◆ are you twisting your hair?
◆ how tightly are you clutching the phone?

One aspect of non-verbal communication which can be problematic relates to touch. For some people touch, even between family members or close friends, is difficult. If our natural instinct is to be tactile, we need to be very careful whether in touching someone – perhaps putting an arm round someone in tears – is meeting our needs, or theirs. Some of the questions we need to ask ourselves about this tricky aspect of non-verbal communication are:

◆ Is the other person's culture of touching the same as mine ('culture' could, in this instance, mean family culture)?

◆ Is touch appropriate between, for example a teacher and pupil? What if a listener and talker are of the opposite sex?

◆ Does age matter?

◆ What does being touched mean for you? How would you know if another person found touch acceptable?

In summary, then, non-verbal communication is a crucial aspect of active listening:

◆ It emphasises verbal communication in a range of ways.

◆ Sometimes it replaces verbal communication.

◆ Attitudes are disclosed by non-verbal communication.

◆ It can be a vital clue to all kinds of emotional states.

ACTIVITY

By watching yourself and others, find examples for all four of these and develop your awareness of how they can sharpen your active listening.

OBSERVING

Good observation skills are very helpful in active listening. Attending is evidenced primarily by our non-verbal behaviour and the obverse of this is that we, as listeners, can sensitively observe the talker's non-verbal behaviour and helpfully make use of what we observe. Observation of a speaker can yield a wealth of information to which we can respond with greater depth than if we respond only to what we *hear*. At the same time, we have to be careful not to see only what we want to see. This is what links observation to suspending value judgements – if we *judge* by what we see, we could be making serious mistakes.

What are your thoughts about a young person who comes to work or college in a heavy coat regardless of the weather, and seems reluctant to take if off even in a comfortably warm room?

It might suggest any number of things.

◆ The young person is too poor to buy more suitable clothes.

◆ S/he is living somewhere where there are inadequate washing facilities.

◆ S/he is attention seeking and winding you up.

◆ S/he is 'going through a phase'.

◆ S/he is hiding something.

Any or none of these may be accurate, but if we have not even *noticed* we are not really listening to all the messages this young person is sending.

Some cultures, particularly in the west, emphasise communication through words, spoken or written. As a result the ability to read non-verbal behaviour is not, in most of us, very highly developed. It is interesting that television sports commentators (especially those commentating on tennis) are increasingly interpreting 'body language'. Whether players' heads are up or down; whether a certain gesture indicates frustration; whether a preoccupied look means a change in tactics all seem to be discussed. Sometimes the commentators seem to read a ludicrous amount into what they observe, and listeners must beware of falling into this pitfall. A pupil who clenches his hand when discussing a maths lesson hasn't necessarily got a deep dislike of the maths teacher – it may just be that he's got cramp! Nevertheless, recognising behavioural clues (a smile, a shift in position, sudden eye contact) is an important part of listening. We can draw inferences from these clues and perhaps feed them back to the talker in a tentative and open-ended way.

Observation can also help us as listeners to modify or adjust our own non-verbals or para-verbals (the ahs, ums, which encourage people to go on talking). Our facial expressions need to be appropriate to the emotional content and tone of what is being said. Often a speaker's non-verbal behaviour will be at odds with what is being said. It is, for example, very common for people to smile or even laugh when they are discussing something sad. If the listener smiles too, it is not very appropriate. Careful observation will allow us to avoid 'mirroring' behaviours that are a mismatch.

ACTIVITY

Find as many examples as you can of when you have noticed:

◆ behavioural 'cues' in people

◆ non-verbals which are at odds with what is being said.

If we are in a position where we are listening to someone over a period of time, being observant can also alert us to changes in their behaviours and attitudes, which could be very significant. A nurse or doctor can watch a patient carefully to check for signs of improvement or deterioration. As listeners, we can usefully learn from this practice, even if we are not (or not usually) looking for signs of physical change.

ACTIVITY

Try to think of instances when, by carefully noticing someone's body language, you were able to detect:

◆ a contradiction between what was said and how the person was feeling

◆ a change

◆ something significant which was not voiced.

LISTENING

How many people do you know who are prepared simply to listen to you – without offering advice, without saying 'I know what you mean because I ...', or 'When that happened to me ...'? People who can really focus on the speaker, whilst setting their own concerns aside and accepting that their experiences may be of no interest to the speaker, are rare. Perhaps these are the genuine 'good listeners'?

Active listening operates at several levels, and even the first level demands a degree of self-discipline.

ACTIVITY

Ask someone you know to talk to you for up to five minutes about something which matters to them. Nod, smile or make any other appropriate non-verbal response, BUT DO NOT SPEAK. Record, preferably on paper, what went through your mind as you listened. Was everything related to the speaker?

Being wholly focused, even for five minutes, takes a great deal of concentration. Words used by the speaker will inevitably trigger a response in the listener. Ideas which are mentioned will resonate with our own and set up a chain of thought. We may disagree with what is said and want to put an alternative point of view. Add to this that there may be noises around us, or that we're hot, hungry or uncomfortable and it is easy to see how staying focused on the speaker becomes hard work.

A further level of active listening is being able to take in the whole of the message, even if we are listening only to content. There are many barriers to this crucial ability of hearing everything. A colleague is talking about work – work which the listener knows well, and where the environment is familiar. The speaker might then say '... and then she just threw the cup at me and stalked off'. What can happen is that the listener 'switches off' – because the situation is known – and then has to pick up on some new factor without really knowing what the link may be. This type of listening is at its worst when it becomes the 'I've heard it all before' syndrome. It is true, of course, that listeners, especially those whose profession is listening, may have heard it (or something like it) before, but good active listeners are aware that for the speaker the experience is unique. Being able to take in the whole content of a message demonstrates the quality of being non-judgemental. We do not assume that what's not important to us is not important to the speaker or vice versa. So we listen to everything that is offered with equal respect.

ACTIVITY

Audiotape someone speaking – a short extract from a radio programme would be ideal – and listen to the content. Either aloud, or on paper, repeat what the person said. Replay the tape and check. Did you hear *every*thing? Did you remember it in order?

A useful way of ensuring that this listening skill is kept sharp is to ask friends or family to tell you about their journey to work, school, shops and even if you know the route as well as they do, to practise listening to what they say about traffic, drivers, other travellers. Another practice exercise is to listen as if you were required to repeat what you heard in court, as a witness. It's important to check whether you heard *everything*, and whether you could remember it in the order the speaker delivered it, rather than in the order you chose to put it in, even if the speaker's order seems muddled.

Sustained focus is both demanding and tiring, but the third level of active listening requires even more effort and energy. We need to be able to listen not only to what is being said but to how it is being said. Hearing the feelings attached to the content is at the heart of active listening.

ACTIVITY

'When you frown like that, you remind of my sister.' The content here is not especially difficult to hear – the listener has a particular way of drawing his/her brows together which brings the speaker's sister to mind. Say the statement in as many different ways as you can, and note the feeling each time.

The speaker may have sounded wistful/sad/amused/challenging/truculent or many other things. The content of the statement then acquires a whole new meaning and will affect the way in which the listener responds. Being able to hear feeling(s), as well as content, and draw sensitive inferences, has sometimes been termed 'listening with the third ear'. It is a highly developed skill, but well worth acquiring and practising because it assures the speaker that not only have they been heard accurately, but also that the listener was genuinely empathic.

What gets in the way of active listening? There seem to be some identifiable obstacles and if we are aware of them it may help us to avoid the pitfalls. You might like to award yourself a score for each one, so that you can practise – but don't worry, we're all guilty some of the time.

◆ **Distractions**: noise, movement, smells, uncomfortable seating and many other external factors can amount to a hubbub which makes it difficult to concentrate.

◆ **Switching on and off**: we think a great deal faster than we speak (four times faster has been calculated). As a result, we fill the time (three-quarters of it if the calculation is correct!) with thinking rather than listening. Slowing our listening to speaking pace helps not to switch-off.

◆ **'Beyond me'**: complex or complicated messages which we find difficult to comprehend often result in a complete shut-off. Afterwards, we may remember nothing of what was said.

◆ **Stuck on facts**: in trying to listen accurately to content, we may try to get the facts into our heads, but can then find that the speaker has gone on to new facts, which we may then lose.

◆ **Pencil and paper**: to make sure that we get the facts we may try to capture them on paper. It is usually impossible to capture everything and the writing can impede the relationship (who will own or see these notes?) and makes eye contact difficult.

◆ **Triggers**: there are words which act as a 'trigger' for all of us. These may vary from the 'red-rag-to-a-bull' words (unions, government, benefits, for example) to words which have a particular emotional connection for us (abortion, bereavement, children). When they are used, we can tune out the speaker.

◆ **'I know'**: we can decide after a couple of sentences that we know what's coming next (and anyway we've heard it before), so there's no point in listening because we won't learn anything new if we do.

◆ **Dreamy**: when we are tired, especially, we can seem to be listening, but are actually somewhere else in thought. We get glassy-eyed eventually and the speaker realises this. Unfortunately, this can sometimes almost become a professional pose – but the speaker is rarely fooled.

◆ **'You're wrong'**: speakers may contradict our pet theories, or strong views, and when this happens, instead of listening, we start planning how to put them right or, at worst, become judgemental.

◆ **Problem versus person**: we can become so concentrated on the details of an issue or problem (and sometimes so concerned to solve it) that we stop listening to the *person* and lose track of how they feel.

The following acrostic may sum up what we have discussed so far about active listening.

L	LOOKING at you (but not staring). LEARNING all I can from observing body language and appearance.
I	I am INTERESTED in you. Maintaining my own IDENTITY, I am willing to be INVOLVED with what you have to say.
S	SENSING your feelings, SENSITIVE to them, SUPPORTING you, keeping your secrets SAFE.
T	TRUSTING you to know what you need, and to make your own decisions, hoping you will TRUST me.
E	ENABLING you to be yourself, EMPOWERING you and EMPATHISING with you.
N	NOT having to solve your problems or give you advice, NOT giving in to my NEED to tell you what to do, but hearing your NEEDS.

RESPONDING

Responding sensitively and appropriately, assures speakers that what they said and how they are feeling have been heard. Being listened to is a novel experience for many and for some can even feel threatening. We need to keep this in mind and make our responses carefully. The basic responding skills which are essential for every listener's 'tool kit' are:

◆ appropriate questioning
◆ paraphrasing
◆ reflecting
◆ summarising.

APPROPRIATE QUESTIONING

Questions are, in one sense, a way of controlling what goes on in a conversation or interview. By asking a question, we turn the focus onto the listener's needs. We may, of course, genuinely need information before we can fully understand what is being said, but, even so, by asking for information the focus is changed and the speaker may feel interrupted. The essence of active listening is 'you talk; I listen' and questions can have the effect of shifting the balance to 'I talk; you listen'.

ACTIVITY

Try to remember some occasions when you have been describing or explaining something and have been asked a question. How helpful to **you** was the question? What were your feelings towards the questioner?

In the general run of conversation, of course, questions can be a way of demonstrating interest, but we do need to ask ourselves whether the question helps the talker or us. Try to decide whether the following questions would be helpful or unhelpful to the speaker.

Student: I'm not getting on very well. My parents really want me to pass and I'm scared of letting them down.

Listener: What are your study skills like?

Patient: I'm dead scared. If I have to have this operation, I don't know who's going to look after me afterwards.

Listener: Have you ever had an operation before?

Colleague: They want to move me and I want to stay. All this uncertainty is getting me down.

Listener: Have you applied for any other jobs?

Young Person: He keeps ringing up just before I go out in the morning and getting upset and threatening all sorts. It's horrible.

Listener: Why don't you take the phone off the hook?

Whether you think the questions are or aren't helpful, you can see that the listener is attempting to control the flow of the conversation and it's important to be aware of this. There are several types of question.

Closed questions: can be used to elicit facts, for example how old are you? They usually elicit the answers YES or NO. Very occasionally this type of question can be useful, especially if a speaker seems confused or muddled.

The great drawback with a closed question is that it tends to halt the flow of conversation and, more often than not, leads to another question and, of course, control of the subject matter is with the listener, who may then be resented by the speaker.

Open questions: are more likely to elicit feelings and can leave much more control with the speaker. A broad open question – 'How were things for you at that time?' invites the speaker to choose where to focus their feelings. Open questions usually begin with Who? How? What? Where?

◆ Try turning these closed questions into open ones.

◆ Have you told your parents about this?

◆ Have you been feeling sad for long?

◆ Are you very upset about this?

◆ Do you always stamp your feet when you're angry?

◆ Do you always just go quiet like this?

Open questions have the merit of enabling the speaker to keep talking, but even so should be used sparingly – question after question can feel like an interrogation!

Leading questions: are a common feature of radio or television interviews. They can usually be spotted as beginning with: Surely ...? or But surely...?, Don't you think ...?, Isn't it time that ...? or they might end with ... weren't you? Leading questions make the assumption that the original speaker is going to agree with the next statement.

◆ Test your own responses to these leading questions.

◆ I'm sure you were very pleased, weren't you?

◆ Aren't you absolutely devastated?

◆ Surely you don't agree with smacking?

◆ But surely you think demonstrating is wrong?

Even if, sometimes, your response was positive it is evident that the questioner *expected* you to agree. If we make this sort of assumption and get it wrong, it can be a clear sign that we are lacking empathy. We are responding from the perspective of how *we* would feel, rather than how the other person feels. There is a real danger in leading questions of pushing a person to feel what others think they should feel or ought to feel, rather than what they *do* feel.

ACTIVITY

Listen to some radio and television interviews, especially with politicians and note the number of times leading questions are used.

Multiple questions: are best avoided, as they often confuse the talker who is uncertain which question to answer. Multiple questions are often detected by their use of 'or' – 'Did you feel sad, or were you just relieved?' An answer to either of these questions would, in effect, mean that the other question was redundant. 'Yes, I did feel very sad' tells us that relief was not the strongest feeling. The skill in using questions lies in helping the speaker to clarify or think before they answer. By supplying alternative answers we are blocking this possibility and, at worst, this is disrespectful because it suggests that we think s/he may be incapable of finding an answer.

A brief word about 'why' questions. Although 'why' questions may be seen as 'open' they often aren't very helpful. They tend to lead to further 'why' questions (rather as children do). Quite often the speaker does not know why (and maybe that's the reason they're speaking to you). 'Why do your parents think you're lazy?' is, in a sense, unanswerable, since only the parents could tell us. 'Why' questions are usually better re-phrased so that they don't lead down a blind alley.

ACTIVITY

Try turning these why? questions into broader open questions. Why does your mother-in-law upset you? Why don't you want to complain? Why do you think he doesn't like her? Why don't you believe her?

'Reasons why' usually lie in the past and if we are trying to help someone, it is not possible for us to change their past, so finding out 'why' may not be very productive.

Questioning, then, can encourage a speaker, but if used insensitively it can do the reverse. Try to get into the habit of checking whether you use questions as some sort of controlling mechanism. If you do, try to question yourself:

◆ why am I asking this?

- ◆ do I really need to know?
- ◆ how does it help the other person?

PARAPHRASING AND REFLECTING

These two responding skills are often described as if they are the same, because both involve a sort of 'playing back' to the speaker what they seem to be communicating. To some degree, too, their purpose is the same – to convey to the speaker that we have heard and understood what was said. Perhaps this idea of 'playing back' has given rise to the myth that this kind of response is just repeating the last four words a person says, as if the listener were some kind of echo. You may have heard the old joke about this type of echoing.

Speaker: I feel awful.

Listener: You feel awful.

Speaker: Yeah, my life isn't worth living.

Listener: Your life isn't worth living.

Speaker: Right, I may as well jump in the river.

Listener: You may as well jump in the river.

(Person leaps into the river, is swept away and seen no more!)

This is not to say that the occasional use of an 'echo' is absolutely taboo; echoing one word can sometimes help the speaker to focus. For instance, in the ludicrous exchange in the joke, if the listener had just replayed the word 'awful' (perhaps on a questioning note) the speaker would have been encouraged to be a bit more specific about what 'awful' actually meant for him/her. Endlessly repeating, however, will make the speaker wonder whether the listener is just applying some kind of technique (or perhaps is mocking them). Paraphrasing and reflecting are much more than 'parrot-ing'.

Paraphrasing

Paraphrasing focuses on the fact(s) or content of what is said. It involves rephrasing, in the **listener's** own words, what was said. This not only allows the speaker to know that they are being listened to accurately, but can help to clarify thinking. If the listener plays back the gist of what was said – adding no inferences and leaving nothing out – the speaker can feel sure that the listener is getting things right. Playing back the essence of a statement in our own words is not as easy as it sounds. Not only do we need to listen in the special way we've explored, but we also need to remember (almost as if we have a tape recorder running in our heads); and to have a good vocabulary so that we can re-phrase the statement without significantly altering its meaning.

ACTIVITY

Try rephrasing the following statements without significantly altering their meaning.

Student: I can't keep up with the amount of work. I've got behind with my assignment. I'll never pass the exams.

Colleague: I keep having these stomach upsets. I don't think it's anything I've eaten. I worry because of the redundancies.

Mother: I do love the children, it's just that sometimes I could do with a bit of adult company, I'm so bored.

Elderly Person: It's not like it was when I was young. Things have really changed, and not always for the better. Sometimes, I feel as if I'm living on another planet.

Nurse: Some patients really seem ungrateful. No matter what you do for them they just moan.

Being able to suspend your values about these statements so that you replay only the content is, in itself, not easy. Rephrasing them so that there is no significant change and, if necessary, shortening them is very skilled work. Good paraphrasing can help people feel much clearer about what they are trying to express. A counselling client once said to me, 'I never know what I'm thinking until you say it back to me', and this perhaps shows the value of paraphrasing. It can also help to slow down someone whose thoughts are spilling out quickly or even chaotically. As listeners, it helps us stay alongside the speaker.

Reflecting

Paraphrasing relates to content, whereas reflecting relates to feelings. Reflecting is the ability to pick up and play back the emotional content of what is said, rather than the factual content. This skill is closely related to empathy; by communicating that we have heard feelings as well as content, we demonstrate that we are really trying to understand the speaker's emotions. Practising reflecting on paper is difficult, because we will all 'hear' the statements differently, but take each of the statements you paraphrased and make a response which begins with 'you sound ...' and name the feeling which you think the speaker was experiencing. It can be quite fun to ask another person to do this exercise with you, as it can sometimes be surprising how differently we 'hear' people – and says a lot about how difficult it is to set aside our own views and biases.

Paraphrasing and reflecting can be usefully used in tandem, letting the speaker know that both content and feeling have been heard. For example:

'Jane, when you were talking about your difficulties in settling in here (paraphrasing) you sounded almost wistful (reflecting) as if perhaps you'd like to feel settled, but don't quite see how to achieve it.

The two skills together act as a kind of mirror for the speaker, not only assuring them of our active listening, and that they have been both heard and understood, but also helping

---

ACTIVITY

Ask a friend or colleague to read the following statements and then reflect back the feeling(s) which seem to be present. Check the accuracy.

(This exercise can usefully be done on audio tape.)

Trainee: It's all very well. You told me to go on that course, and it was rubbish. I learned nothing and I've wasted all that money.

Colleague: It's no good. I'd really like to tell him how I feel, but I just haven't got the confidence. I'm just not assertive.

Young Person: If they go on about my room and my clothes any more, I'll just blow my top. I get that fed up I could smash everything.

Relative: Yes, but now that he's done it for me, I'll have to pay it back and I just don't want to.

Elderly Person: I'm sorry, but I think you're just too young to understand. Nice of you to try dear but it just won't work.

---

them to be more self-aware. Sensitive use of these skills can really help people to clarify thoughts and identify their feelings, and sometimes see how these might appear or sound to another person. This can be especially helpful if the person is confused or if they are concerned that what they are saying and feeling may seem ridiculous to the listener. People often begin to talk about their feelings with 'I know you'll think it's silly, but . . .'

Reflecting that they sound anxious or embarrassed when they talk, can reassure them that we hear the difficulty and can empathise with it, whatever our own views might be.

If we draw an inference as part of reflecting, it's important to make it tentatively so that the speaker can, if need be, disagree. As inference which is given non-tentatively can undo the empathy communicated by good paraphrasing and reflecting. For example, this statement:

It's really miserable. I try so hard to be friendly and I'd really love to be part of the crowd, but whatever I do, I seem to be on the outside looking in. It's as if whatever I do, nobody wants me.

This could be paraphrased and reflected as:

You talk about all your efforts at friendship seeming to lead nowhere, (paraphrasing) and you sound really unhappy and rejected because of that. (reflecting)

The listener might then draw an inference from this and offer it tentatively to the speaker:

Perhaps it would be helpful to look a bit more closely at how you 'try hard', since you said that very strongly.

A stronger inference (based on a more judgemental view) could be:

It's true, people who try too hard often do get the cold shoulder. Perhaps you're trying too hard.

The inference drawn from the paraphrasing/reflecting is, in some senses, the same, but the first builds on the reflection and encourages the speaker to explore their feelings. The second tends to 'take over' the speaker and moves from empathy and respect into 'What you ought to do ...' style.

Paraphrasing and reflecting are valuable skills in the pacing and timing of an interview. Not everyone works at the same pace and using these skills to speed up (concise paraphrasing) or slow down (more detailed reflection of feeling) an interview can be beneficial to the speaker and, often, make optimum use of time if this is at a premium.

A real danger in all listening is that we may make assumptions, based on our own experience or knowledge. If the assumptions are wrong, there can be a variety of consequences from embarrassing to disastrous. I was once confronted by an almost hysterical woman who told me that 'he hadn't come home last night, and that this had never happened before and that she was worried sick and that when he reappeared she intended to let him have it'. My assumptions were that 'he' was husband/father/son/partner and I had thoughts of police, hospitals etc. In the event, it was the woman's cat (a sole companion) who had gone on the prowl. This is, of course, an extreme example, but using paraphrasing or reflecting helped to calm the woman and saved me from the potentially embarrassing action of ringing hospitals. I was very thankful for paraphrasing and reflecting.

In the work of active listening, learning to listen and respond to silence is crucial. At first sight this may seem ridiculous – how can we listen to silence, since there's nothing to hear? Second thoughts suggest something very different. Many silences seem to have a very distinct quality, and although we may hear nothing in a physical sense, we nevertheless know that the silence is definitely saying something.

ACTIVITY

Using this list, describe what might cause different types of silence, for example uncomfortable – trying to think of something to say to someone you hardly know.

comfortable
guilty
frightening
angry
welcome
isolating
heavy

Silence, it seems, can communicate a whole range of feelings and reactions, and being able to 'tune in' to what a person's silence may be saying is a very valuable aspect of active listening. Being able to respond appropriately to silence is equally important. In the UK, and some other cultures, we seem to find silence difficult. We tend to respond in one of two ways; we either jump in quickly, before the silence can become 'awkward' and make some fairly harmless comment (usually about the weather!) or we can become rather stubborn. In groups, especially, people can get into a sort of 'I'm not going to be the first person to speak' frame of mind.

ACTIVITY

Recall experiences of your own where either of these has been your own, or others', response to silence.

Before we can respond appropriately to silence we need to feel comfortable with it ourselves. The term 'silence threshold' is sometimes used to describe the ability to sustain silence. Most of us need to extend this threshold, without allowing it to stray into the stubborn zone.

The old proverb that 'silence is golden', has rather special relevance in active listening. Often if we can wait through a silence, what a speaker will say next is 'golden'. Judging when to break into a silence is never easy – too soon and we may lose the 'gold' that we have been hoping for; too late and we may push the speaker into the stubborn zone, 'Well, I'm not going to talk' mode, and the silence becomes a battle-ground. Being able to read non-verbal signals can be very helpful here. If the person seems to be thinking, or trying to work something out, the silence is best left to run its course. If the speaker looks expectantly, with strong eye contact, then it's probably the time to respond.

Reflecting can sometimes be used as a helpful response to silence – 'You seem to be thinking hard', can reassure that the listener is still paying attention, but at the same time is happy to stay with the silence.

One of the most difficult silences to respond to is silent tears. Our natural instinct to comfort can mean that we break in on crying, when it might be more comforting for the person to cry if they are aware that the listener is comfortable with the tears. (You might remind yourself here about issues relating to touch.)

All the responding skills require a quality of self-awareness and this is a quality which is vital for a good listener.

Summarising

Probably the writer best known for work on helping skills is Gerard Egan (1992). He developed and refined a three-stage or phase model of helping, and sees the ability to summarise as part of active listening.

He says, however:

> A summary is not the mechanical pulling together of a number of facts.

(Egan, 1992)

Just as paraphrasing and reflecting are more than repetition or 'echoing' and provide the speaker with a mirror of how they are, in the same way, good summarising helps the speaker gain a more complete picture of their issues and concerns. Summarising is part of the responding element of active listening because it assures the speaker that the listener is following their story and is 'with' them. It also allows the speaker to correct any mis-understandings or inaccuracies that may have arisen.

Summarising utilises paraphrasing and reflecting, but in a rather condensed way, so that what is fed back to the speaker is the overall picture so far, rather than a response to each individual point.

ACTIVITY

A friend has been talking to you for some time about her boyfriend who has been diagnosed with a heart condition. It is not life threatening, but does limit somewhat his activity. There has been a problem with getting his medication right. Your friend has expressed concern and wants to be supportive. Then she says, 'You know how we always talk about whether we can be responsible for other people like if they drink or take drugs ... Well, since Tom's been ill he keeps saying he doesn't know where he is with me and that it's making him worse. I don't want to make him ill, but I'm not sure if I want to get really serious. I like him as a friend, but he gets upset if I go out with other friends. It's really hard and it's not my fault he's ill.' Try to summarise, without adding or taking away anything and without advising.

There are several ways of summarising and as long as we avoid Egan's 'mechanical pulling together' it is probably best to use whichever method feels comfortable. Summarising is very useful when it feels as if it is time to move an interview or discussion forward. It is also useful if there seem to be too many issues to focus on at once, and can help the talker to tackle one issue at a time. There are three ways of summarising that can be useful in these circumstances.

◆ After feeding back what the talker has communicated, both content and feeling(s), as concisely as possible, you might invite them to choose which aspect they'd like to focus on first. 'Of all the things you've mentioned, which one would it be most helpful to talk about first?' If this method of using a summary to move forward is chosen, it's always worth reassuring the talker that you're happy to talk about any other issues too. If asked to choose one focus people can sometimes become anxious that if they do, other equally important issues might get neglected. So we might amend the response to, 'Of all the things you've mentioned (and we'll come back to each one if you need to), which one would it be most helpful to talk about first?'

◆ Instead of inviting the talker to choose, the listener might offer the talker the possibility of talking about a contrast, in order to widen perspective. At its briefest this could be a simple open question at the end of the summarising, 'What would have to change for things to be different from how they seem now?' If possible courses of action, or choices have been shared by the speaker, then it is possible to invite the talker to weigh up the 'pro's and con's' of what you have summarised, 'How would it be if we looked at the advantages and disadvantages of selling your house and compared them with how it would feel if you stay put?' The advantage here is that it helps the person to focus on what their choices are, without in any way influencing the outcome.

◆ The third method is sometimes called 'figure and ground'. When we look at a picture there is usually something which stands out from the background. This is the 'figure'. When we listen to a person talking, the emphasis they put on certain words or the stronger feelings attached to some statements tend to make some things stand out. The talker may actually be unaware of this, so when we make the summary we can highlight this for them. 'Of all the things you've told me about, the one that seemed to matter most was losing your independence. If I'm right, would it be helpful to discuss that first and then come back to the other issues?' If this method is used, we have to be very careful to offer it sensitively, so that the talker doesn't feel that they must agree with it. They need to be able to contradict, if necessary, especially if, as sometimes happens, hearing the feedback alters their perspective so that something else now seems important.

Summarising is useful at various points during an interview:

◆ 'Mini' summaries can keep an interview on track for both parties, by reminding us where we are and what has been covered so far.

◆ A more structured summary can take place when it feels as if most of the initial or presenting material has been explored.

◆ In order to keep time boundaries in mind, the listener might from time to time indicate the actual time by summarising, 'we're about half way through our time together so perhaps I could summarise where we seem to be'.

Summarising can be especially useful as part of the ending process. We can remind the talker that time is nearly up and summarise, perhaps point to what might still be needed for exploration in future sessions.

If talking with someone is to be more than 'a little chat', the time we spend listening needs to be structured and there is good evidence that structure can, in itself, be helpful. The basic active listening skills looked at in this section help to explore what people want to share with us in a structured way and in a way which demonstrates the underlying values. This is perhaps summed up in this anonymous piece.

YOU ARE NOT LISTENING TO ME WHEN ...	YOU ARE LISTENING TO ME WHEN ...
You do not care about me, and you cannot care about me until you know something about me to care about.	You come quietly into my private world and let me be me.
You say you understand before you know me well enough.	You really try to understand me when I do not make much sense.
You have an answer for my problem before I have finished telling you what my problem is.	You hold back your desire to give me good advice.
You sense that my problem is embarrassing and you are avoiding it.	You don't take my problem from me but trust me to deal with it in my own way.
You get excited and stimulated by what I am saying and want to jump right in before I invite your response.	You give me enough room to discover for myself why I feel upset, and enough time to think for myself what is best.
You are trying to sort out all the details and are not aware of the feelings behind the words.	You allow me the dignity of making my own decisions even though you feel I am wrong.
You are dying to tell me something, or want to correct me.	You don't tell me that funny story you are just bursting to tell me.
You tell me about your experience which makes mine seem unimportant.	You allow me to make my experience one that really matters.
You refuse my thanks by saying you haven't really done anything.	You accept my gift of gratitude by telling me it is good to know I have been helped.
	You realise that the time I take from you leaves you a bit tired and drained.
You need to feel successful.	You grasp my point of view even when it goes against your sincere convictions.
You are disturbed by loaded words or abusive language.	You accept me as I am – warts and all.
You feel critical of my grammar or accent.	You look at me, feel for me, and really want to know me.
You come up with all the clever answers which have little to do with how I feel	
You are communicating with someone else in the room.	You spend a short valuable time with me and make me feel it is forever.
You cut me off before I have finished speaking.	

6

Further counselling skills – Jean Bayliss

In the previous chapter we looked at the basic skills of:

◆ attending
◆ observing
◆ listening
◆ responding.

These skills are the essential foundation of a helping relationship, perhaps of any relationship. The skills demonstrate the core qualities and communicate the values that we bring to the relationship. A deepening relationship needs these skills, but as trust develops a more complex range of skills will also be needed. This chapter looks at these skills and considers how to employ them in a developing relationship.

FEEDBACK

Responding skills could also be called giving feedback. The ability to give feedback, which is neither advice nor criticism, and which can be acted on is an underrated skill. Counselling skills courses usually practise skills in trios – talker, listener/responder and observer. The observer takes no direct part in the exchange between the talker and the listener, but gives feedback on what s/he saw and heard. It is very interesting that observers very often confuse giving feedback with praising. Natural though it may seem to praise someone when we think they have done something well, it is not the same as giving feedback, because when we praise someone, we are giving our opinion as to what was or was not well done; we are, in effect, assessing. This may not matter too much in practice work, but it could be rather dangerous in the 'real' situation. If we praise someone they may feel that they should do things to please us, or that they should act on the praise in ways that aren't very helpful. Praise is different from validation.

Compare the following: 'Well done! It was really brave of you to stand up to him when he was drunk.' with, 'It seems to have taken a great deal of courage to stand up to him when he was drunk'.

In the first response we are responding from our own frame of reference, it is our opinion that the action was brave, it may have been foolhardy! In the second response the action is being validated, but no opinion as to whether it was good or bad is offered. This needs to be kept in mind when we are listening and responding, as when we praise someone, for all the talker knows we may next start criticising.

ACTIVITY

Find examples of when praise and validation have become confused.

In practice work, observers are often very nervous about giving negative feedback, because 'negative' seems to imply criticism and we are (or most of us are) wary about giving criticism, but usually find it easy to praise.

ACTIVITY

How might negative feedback conflict with the core quality of being non-judgemental?

If we see giving feedback to fellow trainees as practice for giving feedback to 'real' talkers it may be easier to develop it as an invaluable skill in advanced active listening.

Although we may see the importance of feedback, we may feel at a loss about how to give it. There are some guidelines, but first:

ACTIVITY

Recall examples of when positive feedback was really useful to you, and when negative feedback was useful, even if not immediately.

Whilst you look at the following guidelines, it may be worth bearing in mind that feedback says at least as much about the giver as it does about the receiver. It's also worth remembering that too much feedback (at any one time) is not particularly helpful. If we hope that people will find our feedback useful we need to remember that everyone has a personal limit as to how much feedback they can take in at one time.

Feedback guidelines

◆ Limit feedback to what you have actually observed or heard, rather than what you assume might have been the attitude behind the behaviour(s) you saw and heard. Even if you 'sense' something, it's best to be cautious – you could be so wrong!

◆ When you describe what you heard or noticed, try to keep the focus on how this felt for you, rather than judging whether it was good, bad or anything else that could be seen as an opinion.

◆ Limit the number of points you think it would be helpful to highlight. This may well mean that you have to choose which aspects to ignore, but being aware of personal limits will help you here.

◆ Feedback is generally more helpful if it is specific. Generalised feedback often gets 'lost'. Try to keep focus; for example 'When you said ...' or 'When you touched on ...', 'I noticed that ...'. This will help the receiver of the feedback to reflect on how someone else sees or hears them.

◆ It is sometimes helpful, as feedback, to use questions. 'Could you please clarify for me what was happening when you ...?' We need to be very careful that the question is genuine, and not a covert way of criticising. If you look back to your earlier work on questioning, you will recall that we discussed the power balance in using questions. The use of genuine questions when giving feedback is very good practice for ensuring that questions are not manipulative.

◆ When we offer feedback, we need to be very aware of whether or not it is likely to be useful to the receiver. If it is unlikely that the behaviour you are commenting on could be changed then it is probably inappropriate to offer it, since it would have no value (or perhaps, even, no relevance) for the receiver. This awareness will sharpen our own listening and observing skills.

◆ It is perhaps a truism that feedback says at least as much about the giver as it does about the receiver, but it's still worth remembering.

CHALLENGING

Giving feedback so that it is heard and accepted and not seen as hostile is very challenging and the more advanced listening and responding skills are often referred to as 'challenging skills'. When we are structuring a helping interview, it is important not to use these challenging skills too soon in the process. The basic skills are used to help the talker feel heard, understood and respected. This takes time. We may be very confident that we are trustworthy, but the talker may need time to know this and believe it. Challenging too soon can interrupt the growth of trust and can mean that the development of the relationship is slowed or, at worst, that it is spoiled. Egan, whose three-stage model of counselling and counselling skills is probably the best known, suggests that helpers have to earn the right to challenge and one of the ways we can earn this right is by being prepared to be challenged ourselves.

ACTIVITY

Recall some times when you have been challenged and ask yourself:
what feelings did the challenge arouse in me? How did I feel about the challenger – at the time? Later? Was the challenge any use/help to me? Did I trust the person who challenged me? Was the timing of the challenge appropriate?

Because counselling skills are based on empathy, respect and on being non-judgemental, challenge can sometimes seem a contradiction in terms.

ACTIVITY

What do you think challenge is for? Why is it a counselling skill? Is it truly a helping skill?

When people seek help from a listener they usually need time to communicate what is troubling them. Those basic skills are essential in enabling the person to explore the difficulty or problem they are experiencing. Feeling that they are understood is very helpful, but at some point more is likely to be needed, if they are to move forward and begin to gain some sense of being able to manage their problem(s) at least a little better. There are many problems which can't be 'solved' and bereavement is an obvious example. Realising this can sometimes make a helper feel rather redundant and de-skilled. Advanced listening and responding skills are especially valuable here, because they challenge us, and the person we are trying to help, to appreciate that a deeper or broader understanding of issues and of ourselves is, in itself, a gift, even if it does not 'solve' problems.

It is unfortunate that challenge, which could be seen as a gift, has often been termed 'confrontation'.

ACTIVITY

What does the term confrontation mean for you?

The dictionaries offer a wide spectrum of meanings and some of them sound quite aggressive. There seem to be overtones, in this more aggressive end of the spectrum, of a sort of self-righteousness; as if some people have to be made to face up to (confront) their flaws and failings.

ACTIVITY

Check how often you hear, 'you ought to ...', 'You should ...', 'You must ...'. How does this resonate with the core quality of being non-judgemental?

Some of the meanings also seem to have an element of blame attached to them, as if confronting is an attempt to make people 'own up'. The deeper level of helping does indeed aim to encourage talkers to disclose more about themselves. But greater personal disclosure and 'owning up' are very different.

A more useful definition is: 'to bring together for contrast', so that if we observe that the person talking to us is showing many signs of tension (wringing of hands, constant fidgeting, hunched shoulders, tense jaw) and what they say is something about being very happy and relaxed, we might 'bring together for contrast' this contradiction. We might say, in a non-accusing way, something like, 'you've told me how happy and relaxed you feel, but I notice that your body seems very tense. Perhaps it would help if we explore that a bit'.

Before we look at using challenging skills in more detail, try to answer these questions.

ACTIVITY

Are you able to challenge? When you challenge, how do you feel? If you are reluctant to challenge, why is this? If you have challenged, has it been worth the risk?

Some people are very reluctant to challenge in a helping relationship because they fear that it will destroy or damage the quality of the relationship. We need to be honest with ourselves about this and check whether our own (very natural) need to be liked is impeding our use of challenge, which could be useful to the person we are trying to help.

Challenging is sometimes made easier if we can feel sure that we can balance the challenge with an equivalent amount of support.

ACTIVITY

Think of a time when you had a challenge to face. If you received solid support, what feelings did this give you? If you had poor support, list the feelings you had.

Generally, people seem to think that although the actual challenge may have remained daunting, the amount of support they received had a significant impact on how they approached their challenge.

An important aim of all helping is to enable the other person's self-reliance. We all need help from time to time, but self-respect and self-esteem depend in part on being reasonably independent. Small children seem to demonstrate that this is, perhaps, an in-built human quality. They delight in doing things for themselves and any interference can produce tears or tantrums. As helpers, we can learn from this. The right amount of support is crucial. Too much and we can end up 'smothering' the person and it shows a lack of respect if we 'take over' and do too much for the person who perhaps really needs to meet a challenge for him/herself.

Challenge, then is a very useful skill, but it should not be used too early in the helping (or indeed any) relationship and needs to be carefully balanced with support. As a relationship of trust develops and the talker begins to disclose more of him/herself, there are some points which it may be especially useful to challenge. As you read each one, try to formulate how you would challenge each of these, keeping that support/challenge balance firmly in mind. An example for you to challenge is given for each.

◆ Many people seem unable to prevent themselves from saying how useless, or hopeless, or bad etc. they are. This kind of negative thinking can impede any change which might help with managing the problem. It also means that people seem unable to recognise and acknowledge the strengths that they *do* have and which they might employ to make a difference. Being able to challenge this negativity and help people to evaluate their strengths, rather than their weaknesses, can help to give a more balanced view of the possibilities. (If you have doubts about challenging and find it rather daunting, perhaps challenging unacknowledged strengths will convince you that it is a positive, not negative, skill.)

  Example: I'm not surprised I didn't pass. I've never been any good at exams. It's like everything else – I'm just not very bright.

◆ If people are to move forward and begin to feel able to make changes, however small and seemingly insignificant, they need help to move away from all the 'shoulds' and 'oughts' which are keeping them stuck. 'I know I ought to visit my parents more often', 'I really should make an effort to lose weight' and similar statements can mean that any action is indefinitely put off. 'Oughts' and 'shoulds' also show that someone has perhaps decided what they really want to achieve, but are stuck with feeling unable to move towards what Egan calls 'the preferred scenario'. The 'current scenario' is the one which is full of 'oughts' and 'shoulds'. The objective of challenging here would be to move the person from ought/should to **could** (and, maybe, to 'I will'). Again, offering to help a person move towards 'could' is not an accusation but an invitation.

  Example: I really should try to find a bit of time to relax instead of endlessly rushing about and achieving nothing.

◆ Many difficulties and much unhappiness in life can be blamed on the past. Most of us can look back and say, 'If only' about at least one thing. If only we had made a different decision; stayed at home; married a different partner; had/not had children; had a better education … the list could go on forever. Even if the blame is realistic, one of the certainties about the past is that it can't be changed. Empathising with 'if only' is, of course, important, but so also is challenging people not to see themselves in an impossible framework where they have no choice. Helping encompasses that over-worked word 'empowering' and, in order to empower, this 'impossible' needs challenging if the person is not to feel a victim.

  Example: My parents got divorced when I was at a very vulnerable age, so I'll never be able to make proper relationships.

◆ During any one day, most of us say things like, 'it makes me mad' or, 'whenever the manager comes he just disrupts the whole office' and so on. This is very natural and part of everyday chatting, but if we never 'own' the problem as our own, or at least as partly our own, then no change is likely to occur. It is often worthwhile challenging ourselves by noting the number of times 'it' makes us do or feel something, and trying to change the thinking to 'I allow myself to be made'. Helping people to change their thinking to 'I don't cope with the manager's visit too well and need to learn how to prevent the disruption he causes', can really empower people to change.

Example: It's driving me potty. If there's another traffic hold up today, it will send me off the deep end.

◆ Albert Ellis, the founder of Rational Emotive Behavioural Therapy (REBT) based his work on the ancient Roman principle (echoed by Shakespeare) that 'Men are not moved by things, but by the view which they take of things'. We are all prone to thinking errors of one sort or another; in the helping relationship, it may be very useful to challenge some of these. Often just reflecting one word may help the person to see the thinking error. For example, 'Why does it always rain when I plan a day out?' Just playing back 'always?' can challenge the thinking. Some of these thinking errors are:

- ◆ over-generalising – I never get anything right
- ◆ filtering out – I didn't have one minute's peace
- ◆ discounting – OK, so I did something right for once, but it will be just as bad again tomorrow
- ◆ all or nothing – if it's not absolutely perfect, I don't want to do it
- ◆ jumping to conclusions – I just *know* it's all going to go pear-shaped
- ◆ labelling (globalising) – We had another argument – I'm the world's worst partner
- ◆ misreading emotion – I feel guilty, so it must be my fault.

None of these is likely to help a person become more self-reliant or begin to regain some sense that they have the power to change their thinking and then, maybe their lives – often if we turn small wheels, big wheels will begin to turn. Challenge can turn small wheels.

◆ Frequently people seem to want two mutually exclusive things at the same time and, just as bringing into the open a contradiction between body language and words can be helpful, so can highlighting two apparently contradictory statements. For example, if someone is telling us that passing their exams is the most important thing at present, but also says that they don't know what they'd do without their social life, we might ask them to look at how these two match up for them. Challenging in this way does not judge whether exam success or a social life is 'best', but invites the person to explore the contradiction. Challenge is especially valuable in this area when people giggle or smile whilst telling us something sad.

Example: I really need a clear head in my job – everything depends on making the right decision. It's teamwork. That's why having a few drinks at lunchtime is important.

Challenging skills involve both listening and responding. We have to listen very carefully in order to spot what actually needs challenging, and then use or adapt the basic counselling skills to make the challenge. Challenging is, perhaps, a rather sophisticated way of giving feedback, since we are feeding back what we hear as a discrepancy, or a contradiction or some errors of thinking. But, rather than pointing these things out as an accusation, we are inviting the person to look at them and reflect on what they might mean.

◆ Sometimes, in a helping interview, there seem to be some behaviours which could be helpfully challenged, but this can seem difficult because they seem to require a rather more personal approach, which might appear to be attacking. For example, some people seem to get so 'wound up' that they rattle away at great pace, in a story that is getting very repetitive and going nowhere, making it very difficult to intervene. Asking the person to stop for a moment, perhaps to take a few deep breaths may initially seem like non-acceptance, but if it is done to enable the person to be better helped, then it seems appropriate.

ACTIVITY

Work out a statement that you could use to help someone slow down, which achieves the aim, but does not offend the talker.

In the previous chapter, we discussed the value of silence. Sometimes people find it hard to talk or they may be avoiding, perhaps because they think the listener will be shocked by what they are thinking or feeling. Being able to challenge silence depends to a large extent on being comfortable with it ourselves. It's often tempting to intervene with questions and then what do we do if the person doesn't answer? Ask yet another question? A useful idea is to challenge the silence rather than the person, 'You seem a bit locked in to being silent, as if you can't decide whether to speak or not. If you feel ready, I'm ready to listen'. We must then have the composure, and courage, to wait. The trouble with silence is that no one really knows what it means. We can interpret it in so many different ways, and end up coming to a wrong conclusion. This is why acknowledging a silence and communicating to the other person that we are not uncomfortable is a useful challenging skill.

ACTIVITY

Practise some interventions you would feel comfortable making in a silence. Ask someone whose views you trust to give you some feedback about how these sound.

There is another type of personal behaviour which we may feel is difficult to challenge and this involves avoidance. If we are alert we can notice that when a certain topic crops up the speaker will try to avoid it, by chatting about something else or, of course, by becoming silent. Confronting avoidance can feel like walking a tightrope. On the one hand we want to respect the person's right to talk about what they want to discuss, but at the same time we might see that opening up a sensitive area could help. We also need to check out whether it is something in us that is causing the person to hold back. Are they afraid that we will be shocked, or disapproving, or think that they are stupid? Again, the challenge can be to the issue, not the person. 'I notice that if sex ever crops up in our conversations you seem to want to shy away from the topic. Would it be useful to look at that?' This type of challenge must always respect the talker's right to retreat, but, if no challenge is given, we may have lost a golden opportunity to bring matters out that would really benefit by airing. Another type of avoidance which we might want to challenge is when someone persistently talks about someone else and avoids expressing how they feel about that someone else. These three 'types' of people who need help can be challenging for the helper, but using the challenging skills can give us a real sense of achievement.

We mentioned that successful use of challenge involves being prepared to be challenged ourselves. One of the ways in which this challenging can happen is when the person we are trying to help asks us a direct question. The question may be to justify something they have said or done, 'Well, wouldn't you have done the same in my position?' The answer, of course, could well be 'yes', but it will not be helpful to the person's self-reliance to indicate this, and if the answer is 'no' we could divert into a discussion of our reasons for doing or not doing something which then moves the focus from the talker. We may also be asked to give our opinion about what someone should do, 'Tell me, what would you do in my shoes?' This is equally dangerous, as not only would we be undermining the other person's autonomy, by telling them what we would do, but we could be so wrong. What's right for us is not necessarily right for someone else. It would be very uncomfortable to have someone return at a subsequent interview and say 'I did what you said, and now everything's even worse'. Responding to this type of question can often be very challenging, especially if we are concerned about the welfare of the other person. For example, responding to the question, 'Do you think I should go back to him?' from a previously battered wife, may create real conflicts for the listener. Questions need to be reflected back to the talker so that they are challenged to answer them themselves. We need to acknowledge that this can make the other person rather frustrated, and they may think (or say), 'Just tell me what to do and I'll do it'. Being firm about challenging questions is not easy, but it is an essential skill and just as challenging for the listener as the talker.

ACTIVITY

Try responding to these questions so that the talker is challenged to think for themselves of an answer.

◆ Do you think I should apologise (after some bad behaviour)?
◆ Look, you're well known here, will you ask him for me?
◆ If somebody helps you, wouldn't you do something in return?
◆ I know you'd agree that it's not fair wouldn't you?
◆ Why do we have to go over and over the same topic?

If there is such a thing as a 'golden rule' about all of these more advanced counselling skills, it is probably 'don't use it too soon'. If we make sure that the relationship is sound and can accept that the other person may not find challenge acceptable, we are likely to use the skills cautiously and with sensitivity. They then move away from being uncomfortably con-frontational and become a gift to the other person, a gift which can open up new per-spectives and understanding and help them move towards their 'preferred scenario'.

IMMEDIACY

Of all the more advanced skills, the one known as **immediacy** is the one which demands most of the helper and calls for the greatest sensitivity. However, before we can use the skill of immediacy the idea of the 'here and now' needs to be explained. If we are sitting in a chair, listening to music that we love, we are, first and foremost, aware of the music. If the chair has a rather 'itchy' covering, we gradually become more aware of the fabric we are sitting on than of the music we are listening to. Similarly if we become hungry or thirsty whilst listening, the urge to get something to eat or drink, will take precedence and although we may still hear the music it will not be in the foreground of our consciousness.

ACTIVITY

Practise awareness of the here and now. Ask: what am I thinking now, this minute? What am I feeling now, this minute?

As we observed when looking at challenging skills, the past is gone and can't be changed. We are unable to predict the future, so if we want to help people we need to be very focused in the present.

Another reason for being very aware of the here and now is that it helps us identify feelings. Inevitably, the stories people tell us will be about what has happened to them, which may be a crisis, or something disturbing or worrying. When the event is described to us it will already have happened and the person may explore many of the feelings they had at the time. Our listening will help us to determine whether those feelings are still present. For example, a young man with an over-protective mother may vividly describe an angry outburst he had with her, re-living his anger and say that he swore at her. How he feels now may be very different, even though his anger then is so vividly described. The helper's task is to pick up on the here and now feeling.

Being alert to the here and now is crucial to effective use of the advanced skill of imme-diacy. Immediacy requires us to acknowledge what we are experiencing in the relationship and to use this to help the other person. Most of us will have experienced irritation or frus-tration with someone who 'beats about the bush' and never seems to get to what they are trying to communicate. In our heads we may be saying something like, 'oh, get on with it'. What we actually say may vary from nothing (but our body language speaks volumes) to something quite aggressively forthright! It will depend on the relationship we have with the other person. In the helping relationship there should be trust and respect, and this will help us to decide whether immediacy is useful and appropriate.

Immediacy involves being able to feed back to another person how we are experiencing them in the here and now. But immediacy should always be for the benefit of the person being helped, it is not an opportunity for us to let off steam. For example, if we found the young man with the over-protective mother rather intimidating when he described his outburst we might feed back to him something like, 'When you shout and bang your fist on the chair like that I feel a bit intimidated. I wonder if your mother experiences you in the same way?' The decision to share this would depend upon whether the helper thought it would be useful for him to take this information on board or whether, if he was for the first time being assertive, it might make him anxious, in which case the helper might use it to open up some discussion about appropriate assertive behaviour.

ACTIVITY

Think of someone to whom you would like to express your feelings (positive or negative). Imagine yourself being open and honest about these. Practise saying things like, 'When you do/say ... I feel ....' Check how doing this for real would be for you.

The use of feedback to express how a helper is feeling, may seem rather contradictory to what we have said so far. Emphasis has been placed on trying always to respond from the other person's frame of reference and on making a real effort not to allow our views or feelings to influence our listening. Yet when we enter into a helping relationship, or indeed any relationship, with someone, it is almost inevitable that both parties will have feelings about each other. If these feelings are not understood then they can seriously impede active listening; immediacy may prevent this happening.

ACTIVITY

Try to find examples of when your own feelings have prevented you from really listening. What sort of feelings were they?

If we are feeling fed up with the other person, perhaps because they haven't done any of the things they had decided would help them; or if we feel rather bored that they are going over the same story for the umpteenth time, how likely is it that we can go on demonstrating the core qualities? Remember the old joke that, 'you can't fake genuineness'? If we're pretending to find these behaviours OK then we are hardly being sincere. By bringing the frustration out into the open we could remove a block not only to our own listening, but also for the other person, and this may enable change. On the other hand, immediacy, if it is not used sensitively, can create a block in the other person, who may hear the feedback as criticism. Insensitive use can also block disclosure in another way: the person may worry that what they are doing, or saying, is upsetting the helper. They may then hold back or feel that they should perhaps protect the helper by not upsetting them. The whole point about immediacy is that it benefits the person we are trying to help. If the focus shifts onto the helper this is clearly not happening.

Try to change the following statements into ones where immediacy is used. Remember – immediacy involves sharing your own feelings, in the here and now.

◆ Why do you keep changing everything round? For heaven's sake leave it alone.
◆ So you think it's OK to educate the boy, but his twin sister doesn't matter?
◆ Look, you've got all the ability in the world, but you just won't work.
◆ If you keep going in this way I dread to think what the outcome will be

---

As with so many responding skills, the way in which immediacy is used is critical for its success. If we comment on how someone's behaviour makes us feel – sad, frustrated, happy etc – we share part of ourselves. We, therefore, have a responsibility not only to increase our self-awareness so that we are sensitive to using immediacy in our day-to-day lives, but also to become aware of how certain behaviours affect us. This awareness will help us express immediacy in terms of feelings rather than judgements.

SELF-DISCLOSURE

Immediacy is a form of helper **self-disclosure**, and there is another form of self-disclosure which can be useful in the helping interview. Just as with immediacy, this self-disclosure must relate to the other person's needs. A very irritating aspect of some interviews is the tendency of some listeners (we hope only a few) to use phrases like, 'I do understand what you mean', or 'I do understand how you feel'. The statement is then followed by an explanation of why they 'understand', and the explanation is usually because they have had what they think is a similar experience. 'I know just how you feel, because when I was your age I had exactly the same problem ...'. In the normal chit chat of everyday life this may not matter and may be part of keeping a conversation going – although it can be irritating even so and can sometimes feel competitive.

ACTIVITY

Recall examples of when someone has sympathised with you by telling you of a similar experience. How did you feel?

In the helping interview this kind of self-disclosure is not appropriate. It moves the focus away from the talker (where it belongs) to the helper (who is, at the time, not needing to be the focus). More seriously, it is the very opposite of empathic; as, far from doing our best to understand how the person experienced an event, we are assuming they felt as we did. There is also an absence of genuine respect as we are, in effect, denying that a person's experience is unique to them.

Even so, helpers bring to their work a wealth of life experience and it may sometimes be useful to share this if it would broaden or deepen understanding. If we ask ourselves, 'why am I sharing this?' we may be able to regulate both the frequency and amount of self-disclosure that we use. For example, a second-year A level student, who is likely to do well, tells his form tutor that he is going to give it all up and get a job. The teacher has 'seen it all before' and, indeed experienced the same wishes herself, at 18. How can she share the information without patronising the student? How could she make the information useful to him?

If she were to tell him, however kindly and, possibly, truthfully, that 'Oh, we've all been through it. I remember feeling the same way, but I stuck with it and managed to get to university', what might his reaction be? He might think, or even, say, 'Yes, all right, but this is me and I want to get a job' or possibly something rather less polite. On the other hand, if the tutor genuinely felt the information and shared experience could be of help, she might say something like, 'I can remember feeling fed up in the run up to A levels, and it seems as if a lot of students do too. For me, it was worth sticking to it because, at bottom, I really did want to go to university. But perhaps it isn't quite the same for you? Perhaps it would help to explore your long-term ambitions.' This might achieve more, because although the tutor is showing the student that he is not alone in this experience, she is careful not to minimise his feelings and indicates an appreciation that his experience may well be different. This seems like more appropriate use of self-disclosure.

ACTIVITY

Try to decide how each approach differs, linking to the core qualities see p. 110.

If you look back at your list of barriers to good listening (pp. 97–98), one of the items will remind you that we can make assumptions that we have 'heard it all before'. This unfortunate habit can be very prevalent in self-disclosure. If the other person tells us something akin to our own experience, we can easily forget that even if the experience is identical, the other person's feelings about the experience will not be the same as ours. It is for this reason that some people do not find support groups helpful, although many people do.

ACTIVITY

Try to think of ways in which support groups could be seen negatively by some people and positively by others.

Examples which came my way recently involved bereaved parents. One felt that the support group was not helpful because, 'I know they've lost a child too, but their grief isn't like mine. I don't know if theirs is more or less, but I don't want to be classed as a grieving parent'. On the other hand, parents who had found their group helpful said, 'Because we've all been through the same thing, horrible though it is, you get a bond that at least someone knows the hell you're going through.'

It seems to be important to get the balance right between helping the person to feel less isolated, and sharing what may be useful information, whilst not moving the focus from the unique nature of the way in which the other person may be experiencing a similar experience.

ACTIVITY

Try turning the following rather general self-disclosures into something more helpful.

◆ I know – we've all been young once, but we get through it.

◆ I do understand, because when we had to move we had the children to think about, changing schools and that.

◆ I know just how you feel – when we lost our dog I was devastated.

◆ It is hard, but I think we all go through these phases and we mustn't let our troubles get on top of us.

◆ Yes, it's horrible being nervous – I remember sitting the driving test. It was awful.

Inappropriate use of self-disclosure can seriously damage rapport. If we say something like, 'I do understand', the other person may think (or, less frequently, say), 'How can you? You aren't old/young; black/white; married/divorced; etc/etc'.

Self-disclosure can have an impact on confidentiality. In order to develop trust, a helper or counsellor will agree the boundaries of confidentiality with the other person. What this often means is that the contract applies to the counsellor or helper, who will make every effort to keep to the boundaries agreed. Quite often, it seems not to apply to the client or other person, who may disclose to family and friends what went on in the interview. Many of us will be familiar with the person who returns for a subsequent interview and cheerfully says something like, 'I told my mother/partner/friend what you said and s/he said ...'. We may have to accept a one-sided contract, it seems! With this in mind, self-disclosure needs careful forethought. Should a manager self-disclose to an employee? Should a teacher to a pupil? A doctor or nurse to a patient? There may be occasions when it would be helpful, but we need to remember that the disclosure may well go outside the room where it could get distorted or re-interpreted.

ACTIVITY

Reflect on instances where self-disclosure might create difficulties, even if originally it was made within firm boundaries.

'Self-disclosure demands self-restraint' may be a good motto for helpers.

CONCRETENESS

What people tell us is often so interesting, and may have so many strands, that it can be difficult to keep focus. The talker may also be rather vague or general about what they are feeling. Helping the other person to be specific and focused is usually called concreteness. Just as some people find 'confrontation' an unfortunate choice of word for a counselling skill, some also find 'concreteness' unfortunate. For them it has the sense of something heavy, or 'set' and they think this is inappropriate in an activity which, by its very nature, is fluid.

Whatever it is called, the skill is aimed at keeping both parties firmly focused and, also, at clarifying what is being talked about. In day-to-day conversation, we often talk about a mysterious 'they'. These are usually the faceless people who make everything go wrong and who ought to 'do something about it'. 'They' may be the government, schools, the Health Service, or any number of anonymous agents who don't seem to be behaving as we might like.

ACTIVITY

Think of examples where 'they' should do something. Who are 'they'? Are 'they' likely to change?

This vagueness is sometimes expressed as 'everyone ...'. 'Everyone knows that teenagers are difficult' or, 'We all know that broken homes have a terrible effect on people'. This kind of statement is not very helpful if we are trying to help someone be specific about their own difficulties. For example if a young person says, in an interview, 'Well, no one gets on with their parents, everyone knows that'. Our task is to explore whether what is actually being said is, 'I don't get on with my parents', which gives us a very different picture. Generalisation and vagueness are often a defence – it may make it less unhappy to be at odds with one's parents if 'everyone' is in the same position. Because generalising may be a defence, we need to use concreteness with care: breaking down defences is a delicate task.

One of the areas where concreteness is probably most difficult to use, but, if handled well, can be most rewarding, is when we are working with loss and grief. The dreadful term 'the grieving process' (as if there's only one) is probably used as much by listeners as by the grieving person, 's/he's going through the grieving process'. If we really want to help a grieving person, we need to be concrete about which process; what we (or the grieving person) mean by 'going through' (or for that matter 'being stuck') and whether the vagueness is blinding us to the true pain of the other person. Concreteness can also be useful when the other person talks at great length about people outside the interview. The factual details about someone who is not present may be necessary (although too many of these can become a distraction). These details may then diverge into what the person we are working with felt about this third person and what they believe the third person was thinking or feeling. Since this is in the past and may also be speculation, the task is to help the person focus on how they are feeling here, in the interview with you.

Reflecting meaning is often a good way of helping a person be more concrete, 'What you are saying seems to be ...' 'The meaning of that for you is ...'. There needs to be a tentative feeling, so that the other person does not feel we are being rather dismissive. It may sometimes be possible to ask the other person to rephrase something they have said so that they express 'ownership'. For example, if someone has said something like, 'They're all the same, men/women', after some discussion about a partner, it may be possible to ask the person to 'own' this by saying something like, 'Could you restate that so that I know which men/women you mean?' or, 'When you say that everything looks bleak and gloomy, could you tell me what things they are?'

Concreteness can help us to face issues more fully and, in the process, begin to take more responsibility. We stay active, rather than passive. For example, if the other person says, 'Sometimes I feel better than others' it will not help him/her to maximise on what is better if the statement isn't made more concrete with responses like:

◆ Which are the times when you feel better?
◆ In what ways are you feeling better?
◆ Could you give me an example of when/how/where you feel better?

You can see here how open questions can be used as a springboard for more advanced skills.

ACTIVITY

Try formulating responses to these statements to help the speaker be more concrete.

◆ Nobody at work treats me properly; they're all against me.
◆ I've had another terrible week.
◆ I feel more positive now.
◆ The kids are driving me up the wall.
◆ I just don't have any confidence.
◆ Sometimes I feel really panicky.
◆ Everything's getting on top of me.
◆ None of the GPs cares how I feel.

Concreteness helps people move towards action, by prioritising where the distress lies. Clearly this kind of work is only possible if a really sound relationship exists, but if we are to help people we can accelerate the process by aiming for really specific aspects that can be tackled.

ACTIVITY

Practise concreteness on yourself. Any time you are vague try to be specific about what you actually mean. Any time your feelings are confused, try to get in touch with the specific feeling(s).

GOAL SETTING

Goal or target setting is another advanced counselling skill. If we have explored a problem area with someone and enabled them to gain insight and greater understanding not only of the 'problem' but also (by our use of challenging skills) how they might be contributing to the problem area, there will come a time when the person will begin to use these insights to plan. Having looked at their 'preferred scenario' they will begin to look for ways of 'getting there'. Helping with this involves a new set of skills. In every helping situation there are issues about power. Is the helper more powerful than the person seeking help? Is the person seeking help weak because they can't, at the moment, see a way forward? Whilst our awareness of the core qualities will make us conscious that these questions should receive a 'no' answer, we need to be aware that to the other person this may not be so evident. Low self-esteem can mean that others often see us as some kind of icon of perfect coping. Paradoxically, this does, in fact, place us in a very powerful position. Nowhere is this more evident than in goal and target setting. We need all the basic and the more advanced skills to ensure that the goal or target is not ours, but is very definitely the other person's. Setting goals with another person can be quite a delicate matter, not only because of the power issue, but because the concept itself is alien to some people. We also have to be alert to people feeling that because they haven't achieved their goals (yet) they are therefore useless and hopeless. This in turn links back to the power issue, because if someone views the helper as a person who (in their imagination) achieves all their goals, it can be very discouraging. It is, however, worthwhile. Research seems to show that those who set goals and work, however slowly, towards them are more successful and have higher self-esteem.

The following list contains a variety of aims and goals, which can be broadly divided into five categories:

A rather grandiose and unlikely, not very likely to be realistic or achievable

B contain some problem related to the person – something negative which needs to be overcome

C a desire for a new skill or for a different state

D there is some plan of action involved relating to something which is relatively easy to complete

E involves changing the actions, or reactions, of other people.

ACTIVITY

Go through the following list and decide which item fits into which category.

> A ...
> B ...
> C ...
> D ...
> E ...

1. Winning the Lottery Jackpot
2. Meeting the Queen/President of the USA
3. Losing weight/Giving up smoking/Getting fit
4. Learning to speak French/Italian/Russian
5. Choosing shrubs for the garden
6. Getting rid of my old clothes
7. Stopping X from delaying me every morning with boring chatter
8. Improving relationships with my relatives
9. Getting promotion
10. Doing something useful for a charity
11. Overcoming my anxiety about anything to do with authority
12. Getting the car serviced
13. Being a bit more assertive
14. Making a million pounds
15. Winning in the next Olympics/Marathon
16. Putting aggressive people in their place
17. Being happier
18. Succeeding at more things
19. Managing stressful situations better
20. Being less inept in social situations.

There have been several attempts to develop a set of criteria, to check whether a goal really is a goal or whether it's a wish. One of the best known of these criteria for goals is known by the acronym **S–M–A–R–T**. Goals should be:

S – Specific, significant and stretching

M – Measurable or verifiable (the person should see themselves achieving step by step)

A – Achievable (goals which are too far out of reach can be a burden rather than an incentive)

R – Realistic (it needs to be in the control of the person whose goal it is)

T – Set within a reasonable time limit.

ACTIVITY

Look back at the list and check which ones best measure up to the criteria.

Clearly there is a great deal of work to be done before even the more specific aims could be said to qualify as goals, but we are perhaps nearer to defining what a goal is.

ACTIVITY

Write down several general goals in your life, for example I'd like to be more confident, I wish I could be more organised. Work to focus the goal until it meets the SMART criteria.

Your work has probably helped you to define what a goal is more clearly.

◆ A goal is a clear statement about what a person intends to do.

◆ It should describe something that will feel like an achievement.

◆ The goal should be within the capabilities of the individual.

Another acronym for criteria for goals is **O–S–C–A–R–S**:

O – Focused on an outcome

S – Specific

C – Challenging

A – Achievable

R – Relevant to the person's values

S – Set in a reasonable time frame

(The acronym is adapted from Egan. Do you like the idea of awarding ourselves, or others, an OSCAR?) Most of the items in OSCARS are the same as those in SMART, but there is a significant addition – R – Relevant to the person's values.

ACTIVITY

Look back at your goals. Do they all sit comfortably with your personal belief-system?

At a recent training session, some teachers pointed out how in school, the school's goals and even the pupils' goals could be seriously at odds with pupil values. The school's (and some of the pupils') goal might be to get good GCSE results, but the pupils' values are that it is not 'cool' to work hard. 'Swots' or 'boffs' are not seen as desirable and so there is a clash of values over the goal. People are unlikely to work towards a goal that violates their personal value system. This highlights the importance of not imposing our goals, which would come from our value base, onto others 'for their own good'.

Having helped the person to devise a goal which meets the criteria, it is then useful to help them look at what might help, or hinder, the achievement. Probably the best known model for this is known as **Force Field Analysis**, or FFA (Egan, 1992). The name relates to the model's process, that by identifying helping and hindering forces a field of movement can be created to help a person move towards the goal.

positive			negative	G
→⟶	⤍⤍⤍	field	←——	O
facilitating	⤍⤍⤍	of	hindering	A
→⟶	forces	movement	←——	L
→⟶	⤍⤍⤍		←——	

Some helpers find it useful to work through the model with the other person, on paper. The person may then want to keep the paperwork, to remind them of their goal and to encourage themselves that the facilitating forces are moving forwards and that the field of movement is beginning to push back the hindering forces. Some helpers dislike working on paper and prefer to guide the other person through the process wholly verbally. Either way it is important not to be so directive that we over-structure what the other person can do and thus impede self-reliance.

GOAL	
FACILITATING FORCES (INTERNAL WORLD)	**HINDERING FORCES (EXTERNAL WORLD)**
skills, resources, strengths 1. 2. 3. etc.	limitations 1. 2. 3. etc.

FACILITATING FORCES (EXTERNAL WORLD)	**HINDERING FORCES (INTERNAL WORD)**
people, places, opportunities etc 1. 2. 3. etc.	People, places, rules etc 1. 2. 3. etc.

You will realise that working through the model requires the helper to use good challenging skills and to be good at asking open and probing questions without overwhelming the other person. Because we are often very good at seeing the negative, hindering forces especially our own limitations, it may be worth having a sort of list of 'prompts' which would open up new possibilities for the other person.

ACTIVITY

Check each of the items on the list against your own goal. Are you using all your resources?

◆ **People**: it seems to be true that many people would love to help, but are afraid of offering. Maybe UK reserve makes us worry that we would be seen as interfering. If we want help with our goal, it could pay dividends to ask for it.

◆ **Models**: some of these people, or some others, could be very good role models. They may have achieved the same goal. As helpers we need to be cautious here, in case we get the, 'It's all right for them' response.

◆ **Places**: this may involve many things, from information centres to a quiet corner to work in.

◆ **Things**: there may be a variety of aids which could help. Computers are an obvious example.

◆ **Organisations**: there are societies for so many problem areas now that it would be hard not to find one that would help.

◆ **Inner resources/Skills**: your 'challenging strengths' work will help here.

Just as the goal needs to be 'owned' by the person being helped, so do the strategies. We are far more likely to work at them if we think we generated them ourselves.

ACTIVITY

With a partner, if possible, choose a goal and spend up to ten minutes generating ideas based on the prompt list, which will help you achieve your goal.

This kind of brainstorming can be energising for both parties, but since it is a novel activity for many, it's important, as helper, not to take over and do all the work yourself!

The third part of the Force Field Analysis model is the **plan of action**. This is essential because it is at this stage that the person commits themselves to setting the field of movement into action.

ACTIVITY

Look back at the criteria for goals and decide what would need to be included in the action plan.

It is unlikely that all the facilitating/hindering forces could (or should) be tackled at once, so it is worth putting some time boundaries on those that have been prioritised. This will encourage the person to see that measurable steps are being taken towards achievement. The plan of action itself could, perhaps, benefit from some criteria.

◆ Is what the person decides to do within their control? There is little point, for example, in attempting to change a whole organisation's policy when we have no executive authority.

◆ The action that a person takes needs to be closely linked to the goal. Some strategies may not be very helpful in maximising the facilitating forces.

◆ Whether the strategies have any appeal in themselves can matter. It is reckoned that over 95% of people who start a weigh-losing diet give up. This suggests that the regime is too strict or the prescribed food is unappealing. Encouraging a strategy that someone actually enjoys can be a powerful move towards the goal.

◆ The question of values is important in the plan of action as well as in the goal itself. Achieving promotion at work, for example, could involve undermining colleagues, but it would not be very ethical.

◆ The world in which a person lives can in itself present obstacles and these need to be considered when strategies are being decided.

The FFA model is sometimes criticised as being useful for more practical problems – like losing weight, getting fit, cutting down on alcohol, but as not very helpful for problems which involve relationships and emotions.

ACTIVITY

Evaluate the model's use for:

◆ a bereaved person

◆ someone in an abusive relationship

◆ a gay person who can't decide whether to come out

◆ the victim of racial violence

◆ exam anxiety

◆ panic attacks.

Whatever your conclusions, it is certainly a useful item to have in the 'kit bag' of counselling skills.

Sometimes people get enthused by their plan of action and neglect to consider the 'what if?' element. Helpers do not want to dampen enthusiasm, but it would be a failure of responsibility not to help the person think through the gains and losses which may result from their action. All change involves some degree of loss and the person has to weigh any losses against the gains.

ACTIVITY

When you have devised your own plan of action, decide: if I follow the strategy what are the gains for me? What are the gains for others? What are the losses for me? What are the losses for others?

The dictionary says of skill that it is:

◆ facility in doing something

◆ practised ability

◆ expertness

◆ tact.

We hope that these two skills chapters will have given greater facility in listening and responding. The only way to be good at skills is to practise (and to go on practising) and we hope you will feel inspired to do this – counselling skills bring great rewards for the user as well as the other person. Practice will lead to the expertness to which we all aspire. Tact is probably a good 'umbrella' word for those core conditions, without which the skills become hollow.

BIBLIOGRAPHY

Egan, G. (1992) *The skilled helper* 4th ed., Monterey Books, Cole.

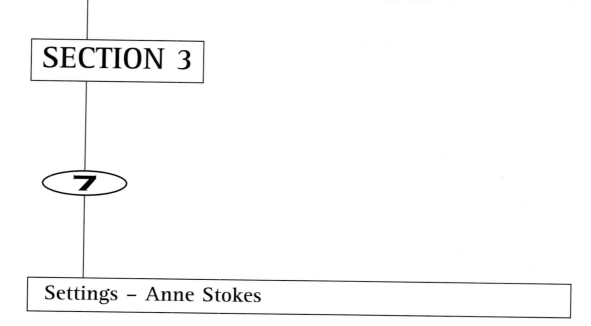

SECTION 3

7

Settings – Anne Stokes

The intention of this chapter is to focus more specifically on those settings in which counselling skills are used, with regard to issues of record keeping, roles and responsibilities, and the practical impact of legislation and professional legislation. Finally, referral to another source of help will be addressed, focusing on why, when, where and how referrals may be made.

Individuals may seek help for a number of reasons. These include:

◆ feeling particularly stressed or anxious
◆ being unable to make a decision
◆ having a difficulty in resolving a specific problem
◆ noticing behavioural or 'mood' changes
◆ going through a life-changing event
◆ wanting to clarify their own views, values or position with a neutral observer.

In addition, those around them may think they could benefit from help and/or support when they are:

◆ not aware of the effect of their behaviour on others
◆ engaged in self-defeating behaviours
◆ not achieving their potential
◆ apparently unaware of the harm they are doing to themselves
◆ taking on additional responsibilities.

Many people are currently realising the value of including counselling skills within their repertoire as an aid to their main functional role, which may be in a paid or voluntary capacity. These helping contacts may have a developmental, problem solving, decision making, crisis or supportive focus at any given time (Nelson-Jones, 1983). Some of the difficulties and ethical dilemmas involved in offering these contacts have been discussed in Chapter one but, despite these limitations, it is widely recognised that individuals can benefit from interventions from well-trained and well-developed professional skills users. A list of such professionals would include:

◆ prison visitors
◆ religious leaders
◆ youth workers
◆ carers
◆ medical workers – doctors, nurses, speech therapists, physiotherapists, midwives, health visitors etc
◆ teachers and lecturers
◆ line managers
◆ mentors
◆ human resource professionals
◆ drugs workers
◆ AIDS workers.

ACTIVITY

Read this list again. Do you agree that all those on it could use counselling skills in some parts of their role? Who has not been included and ought to have been?

OCCUPATIONAL CONTEXTS

The next section looks specifically at the occupational contexts in which counselling skills might be applied. There may be a temptation to read only the part(s) that seem most related to your primary role or function. However, it may be useful to look at others to widen your general understanding and awareness.

ACTIVITY

As you consider the following context(s), which seems the most appropriate to your current primary role? Write down all the job roles within that context where counselling skills could be used. At this stage, don't think so globally that the exercise becomes meaningless. There is an argument for everyone to receive counselling skills training, but this is not the purpose of the exercise! Once you have completed the task, share it with other people in your group, particularly those working in a similar context.

Education

Perhaps the most obvious roles in this context are those of teacher, lecturer or tutor, but there are many other workers who have contact with young people and their families within school, university or college settings. There are administrative staff, welfare support teams, classroom assistants, as well as those employed in overseeing roles such as playground or 'dinner' staff. Anyone who has worked in this context will know that often it can be those people, who are not seen to be so involved in the formal business of teaching and learning, who become 'the listening ear' for many people. They are also frequently overlooked when budgets for counselling or interpersonal skills training are being allocated.

Any child or young person may have a reason for seeking out someone they can talk to about something that is troubling them, So adults in particular educational contexts may find that it is essential to develop counselling skills in order to be able to work effectively. One example would be the area of special educational needs, whether that entails learning difficulties or behavioural problems, or both. This is often a source of anxiety to families as well as to the pupil involved. Not every family whose life is touched by disability needs support. However, many welcome it. In writing about working with children with special educational needs, Sandow and Stokes (1994) suggest that:

> It is acknowledged that many teachers, when working with children and their families, feel that they are bordering on using therapeutic techniques. ... Some of the techniques of the creative therapies may already be in use or hold an appeal for the classroom teacher.

> (Sandow and Stokes, 1994)

They go on to say that, while recognising that there are no clear demarcation lines, and that training is not always necessary to help people, it is worth remembering that such interventions should be used with care. Training, and an understanding of boundaries and the ethical issues involved, can help teachers and others in this context to use counselling skills for the benefit of their students and their families.

Medical and health settings

In the nursing field, the work of community, mental health and practice-based nurses clearly benefits from employing counselling skills. If one thinks of hospital-based practice, then it is also easy to widen this to any nurse working with anxious or frightened patients and relatives. In writing this, there is an acknowledgement of the enormous pressures that nursing staff themselves are under, and many may feel that there simply is not time to engage with patients at more than a superficial level. However, the difference in climate, which is perceptible between units caring for the elderly, frail or the acutely ill where genuine listening is encouraged, and those where it is not, surely indicates that both staff and patient morale is higher in the former.

Until very recently doctors received scant training in counselling, or even interpersonal skills in most instances, as if somehow physical and affective dimensions were separable components of human beings. Fortunately that is changing, and GPs and consultants are more likely to listen as well as to speak to their patients. Perhaps those who find this difficult are inhibited by the fact that there may be times when they cannot offer practical or medical solutions and therefore feel that they are somehow inadequate or failing in their primary roles?

There are many other job functions in health settings where individuals do, or could, enhance their work by using counselling skills. These include the various therapists – occupational, speech and physiotherapists – as well as those working with specific medical conditions such as HIV and AIDS, where some, but not all, of the workers will have a medical background. As discussed in relation to the educational context, there are a number of support roles where counselling skills might be used.

Workplace settings

This term is used to cover those who find that their work with colleagues (whether these are peers, those for whom there is a functional or line responsibility, or even occasionally those to whom they report within the structure) includes an element of support. Again there are the most evident categories, such as personnel or human resource practitioners and welfare staff, as well as a less well defined group, which could incorporate line managers, trade union officials, finance departments etc.

One of the myths in this setting is that people solely bring workplace issues to talk about; those who have been involved in helping people will know that this is far from the truth. Personal relationships, health matters, bereavement and difficulties with children are just a few of the wide spectrum of areas which employees may choose to speak to you about. There is a debate about how appropriate this may be – this is work time, and you and they are being paid to do a particular job. My view is that very often what is going on outside work is likely to have a bearing on that person's ability to perform well within work. If they need ongoing and regular support, you may not be in a position to offer that, and will need to consider how they might find this, but, certainly initially, it can be argued that it may be within your primary function to respond to them.

Social work settings

The training of most social workers will include a counselling skills element. Many find using these skills is an essential part of their work, and often seek further training in this area, to extend or update their knowledge and understanding. Probation officers would come into this category too.

Once more, there are the workers in this context who immediately spring to mind, and those who are more 'hidden'. A major group of the latter are carers, who have regular and ongoing contact with clients. Their work is often of a practical nature; however, the relationship which is built up between themselves and their clients, and sometimes the physical intimacy of some of their tasks, can result in them being the recipient of an unburdening that can leave them feeling inadequate if they have not been trained to work with it in some way.

An interesting and sometimes controversial debate has arisen around training prison officers in counselling skills (and indeed in some instances as counsellors). This has centred on whether the enforcement of a prison regime can be consistent with the values of counselling. In other words, can someone who is responsible for ensuring the authoritarian and disciplinary side of prison life, also be able to be genuinely a listening ear? And even if they have the skills, is it possible for prisoners to be able to see them in this way? There is some evidence that it can happen, given the right training and policies. Pickard (2000) describes the training he offers to prison officers, and goes on to talk about the feedback he has had from prisoners.

> The message was ... (that) the most significant help that any of them received was the care shown by the prison officers. This care consisted of being given time to talk to someone who was prepared to listen and who genuinely showed an interest ... I was amazed at the genuine respect and affection for some of the officers.
>
> (Pickard, 2000)

This has links to the next section, where prison officers might equally belong.

Legal and related settings

What to call this context has been a problem; it is to do with settings involving police officers, solicitors, mediators, victim support workers etc. Police officers often employ counselling skills when interviewing crime witnesses, breaking bad news, supporting those who have been victims of an accident, and there is an ethical minefield here. When is it appropriate to encourage people to talk about something which has happened, and when could it be perceived as manipulative in order to extract information which the speaker might later find they wish they had not given? If you are a police officer, you will need constantly to be aware of role boundaries, of the guidelines of your professional codes, and also perhaps refer back to the chapter on ethics.

Solicitors, particularly those involved in family law, may find themselves in a similar position. Clients may be distressed and the solicitor can offer them genuine and helpful support through the use of effective counselling skills. One extra dimension here is that there is a financial cost involved – would the speaker have freely chosen to talk if they had in the forefront of their mind that solicitors' fees may well be in the region of £120 per hour? Yet in a law practice, time has to be fairly accounted for and costed directly to particular cases.

The role of a trained mediator is to enable parties involved in a legal issue, such as separation or divorce, to find a resolution that is fair and acceptable to both sides. Part of the training will be about learning and appropriately using counselling skills. Both legal and non-legally trained individuals work together as mediators, and a crucial skill here is avoiding being drawn into siding with one party. (This is also a skill that may be necessary in other contexts where mediation, with a small 'm' is taking place.)

Religious settings

Even in this secular day and age, a priest, rabbi, religious leader will be available as a source of help and comfort to those with problems, both to do with issues of faith and those of a more worldly nature. The very nature of this profession can inspire people to confide as they feel that they can trust the discretion of the hearer. Dilemmas inevitably arise here about what role that person is in – is s/he a spiritual director and responsible for giving guidance, or simply a person whom the speaker trusts and who is therefore solely using counselling skills directed towards their autonomy?

There are many organisations that are connected directly or loosely with religious faiths. Those working within them have to be clear with themselves and with their clients about the goal of working with counselling skills.

Voluntary settings

There are likely to be volunteers who are working in several of those settings just described, but since volunteers are a numerically large group of counselling skills users, and play such a vital part in the UK today, they merit a specific section. Some voluntary organisations train their own volunteers in counselling skills and, in particular, the necessary contextual knowledge to underpin work in bereavement counselling or counselling for drugs and alcohol abuse. In some cases these people will be called 'counsellors' within the organisation. Whether they are counsellors as defined in the first chapter, or people using counselling skills, will depend on the extent and depth of their training.

An example of an organisation that is largely made up of volunteers is the national network of Citizens Advice Bureaux (CAB). The CAB advisers will obviously meet clients who are in a wide range of affective states, including those who are, for example, angry, distressed, frightened or despairing. While the adviser is there to give the information or advice that may help them to resolve the problem, it is apparent that counselling skills may be useful in getting clients to a position where they are able to give more of their attention and energy directly to the issue. Advisers go through a basic training that involves demonstrating listening and empathic skills before they are able to work with clients in the bureau.

Other therapeutic settings

As the so-called alternative therapies move into a more central place in our society, many training courses in counselling skills are finding that practitioners are enrolling. Because a core philosophical understanding of the holistic nature of the person is central in many of these therapies, it is often found that such practitioners are ideal listeners as far as their clients are concerned and can help, if they possess the necessary skills and knowledge, in a way that was perhaps not initially envisaged.

Situations in which counselling skills are used within job roles

The contexts in which counselling skills could be used have been discussed, but within those settings there are obviously specific situations where they might be appropriate. You will probably have begun to think about these as you worked through the last activity (p. 134). In the educational context, for example, there may be a bullying incident. It would be appropriate to use the skills to work with the person being bullied to enable them to express their feelings, to find out what coping strategies they can employ and also perhaps how to prevent it happening. The bully could also benefit from being given space to understand what is motivating them to behave in this way, to modify their behaviour and find more fitting ways of both interacting and getting their needs met. Here a clear distinction has to be made between a disciplinary function and a helping function; it may not always be useful for the same person to deal with each role. While in the long run the person who is doing the bullying probably has just as much need of help, unacceptable behaviour has to be stopped.

The example just described might equally apply in a workplace setting, but a different one would be that of an appraisal review meeting. All too often, line managers set the targets without really encouraging the team member to engage in the process. If counselling skills are used, realistic targets (though these are not necessarily lower or very different) can be set because the person who has to achieve them feels that they have been heard and enabled to look at what will help or hinder their achievement. The line manager may also discover skills that the organisation can use, but which they did not even know the employee possessed. In a survey of employees who had been made redundant by the organisation, BUPA discovered the vast array of skills that these ex-employees actually had had all the time.

> This was very humbling because, having categorised all these people into one box ... we had done nothing to unlock their potential, to see them as individuals and to think of them as special in any way ... You say 'where are the stars ... that can grow my business for me' ... They already work for me but we don't realise it.

> (Platt, 1999)

This is a very clear argument to refute those who suggest that using counselling skills with people is for 'soft and woolly' reasons. Those using counselling skills can bring added value to their organisation, whether in the public, the private or the voluntary sector.

ACTIVITY

◆ Work in pairs. Describe to your partner your main job role, and then outline three different situations that have benefitted , or could benefit from the use of counselling skills.

◆ During the next month, add to your list as you are involved in new situations.

◆ Read Chapter one again and reflect on the responsibilities that go alongside each of the situations you have described.

RECORD KEEPING

Counselling skills users will have to make decisions about how and indeed whether they will keep notes of their interactions with clients. There is not a legal requirement to do so, though there are many good reasons why you may decide that you will do this. Counsellors are generally advised to do so unless there is a valid reason such as security that suggests otherwise, but the position is perhaps less straightforward with those who use counselling skills as an adjunct to their main functional role.

The Data Protection Act (1998), gives people the right to access information held about them on computers, and in some instances hand-written records. Therefore if records are being kept they should be written with that Act in mind, and processed according to the law.

Records must be protected against misuse, so it is necessary to think about two main issues. First of all, who else in the organisation has a right of access to any notes that are written about someone you see? Can you ensure that this information will not be abused by a third party? Improper disclosure, even if it was unintentional, can lead to severe penalties. The second issue concerns access by someone who may not have a right to it, for example your files being searched or broken into by another person. Methods of record keeping will be discussed later, but an important consideration is how you are going to ensure that the way in which you write notes, guards the identity of the individual(s) concerned.

If you keep notes, the principles underlying the Data Protection Act require that they are only kept for a specified purpose, so you must have a definite reason for making them. Again these reasons may become clearer later. They also need to be accurate (so what is your evidence for what you write?) and relevant to the matter in hand.

Lastly, they should be up to date, and not kept beyond the point where they might be deemed unnecessary or irrelevant. This is a tricky area. How can you tell whether or not the conversations you have had with someone this month or this year will have any relevance in the future? If in doubt, it might be wise either to decide to keep a condensed version as an aide-memoire, or possibly to shred them if on balance they are unlikely to be needed again. One of the difficulties here is that we can be so busy complying with the Act, and possibly fearful about our clients' right of access to records, that we forget that not only are they useful to us, but that also they can be useful to the client in the future to demonstrate that they have taken steps to try to deal with an issue.

If you work for a global organisation, there is one other factor that you need to be mindful of. The Act specifies that personal data must not be transferred outside the EU without appropriate safeguards. This is because the law in some countries with regard to this information may be very different.

ACTIVITY

◆ Do you know clearly what records your organisation requires you to keep? Who else might have access to those records? Are you sufficiently aware of the Data Protection Act 1998 to know whether any current record keeping complies with it? If not, then take steps to familiarise yourself, and if necessary your organisation, with its implications. At this juncture, are you inclined to keep records or not? If not, why not? Is this solely for your own protection?

◆ After you have thought about the questions above, discuss your answers with someone else who you feel is likely to have a different view from yours.

Having thought about the legal situation with regard to data protection, you may well have thought 'why bother?'. Indeed Houston (1990) acknowledges that if very few clients are seen, it is possible to work effectively without any writing up, as it is possible to carry inter-actions accurately in your head. With reference to a small support scheme that used vol-unteers with training in counselling skills, I also found that if doing so promoted a high degree of anxiety of judgement, or if they are made after a session simply for 'the sake of it' and never referred to again, then the process can be counterproductive. It is, therefore, necessary to be sure that the reasons for keeping them are valid, and their purpose under-stood (Stokes, 1998).

However, there are many ways in which record keeping can support and enhance your work, particularly if you are seeing someone over a period of time. Some of these ways are given as follows:

◆ They are useful in refreshing your memory as you may have seen many other people, and performed a number of other activities to do with your primary role between the times when you see someone.

◆ They give you an opportunity to reflect on your interactions at a later date and think about what you need to do next.

◆ If you have supervision, they can be useful in understanding what you are doing, both with that client and in organisational terms.

◆ If goals are being set, it is easier to monitor their achievement. Even when there are no specific goals, it often helps to see whether there are any changes in the issue under discussion.

◆ They may include a termination summary of what has been discussed, and what actions have been taken both by you and your client.

◆ They could be helpful for both you and/or the client to demonstrate that there has been work to try to resolve an issue.

◆ In organisational terms, it is sometimes discovered that an issue arises over and over again. With statistical evidence, it is possible to look at what the systemic responsibilities are, without having to use individual cases.

There are, of course, arguments against record keeping. The implications of legal liability have already been mentioned, as has confidentiality. Record keeping takes time, and ideally should be done fairly soon after the event. Trust is an important part of many interactions, and if the person who is speaking to you fears that they may be compromised by records which are kept, then they will almost certainly filter what they disclose. An obvious example of this would be someone working with drug users who may face prosecution for supplying or using. There are also non-legal situations, such as when an individual fears that records may end up in the personnel department and jeopardise their chances of promotion, even though the records may simply be a factual account of a conversation.

ACTIVITY

- ◆ Make two lists relating to your use of counselling skills within your primary function, showing reasons for and against keeping records.
- ◆ If possible, discuss this list with someone who has responsibility for your work, to see if they agree and/or can add anything to the list.

The last area to be considered in this section assumes that you have made the decision to keep records. Even if you have not done so, you would be well advised to think about the ways in which they can be best kept, in case you find yourself in a position of needing to do so at a later date.

You may work in an organisation that lays down the way in which you record information, but if you do not, then you will need to find a way that works for you. Consider first what factual information you might want to record, bearing in mind the need for confidentiality.

You must remember that you are legally bound to inform people that you are keeping records and that they have access to them. You, therefore, need to think very carefully about what you write.

LEGISLATION AND PROFESSIONAL REGULATION AFFECTING COUNSELLING SKILLS USERS

Most people using counselling skills are not legal experts, nor are they expected to be. However, they do need to know and understand how the law may affect their work, both for their own and for their clients' protection. We have already considered the impact of the Data Protection Act 1998 on record keeping, which affects people across a wide range of settings. There are other similar broad-ranging Acts and also some which are likely to be much more context specific. This section is designed to draw attention to some of these; it is necessary for each person to consider their own setting and discover what other legislation may affect it, remembering that there are differing legal systems in Northern Ireland and in Scotland, from that which operates in England and Wales. A series of useful questions is posed by Bond (2000).

- What actions are prohibited by law?
- What actions are required to be performed by law?
- What rights and responsibilities does the law protect?

Law is made in different ways. In the first, there is statute law whereby Parliament passes Acts, which include a summary of the main points. These are brief and do not clarify every individual case, though the guidance which is usually provided may be of a little more help. There is also case law, which comes into being through the judgments made in courts, either in the UK or in the European Court of Human Rights and sets a precedent for similar cases, and common law which is made by judges over time. Currently counsellors and those using counselling skills are not regulated by specific law, and therefore have to be mindful of how various parts of it apply to their work in any particular situation. Those using counselling skills also have to be aware that their actions may not be seen simply as those of an individual, but have implications for the context in which they work – in other words, what are the organisational implications if you are ignorant of, or unwisely choose to ignore, the law? Remember once again your primary role function.

The law is constantly changing, so what is written here may well be out of date by the time you are reading it. On the whole, agencies and individuals do not have to disclose information even if it involves a crime, with the exception of terrorist activities, or if ordered by a court to reveal it. For those employed by organisations, the matter is more complex, since the law may require them to operate (or not operate) in particular ways. If withholding information could be seen as a way of trying to avoid statutory responsibilities, there may well be severe penalties.

The Acts that apply across the board for those in organisations include various discrimination Acts – the Sex Discrimination Act 1986, the Race Relations Act 1976 and the Disability Discrimination Act 1995. Commissions have been set up to monitor the working of these Acts and to enforce them, namely the Equal Opportunities Commission, the Race Relations Commission and the Disability Rights Commission.

As an employee or voluntary worker, you need to be mindful of these both in your practice and also in relation to your wider context in most cases. There may be a few specific instances where these Acts might not apply; for example in certain training situations which might be targeted at under-represented groups within management levels, or an organisation which has been set up to work with men who have been victims of violence perpetrated by women. However, in the main it is a legal necessity to conform to the Acts.

The information you may hear when using your counselling skills cannot be totally bracketed off from your primary role. If you are aware that a person is being sexually or racially harassed, for example, it is your responsibility to ensure that some action is taken. That does not necessarily mean that you have to tell someone else immediately, or begin an investigation, but you should be able to demonstrate that you are either helping the individual involved to take the steps they need to bring the matter to light themselves, and/or are working with them as to the best way of you taking it forward.

In the same way, you may become aware of discrimination within the organisation, in career development terms, against individuals. The Sex Discrimination Act 1986 currently does not apply to volunteers in most cases, although it may be a basis for the organisational code of a voluntary organisation. You may feel that any discrimination within your organisation is unintentional; however, that does not prevent it from being illegal. Those using counselling skills often find themselves in the uncomfortable position of being amongst the first to realise that this is an issue and they have a duty to bring it to light at a systems level.

ACTIVITY

The discussion just in this section relates to clients presenting you with information that appears to contravene the law. However, it is equally important to ensure that your own counselling skills practice is non-discriminatory. With a partner, outline how you monitor your work, and identify any areas that might cause you difficulties at a personal level.

The Health and Safety Act 1974 may also affect your work. Stress and poor working practices are referred to almost weekly in the media. There may be other areas that also affect how you react to disclosures by those who seek your help. If unsafe practices are being encouraged, for example, then your primary role function must override your counselling skills role. Of course, implementation of health and safety regulations is not solely the responsibility of the employer; employees have to look after their own safety too.

There are a number of Acts that will relate to specific contexts. For example ,those working in education, social work, some parts of medical settings and youth work will need to be aware of the Children Act 1989. Although it is an Act that covers a huge area, with numerous volumes of guidance about its implementation in practice, there are two main areas that have particular relevance for those using counselling skills with children and young people. The first relates to suspected child abuse. Teachers, those within social services, health settings and some voluntary agencies will probably find that they have no choice but to report this.

The second concerns the right of parents to know about information concerning a child under 16, including whether they have the right to know that they are being seen within a counselling context. This is not in fact the case and, although it may be wise to obtain parental permission, there has been no clear-cut case which has established that this is an absolute necessity. If the process would be undermined, to the detriment of the child, then it seems possible that the decision not to inform the parents might be upheld. Many pastoral staff know that if young people felt that what they talked about in terms of their sexuality would automatically have to be told to their parents, then they would not talk in the first place. That doesn't mean to say that parents should not be informed. It may well be more productive to work with a teenager who is engaging in underage sex, is pregnant, or is mixing with anti-social peers, to find ways of helping them to address the issues with their parents, than to contact their parents immediately.

What becomes apparent in addressing such issues is the need for you to make sure that you are both fully aware of legislation that might relate to your context, and able to find out what your organisation's policies and procedures are with regard to particular aspects of it. You may find that your professional body and your trade union can also supply you with guidance. Another source would be BACP's specialist divisions – for example Counselling in Education or Counselling in Medical Settings.

The Mental Health Act 1983 protects the rights of people with mental health problems. While counselling skills users would certainly not be expected to be able to diagnose someone they were working with (although there could be exceptions for those working in health settings), it is useful to understand the Act and how mental health services operate, in order to help those you are working with who might be affected by this legislation.

Some employment and voluntary settings give very clear guidelines about how to proceed if someone is suicidal. Again, if this applies in your context, make sure you understand not only what has to be done, but also the underlying reasons for the action. The law does not require this information to be passed on, since adults have a right to refuse medical treatment and an implied right to self-determination. Indeed, it is possible that if you do disclose this information to a third party, and then the person who was suicidal finds at a later stage that the information is being used against them in some way, such as being passed over for promotion, they might have a legitimate claim against you.

From the example just discussed, there is a set of principles emerging that have wider application.

- Counselling skills users should ensure that they are aware of:
  - general legislation that affects their role
  - any context-specific legislation
  - professional regulations and guidelines
  - policies and procedures relating to their agency or organisation.
- They should also be clear to those with whom they are working about what will happen if there is an issue relating to legislation, regulations and policies.
- They should ensure that individuals know what will happen if it is thought that they are at risk themselves, or likely to put others at risk.

ACTIVITY

- Make three lists, one each for the legislation, policies and procedures, and regulations which will affect how you use your counselling skills in your specific setting.
- Share this list with someone on your training course who works in the same or a similar context. Are there any fundamental differences between your lists?
- Are there any areas that you need more information about?

In practice, most counselling skills users do not find themselves having to wrestle with such issues during the majority of their interactions. However, when they do arise, they can feel very stressful, so it is sensible to have at least a theoretical understanding of the position in advance. Another way is to reflect on particular cases.

ACTIVITY

◆ Each person in the training group should bring with them four copies of a written scenario, outlining a legal policy or regulatory issue which has arisen in a counselling skills context.

◆ In groups of four, consider each scenario in turn. The person to whom it belongs does not join in the discussion, simply providing factual information if asked. Decide on the main issues involved, what action (if any) is needed, and the best way of implementing it. Try to foresee consequences.

◆ After the discussion has taken place, the owner of the scenario explains what s/he did, and reflects on the discussion which has taken place.

◆ Once all the scenarios have been discussed, make a list of guiding principles for dealing with the practical implications of legislation, regulations and policies.

REFERRAL

When someone is uncertain of their ability to use their counselling skills to help another person, there are two main options, neither of which is mutually exclusive. They can consult someone else who might have more experience and who knows the capabilities of the skills user, and/or they can refer the client on to a more suitable source of help. Some of the reasons for having this dilemma might include:

◆ the issue being beyond the level of your counselling skills

◆ lack of time available to continue to help the person

◆ the issue needing specialist help or guidance

◆ a personality clash

◆ particular guidelines for dealing with an issue which apply in that setting

◆ a boundary issue, such as being involved already, or likely to be involved in the future, in your primary role function – a disciplinary matter might be an example

◆ the issue touching on something which is also currently affecting your life, such as a bereavement

◆ a clash of fundamental beliefs or values which make it hard for you to be empathic, for example a decision to terminate a pregnancy

◆ the person involved might request it.

ACTIVITY

Look at this list and add any other reasons for referral that you think might apply to your setting. Taking each one in turn, think of a specific case in which this has been necessary, or one that might occur in the future. Notice any feelings that arise as you reflect on the situation – for example there might be discomfort, relief, anxiety, ambivalence etc. With a partner, explore these feelings further to help you clarify the source of these feelings.

Given the fact that most people need at some time to refer to another source of help or support, it is useful to ensure that you are aware of possible sources and contacts. While some information can be carried in your head, it is sensible to have a folder of names, addresses and telephone numbers of individuals and organisations that you could use, which you can add to as you come across new ones. If you decide to do this, then, from time to time, go through to check that the information is up to date, and throw out old leaflets as you obtain new copies! If you find that you are storing quite a lot of information, then devise a simple filing and cross-referencing system which suits the way you work. This may sound blindingly obvious, but many of us have good intentions, or start off in an organised manner, only to discover that when we really need to find something in a hurry we are rummaging helplessly through heaps of irrelevant material.

Depending on your main role, and also appropriateness to your situation, you may want to display some sources of help, or make it available to others in some form that can be accessed without reference to you. If you do make it available, it is worth considering whether you also want to keep your own back-up system, so that you can still find what you need if a leaflet has been removed from the general set. If there are 'awareness weeks', such as for breast cancer or age awareness, happening at a national or local level, you might target information to reflect this. Organisational newsletters are also a way of enabling people to know where they might self-refer.

Local libraries, the CAB, the BACP directory and doctors' surgeries are all good sources of obtaining referral information. Your file might include information on:

- the Samaritans
- Victim Support
- bereavement agencies
- Rape Crisis centres
- drug and alcohol agencies
- groups concerned with specific medical conditions such as infertility, cystic fibrosis, Alzheimer's, the Miscarriage Association, or Lupus UK
- relationship organisations such as Relate, Marriage Care, or lesbian and gay support groups
- groups which support those with personal or families issues, such as the Carers National Association, Disabled Living Foundation, Families Need Fathers, or local refuges

◆ the Consumers Association, the Press Complaints Commission etc
◆ local counsellors and counselling agencies (if possible with some idea of fees and availability/waiting list times)
◆ memos to yourself about who else within your organisation has specialist knowledge or has counselling skills training – do not overlook this more obvious source of referral simply because it is under your nose.

You may not consider that all of these are actually referral options; for example the Consumers Association is likely to simply give information, rather than be a place where people will be supported through the personal and emotional aspects of an issue. However, it is not unknown that, even though someone has been distressed when they speak to you, after having felt listened to and understood by you, the factual information is all they then need to take themselves forward.

ACTIVITY

Decide how you are going to compile your possible sources of referral. Begin to gather the information you will need through Yellow Pages, Thomson Local directories (try under counselling, advice, helplines), libraries etc. Send for information from any national or local organisations that you think might be useful. You might consider telephoning local counsellors to find out whether, in principle, they take referrals, and to obtain information about how they work. When you have made a reasonable start to this task, compare notes with someone else. Be aware of what else they have included. Would this be useful for you? Be prepared to share your information with them.

So far, the emphasis has been on knowing when you might need to refer and being prepared in advance. That is possibly the easiest part. More difficult for many people, is handling a referral well, so that both parties involved feel satisfied with the outcome. If the values which underlie the use of counselling skills are to be upheld, then respect, support and care must be demonstrated, so that the client does not feel like an unwanted parcel being passed down the line, or that their issue is so overwhelming that it cannot be contained. Ideally, referral should be an empowering process that involves the client as well as yourself. It is your task to give information and it is then up to them to accept or decline.

ACTIVITY

Imagine, or recall, a situation where you have talked to someone about an issue that is affecting you. During the conversation, they suggest that there would be people better able to help them than themselves.

◆ What would you need to know about their reasons for saying this?
◆ What might you feel?
◆ Would you want any information about whoever it is they are suggesting?
◆ How might you like the referral handled?
◆ Is there anything else that you need from the person you are talking to?

In undertaking this activity, you will have begun to consider some of the key factors in handling a referral well. Obviously it is important to bear in mind that each individual is different, and so there is not one magic formula which works for every counselling skills user or every person receiving counselling skills. At the outset of any supportive relationship, the questions 'Can I help this person?', 'Should I help them?' and 'Am I the best person to help?' should be asked. Rather than dismiss any doubts or fleeting fears, the answers need to be examined. If talking to you is not an appropriate or useful step, then it is probably better to look at other options rather than engage in a process which will need to be terminated, with the client having to go through the same thing with someone else.

However, there is often not a definite 'yes' or 'no' to those questions, unless you have a very apparent clash of boundaries. If your functional role would mean that it is inappropriate for you to support someone in this particular way, then that has to be said clearly, though not in a manner which dismisses the importance of the issue. The task here would be to discuss with them who else they would be able to talk to. So that people do not feel rejected as individuals, or their future relationships suffer damage, in most cases it is better not to fudge this by making excuses for not being available.

It is more difficult to be open when there is a more personal reason for feeling that you are unable to support someone. If you are in the middle of an acrimonious break-up of a relationship, and this is the issue that is being brought, then you may well consider that your own feelings are likely to get in the way, and yet, perfectly appropriately, not want this to be common knowledge within the organisation. A partial truth could be offered, such as 'There's a very similar situation within my family group at the moment, and I think that might interfere with my ability to help you', though this may have the opposite effect from that which you intended, and make the speaker feel that you would really have insight. Another possibility might be to listen, but focus on picking up any other sources of support that are mentioned, and look at ways for the person to maximise these. A third option would be to ask 'What is it that s/he needs from this interview, and how can we find ways of meeting that need, which may not involve my continued involvement?'

ACTIVITY

Work in groups of three, taking on the roles of counselling skills user, speaker and observer. Use the scenario from the previous text, or a similar one from your own work, and role play the interaction between counselling skills user and speaker. At the end, the observer gives feedback, remembering the best way to do this is to be clear, specific and respectful. After the observer has spoken, the speaker first and then the counselling skills user also comment on the interaction. To end the exercise, the counselling skills user summarises what has been heard and makes his/her decision about what, if anything, would be done differently another time.

In many cases it may not be apparent at the start that a referral may be appropriate. It can be difficult to suggest to someone who has confided in you, that they may be better off talking to someone else. It is sometimes useful to ask the question, 'Am I the best person to help you?' People may feel disappointed or rejected if they need to move on to talking to someone else. It may have taken them time to summon up the courage to seek help in the first place, and they are going to have to do the same thing all over again. Of course, the opposite could also be the case; having managed to bring the issue out into the open once, it may seem easier to do so again.

Having a good experience of being listened to, and being helped to clarify what they would like to do next, may enable that individual to contemplate contacting a specialist agency, whereas if the suggestion of a referral had been made too early, they might simply have decided that they had such an enormous problem that they could not be helped, and have retreated.

In a similar vein, it may be apparent that it would be beneficial to enter into counselling either within an occupational scheme, or with an independent counsellor. The person has to get to that point themselves, and so, within the limitations of what support can be offered by a counselling skills user in terms of available time and also the level of competence, it might be more valuable to continue to hold and support the person until they are ready to hear the suggestion, or, better still, make it themselves.

It is always appropriate that referral is a joint decision, even when the initial suggestion comes from the counselling skills user. It is also much better that it is a considered and not a hasty decision. People may sometimes agree to a referral even if that is not really what they want to happen. They may be compliant by nature, feel they have no choice, or if they are in work, medical or educational settings, for example, worry that if they refuse, it will be held against them in some way. They may also lack the energy to do anything other than agree. Because this could happen, the skills of empathic understanding, listening, reflecting and clarifying are as vital here as they are in other situations.

There can be such a feeling of relief when someone has agreed to a referral, particularly if the listener has been feeling out of their depth, that this stage is rushed. Reflect again on what you decided you would need to ensure a good referral process. Would you have wanted the process rushed? Options can be explored and the possible consequences of following those options, including not seeking other support, teased out. Often imagining 'worst possible scenarios' of doing or not doing something can be useful in bringing out the fears and fantasies which are causing anxiety. Factual information is likely to be needed at this stage, and while it is preferable to be able to supply the information at once, it is better for it to be checked out first than to mislead the person in some way.

On the whole it is probably better for the individual to make the contact with the person or agency involved; indeed some will not accept clients on anything other than a self-referred basis. Occasionally, the opposite is true, and an employer or an organisation such as a school, GP surgery, or social work agency has to make the referral. One of the main reasons for preferring the individual involved to make the contact is to do with the client's right to autonomy. If they make the appointment, there is a greater likelihood that they are freely choosing to take this path, and will be committed to it. This does not mean that the counselling skills user should not offer support during the referral. This may be with information about how the process works, if that is known, factual information, and being available to listen to the client's feelings as they move through a referral process.

After a referral is made, it is likely that formal contact over this particular issue would end. This is particularly true if the individual is now seeing a counsellor. Having two people actively involved in this way is generally counter-productive for the client. However, this may not be the end of informal contact if the two in the original relationship are in the same organisation, and it is sensible to tread the line carefully – between appearing to need to know everything that is going on, and having no apparent interest. It may be hard for you to let go of your involvement, and to know that you may never hear the 'end of the story', but that is also often the reality.

There may be some instances where it is right to go on supporting the individual even if they have made contact with another agency. If, for example, the referral was a medical one, the condition may well be being dealt with, but perhaps the emotions or family issues that are attached to it are not being looked at. In an education setting, a young person may have now been allocated a social worker because of a family issue, but still find it helpful to talk to their tutor about the situation as it affects them at school. Like many aspects of using counselling skills, there is no one correct answer to the question.

ACTIVITY

Pat manages a project that encourages young managers from a variety of local companies to act as mentors for 'disadvantaged' adolescents, to encourage them to fulfil their potential. One of these volunteer mentors, Bill, has quite often talked to Pat about his own life and ambitions, and they have built up a good relationship. One day he seems rather down, and Pat asks him if there is anything wrong. He talks for a while and then says that although he is currently in a heterosexual relationship, he is struggling with a belief that he may be gay. Pat has been trained in counselling skills but is unsure about whether he should encourage Bill to seek support from another source.

In a small group, brainstorm reasons why Pat might think that he should refer Bill elsewhere, and also any reasons for not doing so. Assuming that Pat feels he cannot support him, work out ways of managing this process, so that Bill does not feel rejected. Compare your ideas with other groups. What issues does this case study raise for you?

Even if you are handling the issues surrounding referral well, it is often useful to seek support for yourself, so that you can think through all the implications. Finally, at the end of this section, spend a few minutes reflecting on your particular situation and how able you now feel to deal with referral issues.

Can I make this referral so that the client's life and experience is added to rather than taken away from, and so that they experience it as affirming rather than negative and rejecting?

(Williams, 1993)

This chapter has looked at the settings in which counselling skills users may work, and some of the professional and legal issues of which they need to be aware. The next two chapters focus on discrete areas that arise in those settings and the impact and value of using those skills to empower individuals.

BIBLIOGRAPHY

Bond, T. (2000) *Standards and ethics for counselling in action*, London: Sage.

Houston, G. (1990) *Supervision and counselling*, Rochester: The Rochester Foundation.

Nelson-Jones, R. (1983) *Practical counselling skills*, London: Holt Psychology.

Pickard, P. (2000) 'An inside job' in *Counselling News*, March, London.

Platt, A. (1999) 'Counselling in a commercial world' in *Counselling at Work*, summer, no 25, Rugby: Association for Counselling at Work.

Sandow, S., and Stokes, A. (1994) 'It's not about happy endings: individual and family therapies' in S. Sandow (ed.), *Whose special need? Some perceptions of special educational needs*, London: Paul Chapman Publishing.

Stokes, A. (1998) 'Training volunteers in a non-counselling setting' in H. John (ed.), *Balancing acts: studies in counselling training* (ed. Johns, H.), London: Routledge.

Williams, S. (1993) *An incomplete guide to referral issues for counsellors*, Manchester: PCCS Books.

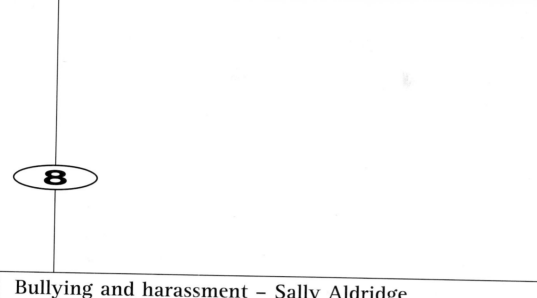

Bullying and harassment – Sally Aldridge

INTRODUCTION

You might wonder why a textbook on counselling skills includes a chapter on harassment and bullying and where this subject fits into the book. In recent years, the acknowledgement of the prevalence of such behaviour has led to government action at both national and European level, to make clear that such behaviour is antisocial, unacceptable and has a high cost to individuals and society. Despite this, it is clear from surveys, media reports and statistics on the causes of absenteeism at work and truancy in schools, that many of us, both children and adults, are the victims of bullying behaviour. In one term 27% of children in primary and 10% in secondary school reported having been bullied (Sharp and Cowie, 1998). Research for the BBC in 1995 found that in a sample of 1137 employees, 79% had witnessed bullying and 59% had experienced it themselves. There are, therefore, a very large number of people suffering from the effects of harassment and bullying in society, and also a large number of people who regularly use bullying behaviour.

This chapter has three sections: the first looks at what constitutes bullying, racial and sexual harassment; how and why some of us become bullies and others victims; and how this affects us. The second section looks at the difference and similarities between bullying and discrimination and the legislation that exists to protect us. The final section outlines the approaches and strategies that can be used to counter bullying and harassment.

The behaviours described in this chapter are found in everyday life, from childhood onwards, and most of us can recall some encounter with harassing and bullying behaviour during our schooldays. Understanding the nature and causes of bullying behaviour calls for an understanding of what makes us develop as we do. Recognising the effects of these behaviours and knowing how to deal with them relies heavily on the use of counselling skills. The knowledge and skills in this book will equip you to understand and deal better with bullying and harassment, whenever and however you find it.

DEFINITIONS OF BULLYING AND HARASSMENT

There are few agreed definitions of what constitutes harassment and bullying. The word 'bullying' has associations with childhood and the school playground, whereas the word 'harassment' is linked more to adulthood, the workplace and the community. In this chapter the terms 'harassment' and 'bullying' are used interchangeably. Racial and sexual harassment are perhaps the most clearly defined and understood forms of bullying. Most adults and children can easily draw up a list of behaviours they would describe as bullying and harassment. Some adults might hesitate before including some of the behaviours of managers on the list. However, excessive work demands, public criticism, disadvantageous manipulation of holiday schedules, can all be examples of workplace bullying.

Cary Cooper, BUPA professor of organisational psychology and health at the University of Manchester Institute of Science and Technology (UMIST), in an article in the *Times Higher Educational Supplement*, described bullying as:

> Basically, bullying is persistent harassment, physical or psychological, that demeans, devalues and humiliates the victim. Bullies who shout and publicly humiliate their subordinates or colleagues are easy to identify, but there are more underhand forms of bullying too. Subtle bullies set their staff up to fail by withholding or manipulating information, calling meetings when staff are not available, isolating workers from colleagues, criticising them for minor mistakes and undermining their self-confidence by ignoring their successes ... the big increase in bullies today is among the 'overloaded' bullies – those unable to cope with their workload, with difficult staff, with their or others' careers problems or with autocratic superiors. These people use bullying as a management style.
>
> (Cooper, 2000)

Racial harassment

Racial harassment is defined as verbal or physical aggression towards an individual or group, on account of their race or colour. It can include such things as assault on the person or their property, verbal abuse, jokes, offensive remarks, racist graffiti, racist literature, offensive mail or obscene phone calls, intimidation at work on account of a person's race or colour. It can range from the humiliating and annoying, to life-threatening behaviours and murder. Surveys have shown that children from ethnic minorities are far more likely to be the victims of racial bullying than other children. Surveys in east London schools found that nearly half of the Bengali and more than a quarter of the Afro-Caribbean pupils had been bullied in a three-month period (Sharp and Cowie, 1998). In particular, Asian children were subject to name calling and taunts. Many black children regard racist bullying outside the school gates as part of everyday life (Randal, 1997). Racial harassment continues in the workplace: overtly, as in the racial taunts heard at football grounds and arson attacks on the businesses and homes of members of ethnic minorities and, more covertly, within what has come to be described as 'institutional racism.'

Sexual harassment

Sexual harassment has been clearly defined, by the European Commission Code of Practice on protecting the dignity of women and men at work (No 49/1 24 February 1992) as:

> unwanted conduct of a sexual nature or other conduct based on sex affecting the dignity of women and men at work.

Randal (1997) describes sexual harassment:

> as any non-work related behaviour having a sexual component ... and is one of the most common forms of harassment behaviours in the workplace world wide.

Both sexes are victims of sexual harassment, but it is predominantly men who are perpetrators and women who are victims. There are significant differences in the perception of what constitutes sexually harassing behaviour between men and women. Men tend to think that it requires a physical element. Men also think that sexual harassment is a rare and exceptional thing, whereas women in surveys consistently report sexual harassment as a common workplace experience. For example, in a survey of trade union branch members, 73% of the women surveyed reported some form of sexual harassment at work (Costigan, 1998). Sexual and racial harassment can range from the humiliating and annoying to life- threatening behaviour. A wide range of behaviours come under this term; from a genuine lack of awareness, to the cumulative effects of sexual jokes and comments, to physical assault and rape. There are some behaviours that are explicitly sexual harassment; for example invasion of personal space, unpleasant and unwanted sexual advances, unwanted touching and groping, making sexual jokes, the deliberate use of sexual material such as posters, calendars, emails. In the USA in 1991 an attempt was made to define sexual harassment, with the introduction of what was known as the 'reasonable woman' standard. That is, 'Would a reasonable woman find it offensive?' This was not a success as there were disagreements over, among other things, what constituted 'reasonable'.

ACTIVITY

What problems can you see with using 'the reasonable woman standard' to define sexual harassment?

ACTIVITY

If you are reading this book while doing a counselling skills course use fellow course members to do the following experiment. If you are reading it on your own, try this with family or friends, but remember the result will be different if you do this with a group of people you know. Make two rows of people as far apart as you can and first place a man facing a woman.

◆ Ask the man to walk towards the woman and keep going until told to stop.

◆ Ask the woman to say stop when the man feels too close for comfort.

◆ Do the exercise again, and this time, ignore the command to stop, keep walking towards the other person and see what happens.

◆ Repeat this with the woman walking towards the man and the man saying stop.

◆ Repeat this with members of the same sex walking towards each other.

◆ Was there a difference in where you asked the member of your own sex to stop, compared to the member of the other sex?

◆ How did you feel when the person did not stop coming towards you?

◆ What did you do?

What is meant by bullying behaviour?

The behaviours range from those generally regarded as socially unacceptable, to those which would be found offensive and hurtful by a minority of people.

All these behaviours, whether involving children or adults have the following in common.

◆ The behaviour is deliberate.

◆ The intention is to hurt or damage the target person.

◆ The behaviour is carried out by a more powerful person, the bully.

ACTIVITY

◆ Brainstorm a list of behaviours you would call harassment or bullying.

◆ If you have school age children at home ask them to draw up a list of their own.

◆ Compare the behaviours listed.

◆ Have you seen any of these things being done?

◆ If so, where? When? To whom?

There are differences between the sexes in how harassment and bullying are carried out. These differences are particularly apparent among children and tend to lessen with adults. In schools, boys tend to use more open physical aggression, hitting victims, or threatening physical violence, and name calling. Girls tend to use social exclusion. The isolation of the victim from his/her peers is achieved by such things as rumour spreading, gossip and 'sending to Coventry'. As children grow older, the behaviour becomes more subtle and indirect, as the perpetrators have learnt that this behaviour is socially unacceptable and do not wish it to be noticed by adults or peers who disapprove. School bullies of both sexes often need an audience of onlookers from the peer group who, actively or passively, encourage the behaviour. It is often safer to be a member of the gang than to risk becoming a future victim. In adulthood, female behaviour changes little, and women continue to use social exclusion. Men change to the covert use of aggression; for example the invasion of personal space or verbal aggression. Workplace bullies of both sexes tend to use subtle and covert forms of bullying and harassment against work colleagues. In adulthood, the need for peer group support continues, if the aim of the bully is the social exclusion of the victim.

Workplace bullies are often, though not exclusively, in supervisory or management positions, and thus have the advantage of being in positions of authority. The BBC survey (BBC, 1995) found that of the employees who had experienced bullying, 41% had been bullied by their line manager and 30% by senior managers. In these roles, the workplace bully shows contempt for the victim and uses unfair criticisms, unreasonable work demands, snide remarks and may humiliate victims in front of other colleagues. Workplace bullying is often covert and some bullies will use other malleable staff to do the bullying at their behest.

ACTIVITY

Look at the list of behaviours you made in the last activity. Put them into one of these boxes. There are already examples in each box to start you off.

BULLYING AND HARASSING BEHAVIOUR

	DIRECT	INDIRECT
VERBAL	teasing	sending an offensive sexual email
NON-VERBAL	damaging belongings	'sending to Coventry'

Causes of bullying – how bullies are made

We all have the potential to be both bullies and victims. We all have bad days when we snap at a colleague. We all know people to whom we have behaved less than well, and have relationships in which sometimes our behaviour, with hindsight, could be seen as bullying. Most of us feel uncomfortable when we review these aspects of our behaviour, some of us don't.

Neil Crawford in an interview in 1994 said:

> The bully is basically a child dressed up as an adult. Their relationships in adulthood are informed by aggression, the need to be sadistic and the need to humiliate. When you ask them why they need to behave like this, you frequently hear a tale of a broken home, of broken relationships, of complicated relationships with their partners: basically not a stable situation.
>
> (Guardian Obit, 6 November 2000)

Research (Randall, 1997) seems to support the idea that bullies are made not born, and that the tendency to use bullying in relationships begins in childhood. Bullies appear not to have learnt how to control childhood aggression and this develops into antisocial behaviour, with little or no respect for other people. Bullying behaviour is very common in childhood, and it seems that it must meet some common needs. If bullying behaviour is learnt, then it must be learnt for a purpose and to be continued it must meet that purpose. In other words, if a bully got no reward or pay-off from bullying, he/she would not continue to do it. Therefore, for both children and adults, it is a repetitive behaviour, and the more it works the more entrenched the behaviour pattern becomes. However, many children who use bullying behaviour at school grow out of it, and do not become adult bullies. This would indicate that adult bullies bully more people than child bullies.

It has been suggested that some kinds of inconsistent parenting make it more likely for children to develop into bullies. Inconsistency from parents can lead to the child developing a sense of helplessness and becoming out of control. Bullying is the way a child copes with this, as bullying provides a sense of power and control over others and this, in turn, boosts the child's self-esteem and confidence. This may be the only way that a child can find to gain any sense of control in their life. In childhood, bullying is often done in front of an audience, which increases the bully's self-esteem and self-respect. Children will join the bully's gang; they have seen the consequences of becoming a victim.

Bullies, both child and adult, are quick to perceive put downs and imagined slights from others, and often see themselves as victims. They regard their behaviour as a reasonable response to the provocative behaviour of their victim, and are motivated by a desire to get revenge or get even. Jealousy and envy can also be powerful motives for bullying.

Bullying has positive rewards for the bully. It provides respect from the peer group, self-confidence and a sense of control. It does not matter to the bully if this apparent respect is based on fear. The feedback the bully receives is that he/she is powerful and important, and this leads to bullies having a high opinion of themselves. Although many child bullies do not continue to bully as adults, some do. If the childhood behaviour has been successful and no other strategies have been learnt to achieve the same end, then the behaviour continues into adulthood as there is no reason to change it.

ACTIVITY

Recall a time when you have behaved in a way that could be seen as bullying or sexually harassing.

◆ What motivated your behaviour?
◆ How did you feel while doing it?
◆ How did you feel afterwards?
◆ What were the results of your behaviour?

Case study

At the age of 11, Christine was a fat unattractive child who wore thick glasses and had few friends. Her solicitor father was disappointed in her and constantly criticised her performance at school, both academically and in sports. He compared her unfavourably to her younger brother. Her father became especially angry that summer when Christine would not go in the swimming pool on holiday. In September he told the school that Christine must learn to swim before Christmas. In swimming lessons the teacher put Christine in a harness and dragged her round the pool. Christine learnt to swim and to hate her father and the teacher. Christine began to bully younger children at school and get them to hand over their pocket money, which she spent on sweets. They were too frightened of her to tell anyone.

ACTIVITY

◆ How many examples of bullying behaviour are there in this story?
◆ How do you think Christine felt in the swimming lessons?
◆ What might have motivated Christine to bully the younger children?
◆ What sort of interventions at school could have helped Christine?

Bullying behaviour in adulthood can be as rewarding as in childhood. Bullies who get results are seen as effective useful employees, contributing to the success of the company. As adults in the workplace, in particular as bosses, bullies use threats, abuse, sexism, racism, isolation and ridicule of selected employees, to reinforce their control and power. Often bullies can only get self-esteem from the aggressive manipulation of others. This can be the only form of self-esteem they appreciate. Bullying can be triggered by current events such as threat of job loss, and victims of bullying can themselves bully those beneath them.

Costigan (1998) lists the following behaviour traits of adult bullies:

◆ need to always be in control
◆ they make life difficult for those people they dislike
◆ refuse to delegate, because they believe that no-one else can be trusted
◆ feel insecure and inadequate
◆ never admit they are wrong
◆ demonstrate poor communication skills
◆ feel under stress themselves
◆ set tasks they know are unreasonable and beyond the employee's capabilities
◆ refuse reasonable requests
◆ take credit for other people's work
◆ are vindictive, tyrannical, devious and/or dishonest
◆ appear charming to outsiders and superiors
◆ can be unbalanced emotionally and prone to bouts of ferocious anger.

Racial harassment

Much racial harassment involves similar behaviours as are found in other kinds of harassment and bullying, but aimed specifically and exclusively at members of a particular racial, ethnic, religious or national group because of their membership of that group. The membership of a particular group gives rise to special sets of insults and offensive behaviour by the harassers. For example, in a recent case a Jewish employee was forced to wear a Nazi uniform as an office penalty for arriving late. Racial harassment can also take the form of group bullying and mobbing, and this can escalate to gang violence, in schools, playgrounds and in the community.

Sexual harassment

There are more men than women who sexually harass. Studies have shown that whereas it is possible to identify likely bullies in the workplace, it is more difficult to identify likely harassers. Some research suggests that there are no distinguishing characteristics between men who sexually harass and men who don't. When the sexual harassment is deliberate and repetitive, the motivations are often similar in both sexes. As with bullying, there is often a need for power and control and a desire, conscious or otherwise, to humiliate the opposite sex. Male harassers may be insecure in their sexuality and attractiveness, and so use coercion to avoid rejection. They may have hostile feelings towards women and express these through sexual harassment. Sexual harassment is also used to put down 'rivals' of the opposite sex at work, in order to undermine the self-confidence and reputation of the 'rival', and thus remove the threat. Women who sexually harass men often pick on apparently vulnerable and isolated young men. There are also sexual harassers who have no idea that their behaviour constitutes sexual harassment and is objectionable, for example the middle-aged man walking the dog who daily passes women joggers and without fail shouts 'keep those tits and thighs moving'.

Stalking

Stalking is a particular form of harassment, predominantly, but not exclusively, by men of women. There is no single psychological or behavioural profile for stalkers, therefore, every stalker is different. A common cause of stalking is that the stalker believes that there is a relationship with the victim, or seeks revenge for the ending of a relationship, real or imaginary. Recently, two cases in the press in the same week demonstrated this. In one high-profile case, the stalker, a female fan of a female pop star, believed that the star had given her a 'sly dirty look' and as a result made 13 phone calls threatening to kill and dismember the star and her parents. In the same week, a 61-year-old man was issued with a restraining order after stalking a woman he had made advances to 30 years earlier when she was 13. After 30 years without any contact, his obsession had re-emerged and he had harassed and stalked her at work and at home over an 18-month period.

Some of the things stalkers do are against the law – obscene phones calls, acts of violence to the victim's possessions or the victim. Other things seem very ordinary, such as sending cards and flowers, sending emails, frequenting places the victim goes. The Internet has become one of the places frequented by stalkers. It is the obsessive persistent nature of the behaviour, and the fact that this attention is unwanted by the victim, that makes it stalking.

ACTIVITY

Recall a time when you were an onlooker to bullying or racial or sexual harassment.

◆ How did you feel while watching?

◆ Did you want to intervene?

◆ If you did intervene, what did you do?

◆ What were the consequences if any?

◆ If you did not intervene, how did you feel?

◆ What stopped you?

◆ What did you feel afterwards?

◆ What were the consequences if any?

EFFECTS OF BULLYING AND HARASSMENT

This section considers the effect of bullying and harassment on young people and adults. It is suggested that just as potential bullies can be identified, so too can potential victims. The impact of bullying on both victims and perpetrators is outlined.

Making of victims

It has been suggested that in some cases there is a formation dance between bully and victim, and that just as bullies are made not born, so too are some victims. It is certainly true that the response of the victim can reinforce the bullying behaviour. Just as bullies may have inconsistent parenting, leaving them with the need to be in control, so too victims may have had parenting that left them unable to deal with bullies. For example, the child victim may fear rejection and isolation and so will try to placate the bully. Children may lack any strategies for asserting themselves. Such assertive behaviour may have been seen as unacceptable at home. Evidence suggests that young people from ethnic minority and gay, lesbian and bisexual groups are more likely to be recipients of bullying behaviours than other groups.

Research (Randall, 1997) over a 20-year period found that child victims shared the following traits:

◆ insecurity
◆ timidity
◆ sensitivity
◆ anxiety
◆ cautiousness
◆ low self-esteem.

Costigan (1998) identifies two types of adult victims from the point of view of why they would be selected by the workplace bully. The first represent a threat to the bully. These people are called the 'conscientious victims'. They are hard-working efficient high achievers, confident and popular with colleagues. They may be better qualified than the bully, have better social skills, be creative with natural flair and possibly younger than the bully. In a way, these victims represent what the bully would like to be and have and are therefore obvious targets for envy and jealousy.

The second group are called the 'vulnerable victims'. They are easy targets on whom the bully can prey in order to feed their sense of control and power. These people are already somewhat isolated in the workplace, different from the rest of the staff in some way; for example age, social status, background, ethnic origin, sexual orientation or physical disability. They may also be vulnerable because of their personal circumstances – bereavement, return from maternity leave or prolonged sickness. They may have poor social skills; for example timidity and shyness. In some ways, this group represents how the bully may feel inside – isolated and lacking in social skills.

Effects of bullying and harassment on the victims

As stated in the introduction, bullying is a fairly common experience of childhood and adolescence. Most victims will survive the experience and go on to develop social and interpersonal skills. Bullying remains a fairly common experience in adulthood. An IPD survey in 1996 found that 1 in 8 employees had been the victim of bullying and over half stated that bullying was common in their organisation (Costigan, 1998). A bully in the workplace or playground reduces any sense of well-being in the whole environment. Therefore the impact is far wider than the effect on an individual victim. In both children and adult victims there is a developing sense of helplessness, of being in a 'no win' situation. If the victim gives importance to the bullying, this makes it more important, makes it a problem and may reinforce it. This may also show to the bully that their behaviour has had the sought after effect on the victim and thus reinforce the bully's behaviour. If the victim is already prone to the victim traits outlined in the earlier paragraph, then these will be reinforced.

Bullying produces in many victims the very emotions from which the bully is trying to protect himself:

◆ a sense of helplessness
◆ a sense of being out of control
◆ a loss of self-confidence
◆ a loss of self-esteem
◆ loss or damage to relationships.

Effects of bullying on children and young people

The effects of bullying on children differ from the effects on adults in several ways. Children at the receiving end of bullying behaviour may not understand what is happening to them beyond the immediate attack. Often an instinctive reaction is towards an escape route, for example in the form of truancy. A high proportion of gay, lesbian and bisexual young people who are victims of bullying consider suicide as an escape. If the bully is known, there may be a resigned acceptance of the fact that it is 'my turn now'. Bullies can be powerful people, gang leaders, and some victims, whilst hating being bullied, still want to be friends with the perpetrator. Existing difficulties at school can be made worse by bullying. Some well-known effects are truancy, 'illness', unwillingness to go to school, negative self-view, poor self-esteem and serious long-term psychological, educational and emotional consequences. Children sometimes try to cope by laughing along with the bullies, in the hope that this will either stop the behaviour or at least make it get no worse. If there are witnesses, this response makes it more difficult if the child reports the bullying later, because to an observer it appeared to be a game that all participants were enjoying. Children can join with the bully in picking on vulnerable peers because they hate wimps. Bullying can have a lifelong negative effect on a child's educational development; on the other hand, some children cope with the bullying and isolation by flight into study.

ACTIVITY

Recall a time when you were at the receiving end of some bullying behaviour at school.

◆ What happened?

◆ How did you feel at the time?

◆ What did you do at the time?

◆ How did you feel afterwards?

◆ What did you do afterwards if anything?

◆ Did it change your behaviour? If so how?

Effects of bullying and harassment on adults

Research as long ago as 1951 (Randal, 1997) found that 75% of us will react to bullying with stunned bewilderment and emotional, psychological and physical stress reactions. Adult victims work less well; self-esteem falls. They may be angry with the employer who has not protected them. Victims may feel obliged to give up a chosen career or job. The impact of the bullying can leak into other relationships, and the victim may turn into a bully. The individual victim may feel angry, anxious, guilty and be prone to mood swings. Physical symptoms can include nausea on approaching work, vomiting before leaving home, uncontrollable crying, high blood pressure, clinical depression, panic attacks, the desire to kill or injure the bully, nightmares, disturbed sleep.

The sense of helplessness is increased by the difficulty of being taken seriously as in:

◆ 'grown ups don't get bullied'

◆ 'it's your fault'

◆ 'it's just a clash of personalities'.

Victims who complain about bullying often end up being moved to other jobs and being seen as the problem rather than the bully; especially where the bully is perceived to be successful. This may be the least bad option in some ways, but it leaves the victim with a sense of injustice and anger against the employer.

ACTIVITY

Recall a time when you have been on the receiving end of unpleasant or hurtful behaviour. Did you ever have any of the following thoughts?

◆ 'Why is this happening to me?'

◆ 'I must be a real wimp if I can let this happen to me.'

◆ 'I must be useless and no good if someone want to do this to me'.

◆ 'I'll never get on with anyone at work, if it's all gone wrong here'.

Did you have any other thoughts? If so what were they?

The activity shows the common internal reactions of victims of bullying which reflect:

◆ the deep sense of shock many of us feel when we are first victimised
◆ our sense of failure, that we don't seem able to stop it happening
◆ the low self-esteem that results from persistent bullying
◆ our fear that we are not going to be able to make good relationships ever again.

Effect of bullying and harassment on bullies

Bullying is a source of power in social relations both for childhood and adult bullies. Bullies have an accurate view of their own power and the behaviours they use to achieve this. Bullying behaviour is used to build and to win status in the group, and also to keep the group strong and together. Outsiders are punished by bullying, in particular by humiliation and exclusion. This is seen in playground and teenage gangs. Bullying gives membership of the group, leadership and status in the group. Bullying influences the behaviour of group members; they have to conform to the attitudes and behaviours of the leader. Some causes of bullying, especially racist bullying, lie in the values and attitudes of the community and go back through several generations. These values and culture may be imported into the schools in the community through such bullying gang leaders.

It is not necessary to play the main role to take part in bullying, and lesser involvement is still bullying behaviour. Children who have colluded with bullies by joining in and ganging up on victims can suffer from feelings of shame and guilt later in life, when they look back at their behaviour. Observations of playground behaviour identified four roles that children play when seeing bullying taking place (Sharp and Cowie, 1998).

◆ **Assistant** – these children do not begin the bullying but join in and help the bully.
◆ **Reinforcer** – these children act as an audience, incite the bully to do more and call over others to watch. 'Come on, someone's really getting it.'
◆ **Outsider** – these children do not get involved and pretend not to see what is happening. 'It's nothing to do with me.'
◆ **Defender** – these children are likely to confront the bully, comfort the victim and call for adult help.

ACTIVITY

Think back to your time at school.

◆ Do you recognise any of these roles?
◆ What roles did you play?
◆ In your experience, do any of these roles translate to adult behaviour?

This behaviour continues into adulthood for successful bullies. Such bullies are often successful in their jobs and in charge of other people. Bullies see themselves as powerful and successful. When in a management position they may be seen as the managers 'who get results'. The bully is often seen by the senior management as contributing to the goals of the company. Bullies feel superior to others and behave in ways to reinforce this. This behaviour is in turn either tacitly or explicitly supported by the responses of employers and senior management. This feedback naturally reinforces the bullying behaviour. The perception of the colleagues working with, and for, the bully is far removed from the bully's view of themselves. Victims see the bully as aggressive and unfair. Bullies in the school, workplace or community are usually well known. They rarely bully only one person, but may be sequential bullies, always needing one victim in place to boost their self-esteem.

Some bullies are unsuccessful. Murano (1997) identifies the unsuccessful bully as one whose behaviour was so overt and blatant that it soon failed and the aggression backfired onto the bully (Randal, 1997). Although research shows that bullies have low self-esteem, and live in fear of loss of control and humiliation, it may be very difficult to discern this in their behaviour and public presentation. Indeed, the bully themselves may have no insight into the deeper motives for their behaviour. They believe that to achieve and enhance their own progression at work, they must be 'tough managers' and force subordinates to carry out their wishes. 'If the staff can't cope, then the staff aren't up to the job.'

Some bullies are unsatisfied with their work. This dissatisfaction may arise from perceived insults, slights and envy. Other staff are perceived to be denigrating the bully, or doing better or sabotaging his/her efforts by not performing as the bully wishes. Some bullies seem to keep the bullying behaviour to one area of their lives, for example some people are bullies at work and appear to have ordinary relationships outside work. Others are bullies at home, and regarded by everyone else as charming pleasant people.

Bullies achieve satisfaction only through the domination of other people. They have no respect for other people. They do not see the effect of their behaviour on others, or if they do see it, believe that the victim deserves it or asked for it. Bullies see other people joining their group/gang as evidence of their popularity and success. They do not see these people as motivated by fear. It is difficult for bullies to change their behaviour. They see no reason to because it is successful. Change is also difficult because the bully has constructed a lifestyle and way of operating based on bullying behaviour, there is therefore too much to lose.

DISCRIMINATION, BULLYING AND HARASSMENT

It is helpful to consider the distinction between discrimination, and bullying and harassment. At the same time, we must recognise that there are also some similarities. Discrimination can be defined as when a person is treated less favourably (without justification) because of his/her sex, disability, or membership (or presumed membership), of a racial group. This discrimination can be for example, in terms of employment, training, and access to goods and services. Thus sexual harassment and racial bullying can be seen to fit into this definition. However, bullying and harassment are not necessarily focused exclusively on the members of one distinct group.

Discrimination and harassment are sometimes found together in legislation. For example, the two directives arising from Article 13 of the Treaty of Amsterdam (1997) stated that 'harassment on the grounds of ethnic or racial origin which creates a hostile environment should be regarded as a form of discrimination'. In some legislation, harassment is seen as a subset of conduct within the broader definition of discrimination, for example the Race Relations Act 1975 and racial harassment in the Crime and Disorder Act 1998. The main Acts in UK law that make it illegal for someone to be discriminated against on account of their sex, racial group or disability are: the Sex Discrimination Act 1975 and 1986, the Race Relations Act 1976 and 1995 and the Disability Discrimination Act 1995. The origins and nature of discrimination are discussed in the chapter on values, attitudes and beliefs.

Legislation relating to the prevention of bullying and harassment

There are two aspects to consider in looking at the legislation that relates to bullying and harassment in the UK and the European Union. The first is legislation that protects us directly from bullying and harassment by another person, the second is the duty of the employer to protect employees from risk and of schools to protect pupils from bullying. The kinds of behaviour that constitute harassment and bullying can be any one of several offences and be covered by several Acts.

Summary of legislation against harassment

ACT	OFFENCE	BEHAVIOUR
Offences Against the Person Act 1861	Threats to kill	Making a threat to another, intending the other would fear it would be carried out, to kill any person
Offences Against the Person Act 1861	Actual or grievous bodily harm	Actual bodily harm or good medical evidence of psychological injury
Public Order Act 1986	Intentional harassment, or intentionally causing alarm or distress	Threatening, abusive, insulting words, behaviour, signs etc within hearing or sight of person likely to be caused harassment, alarm or distress

ACT	OFFENCE	BEHAVIOUR
Public Order Act 1986	Fear or provocation of violence	Being threatening, abusive, using insulting words, behaviour, signs etc with the intention of causing a person to believe that immediate unlawful violence will be used or to provoke such violence
Telecommunications Act 1986	Improper use of telecommunications system	Using public telecommunications to send a message or matter that is grossly offensive, indecent, obscene or menacing for the purpose of causing annoyance, inconvenience or needless anxiety
Protection from Harassment Act 1997	Putting people in fear of violence	A course of conduct that causes another to fear, on at least two occasions, that violence will be used against him/her
Protection from Harassment Act 1997	Causing harassment	A course of conduct that amounts to harassment of another
Malicious Communications Act 1998	Sending letter or articles with intent to cause distress or anxiety	Sending grossly offensive letter/article intended to cause distress
Crime and Disorder Act 1998	Causing racially aggravated harassment	A course of conduct that amounts to harassment of another and is racially aggravated
Crime and Disorder Act 1998	Causing racially aggravated fear of violence	A course of conduct that causes another to fear, on at least two occasions, that violence will be used against him/her, and that is racially aggravated

The 1997 Protection from Harassment Act

The 1997 Protection from Harassment Act 'makes provision for protecting persons from harassment and similar conduct'. It is often referred to as the anti-stalking Act, however, it has a much wider remit. The Act defines two criminal offences: harassment of another person and putting a person in fear of violence. Both are punishable by prison sentences, fines or both. The offence of harassment is punishable by imprisonment of up to six months; for the offence of putting people in fear of violence the sentence can be up to five years. The Act also gives the plaintiff the right to seek civil remedy for damages for, among other things, anxiety and financial loss caused by the harassment.

Harassment occurs when a person pursues *a course of conduct* which either 'amounts to harassment of another' or 'which he or she knows or ought to know amounts to harassment of the other'.

The prohibition on harassment does not apply during the prevention or detection of a crime. This means that police actions are excluded. Also the Act excludes circumstances when such behaviour was 'reasonable' and was complying with some other legal directive.

The offence of putting people in fear of violence occurs when a person pursues *a course of conduct* 'which amounts to harassment of another' or 'which he knows or ought to know amounts to harassment of the other'.

The Act defines what is meant by several of these terms.

◆ *'Course of conduct'* means that the behaviour must have been done on at least two occasions.
◆ *'Conduct'* includes speech.
◆ *'Harassing'* a person can include alarming a person or causing personal distress.
◆ *'Ought to know amounts to harassment of another'* is defined as 'if a reasonable person in possession of the same information would think the course of conduct amounted to the harassment of the other'.

Case study

Mike was a lecturer in the geography department of the local university and year tutor to the first year of the degree. He enjoyed the job, especially seeing the way first-year students grew up during the year. In November 1995, he began to receive anonymous printed notes through the post at home. They said such things as 'You were a long time on the phone last night. Have you a girlfriend at last?' He was thinking of changing his car, and spent one weekend going round car showrooms. Soon after a note arrived that said 'You would look good driving a BMW'. Mike began looking over his shoulder when he went out, to see if he could spot someone following him. He didn't tell anyone because he felt a bit silly.

There was a lull over Christmas and Mike hoped whoever it was had got tired of the game. However, in January, not long after term started, he began to get silent phone calls and more notes. In February he put some tubs planted with bulbs outside his kitchen door. The tubs could only be seen if you were in the house or had come into the back garden through the high garden gate that was kept bolted. Mike got a note saying 'I like the tulips and daffodils outside the kitchen'.

This really frightened Mike. The person must have gone into his garden, probably looked into his house, and he began to make sure that he drew the curtains as soon as he got home. Then he began to feel angry at himself and at whoever was doing it. The break over Christmas convinced him that the stalker must be a student.

Mike told his head of department who suggested that he contact one of the university's harassment advisers. Mike did, but at first he felt embarrassed that he, a grown man, should be so unnerved by this, and had let it go on for five months without doing anything.

The adviser got Mike to tell her the whole story. She heard and saw his ambivalence about his own response to the situation: anxiety, fear, embarrassment, anger, his sense of powerlessness. He didn't know who was doing this to him, what they wanted and what they might do next. She asked him to go back and tell her everything from the very start, and asked if he had kept any of the notes. They then looked at strategies for dealing with it: what Mike could do and how to identify the person responsible. Mike would keep a log of all future notes, calls etc and keep these with the previous notes he had kept. He would approach BT for their intercept service for nuisance calls.

That weekend Mike bought some wine in a supermarket and caught sight of one of his students there. On Monday a note arrived 'Three bottles of wine is a lot to drink on your own. Be careful.' Mike asked the head of department to see the student and ask her if she was responsible for the note. He didn't feel able to deal with it himself. He was frightened of what he might do if the student admitted it.

At the meeting, when the student was asked if she was responsible for the notes and phone calls, she immediately said that she was. She was bored she said, and this made life interesting. It was a game she liked playing. Only 'little people' got upset by it. The head of department was rather nonplussed by this response. He decided to discipline the student and warned her that the behaviour must stop or she would be asked to leave the course. He suggested that she might like to use the counselling service. Her reply was that she did not have a problem.

The student did not repeat the behaviour with any other staff or students and left at the end of the first year. It later emerged that she had behaved in a similar way to a presenter of a local radio station in her home town.

ACTIVITY

◆ At the date that these events took place, 1995/96, with what if any offences could the student have been charged?

◆ Would more recent legislation change the responses and behaviour of Mike, the head of department and the harassment adviser?

◆ Find out what service BT offers to people receiving nuisance calls

1998 Crime and Disorder Act

In this Act the government recognised that racial harassment had an impact not only on the immediate victim, but also on the victim's family and eroded 'the standard of decency of the wider community' (Crime and Disorder Act 1998, Home Office Race Equality Unity 1998). This Act added to the two offences from the Harassment Act the possibility that each might be racially aggravated and introduced heavier penalties. In the Act racial group means a group of persons defined by reference to race, colour, nationality (including citizenship) or ethnic or national origin.

The offence of racially aggravated harassment is when a person pursues *a course of racially aggravated conduct* 'which amounts to harassment of another' and 'is intended to amount to harassment of that person' or 'occurs in circumstances where it would appear to a reasonable person that it would amount to harassment of that person' or 'acts in a manner which is racially aggravated and which causes, or is intended to cause, a person alarm or distress'.

The second offence is one of racially aggravated harassment putting people in fear of violence. This offence requires that the offender knows or ought to know that their course of conduct was likely to cause the victim to fear that violence would be used against them.

For the purpose of the Act, a course of conduct or action is racially aggravated if 'immediately before, during or immediately after carrying out the course of conduct or action the offender evinces towards the person affected malice and ill-will based on that person's membership (or presumed membership) of a racial group' and 'the course of conduct is motivated partly or wholly by malice and ill-will towards members of a racial group based on their membership of that group'.

ACTIVITY

If you are faced with dealing with bullying or harassment that seems to fit with descriptions given in the Acts, then you are dealing with a criminal offence.

Does this change the way you should behave?

Legislation affecting schools

The Race Relations Act 1976 gives schools and governing bodies the duty to 'ensure procedures are implemented to eliminate unlawful acts of racial discrimination and harassment.' School governors and head teachers have legislation of their own to comply with in this area. The 1998 School Standards and Framework Act specified the responsibilities of governors and head teachers with regard to discipline. One clause specifically mentions bullying:

> Head teacher shall determine measures (which may include the making of rules and provision for enforcing them), to be taken with a view to ... encouraging good behaviour and respect for others on the part of pupils, and, in particular, preventing all forms of bullying among pupils.

This presented a problem to head teachers of schools under local authority control with regard to the bullying of homosexual pupils. The Local Government Act of 1986 prohibited local authorities from 'intentionally promoting homosexuality, from publishing materials with that intention, or from promoting the teaching in maintained schools of the acceptability of homosexuality as a "pretended family relationship"'.

There appeared to be two contradictory pieces of legislation. How could a school protect its homosexual pupils from bullying without falling foul of the 1986 Act? The government recognised the problem and in the Local Government Act 2000 amended the clause in the 1986 Act by adding a note of clarification (Section 104, 252) that 'this does not prevent head teachers, teachers or governors of maintained schools from taking steps to prevent bullying'.

ACTIVITY

How could a headmaster address the bullying of gay and lesbian pupils and at the same time not promote homosexuality?

Legislation affecting employers

Employers have a legal duty under the health and safety at work legislation to ensure that employees are not made ill by their work. It is accepted in the legislation that stress, of which bullying and harassment are major causes, can make employees ill.

Where stress is caused by or made worse by work and could lead to ill health, an employer is obliged by law to assess the risk. S/he must assess the risk by looking at the pressure that could cause the stress, decide who might be harmed by it and decide whether he/she is doing enough to prevent the harm. If necessary the employer must take reasonable steps to deal with the pressures. The Health and Safety Executive's publication *Help on work related stress – a short guide for employers* makes it clear that both bullying and racial and sexual harassment fall within the definition of stress in the workplace.

STRATEGIES AND APPROACHES FOR DEALING WITH BULLYING AND HARASSMENT

This section looks at how you can use the knowledge and skills in this book in dealing with harassment and bullying. It is divided into two sections: strategies and approaches to be used with and by the individual (either as a victim or as someone dealing with bullying and harassment), and those to be employed in schools, organisations and the community. Some of the approaches outlined are helpful to both children and adult victims.

Strategies for individuals

All the strategies for dealing with bullying and harassment are based on the victim taking back some power and control to him/herself, which has been systematically removed by the bully.

Being the victim of bullying or sexual harassment can be a terrifying and disempowering experience. Sometimes an individual who is being bullied needs common-sense advice about what to do and concrete strategies to use. Organisational policies and procedures and an anti-bullying environment can be as important as personal support and the acquisition of assertiveness skills. Other people need more support to rebuild confidence. Any individual who is being bullied or harassed, adult or young person, needs support and encouragement to regain some self-esteem and control. However, when the bullying is well established and persistent, in many cases, the individual needs more than this to be able to cope with and survive the bullying. Sometimes the victim needs an advocate. This requires a careful balance to ensure that acting on behalf of the victim of bullying is not reinforcing their sense of powerlessness. It is important to work 'with' not 'for' the victim.

Bullying, especial covert bullying, needs first to be recognised and owned. Bullying and harassment thrive in secret. Many victims say nothing because of a sense of shame, and thus inadvertently perpetuate a bullying culture. Becoming the target of a bully is nothing to be ashamed of. Being at the receiving end of unpleasant and frightening behaviour such as harassment does not make you a less worthwhile person.

ACTIVITY

If you have ever been a victim of bullying and harassment, ask yourself the following questions.

◆ Is there anything in your past that makes you vulnerable to this behaviour?
◆ Is there anything in your current circumstances that makes you a likely target?
◆ What stops you from changing in order to deal with the bullying better?

Practical strategies

Strategies for dealing with harassment and bullying revolve around empowering the victim to take back some control. These do not have to be psychological help or training in assertive interpersonal skills, many are very simple everyday activities.

Recognise and name the behaviour

A first step is for the victim to recognise and name what is happening to them. This can take adult victims a very long time, because it is so unexpected, and feels shameful to admit.

Keep a log

The victim should keep a log of events, conversations etc, to provide concrete evidence of the behaviour to which they are being subjected. It is advisable to log and date every encounter: physical, phone, written. Log what happens, when it happens and if there were any witnesses present.

Collect evidence

It is advisable to keep copies of all correspondence including emails. If professional competence is under attack, copies of previous appraisal reports on performance, references etc which show previous efficiency and competence are useful evidence. An additional benefit to keeping a log and collecting evidence is that it can be a helpful first step towards empowerment.

Learn and practise assertiveness skills

It is a good idea for someone who plans to challenge a bully, to rehearse that statement they wish to make, in advance with a trusted friend. The words should be congruent with the non-verbal behaviour. The bully will respond to body language that shows anxiety, or tone of voice which lacks confidence.

There are assertiveness techniques that can be very useful in these situations. These begin with the active listening skills you have already learnt in this book and add other specific skills and techniques. Assertiveness classes are held in many colleges, and provide a safe place for victims to learn and practise the skills needed to deal with bullying.

ACTIVITY

Pretend you are going to challenge someone of whom you are frightened. Write down what you want to say. Then say it in front of a mirror. How are you standing? Record your voice or ask a friend to give feedback. How does you voice sound? How do you feel? What could you change to look and sound more confident?

◆ the words you say

◆ the way you say them

◆ the way you are standing.

Tell someone about it

Persistent demeaning criticism will lead to anyone beginning to doubt the quality of their work. Sometimes bullying undermines the victim's self-confidence so much that they are no longer sure they are competent to do the job, or that their work is good enough. In these circumstances it is helpful and supportive to show the work and the bully's comments to a trusted friend or colleague, and ask for their opinion.

Challenge the bully's behaviour

This may be a sensible tactic in some circumstances but in others it is not. If someone suspects they are being stalked, it is unwise to challenge or have any direct contact with the alleged stalker. Any such contact is likely to reinforce the obsessive behaviour. Challenging a bully calls for a degree of courage and strength that many people do not have when at the receiving end of persistent bullying. If you are going to challenge a bully's behaviour face to face, think carefully about the best time and place to do this. If the bully always needs an audience, then the best place would be to find them when they are alone, lacking in the support of cronies.

The bully should be confronted with the specific behaviours and asked that these stop. In brief the victim should:

◆ state the behaviour they want stopped

◆ focus on the behaviour of the bully not on the bully as a person

◆ say they find the behaviour offensive, demeaning, etc

◆ state that there will be serious consequences if the behaviour does not stop, and that the senior manager will be informed

◆ follow up the meeting with a written memo stating the same thing.

Sometimes this is enough and the behaviour stops or at least moves on to someone else. The approach of confronting the perpetrator with the specific behaviour that you want stopped, often works in cases of sexual harassment, especially if the perpetrator is genuinely unaware that the behaviour is offensive.

ACTIVITY

What are the advantages and disadvantages of challenging a bully in the following places?

◆ in a private place, for example in his/her office

◆ in a public place, for example canteen, office corridor or car park.

Get support and help

It may not be possible for someone to challenge and confront the bully themselves. It may seem too hard, or feel as if it is demanding too much. It may be too frightening to contemplate. The victim may not want to risk the bully seeing that their behaviour is upsetting, in case this reinforces the bullying. If this is the case, then help can be sought from someone such as a trade union representative, personnel officer, equal opportunities officer or welfare adviser, if the organisation has one. This person can be asked to speak to the bully on behalf of the victim. The disadvantage of having a third party intervene is that the victim will not have the same sense of having taken control back, and the feeling of empowerment that this brings. In this case, the victim is likely to need further support.

Helping someone who is a victim of bullying and harassment

You may find yourself involved in a formal capacity, helping victims of bullying and harassment, as a member of a voluntary welfare advisers team or in your employment role. If you are called upon to address and deal with complaints of bullying and harassment, the skills and attitudes you have learnt from this book will stand you in good stead. Bullying, because it can be complex, includes a wide range of behaviours and is often covert. It is, therefore, more difficult to identify and deal with than racial or sexual harassment. In all bullying and harassment, it is the reactions of, and impact on the victim that is important, rather than the intention of the perpetrator. Alleged perpetrators often defend themselves by saying such things as, 'It was only a joke', 'He/she always takes things too personally'. If cases are taken to formal or legal procedures, and it emerges that the alleged perpetrator was told of the impact of their behaviour on the victim and persisted in the behaviour, then the intention to bully and harass is clear.

When dealing with the victim, it is important to listen empathically, to clarify what has happened, how the victim feels and what they wish to do. Sometimes a victim does not want to take any action, the very fact of sharing the secret with someone who listens and accepts is enough. This may leave you seething and wanting to deal with the bully. However, many people who have suffered persistent bullying cannot act in the same way, with the same energy and confidence as you. You will need to recognise that the desire to confront the bully directly, in no uncertain terms, at this stage belongs to you, and not the victim. In your role as trusted friend, colleague or adviser, it is for you to help the victim to decide what he/she wishes to do and then support them in whatever course of action or inaction they choose. It is also necessary for you to be fully aware of the legal position with regard to yourself and the victim.

If you are called upon to investigate a complaint, you need to bear in mind that sometimes complaints are malicious, and sometimes the victim can turn out to be the bully. You will need to listen carefully to both complainant and alleged bully, using the skills from Chapters four and five of listening empathically, clarifying, paraphrasing, summarising. Encourage both parties to use 'I' statements and be concrete about what has happened.

It is important to be **empathic** but not **sympathetic** with the victim, and to guard against identifying with either party, especially if you have had a similar experience yourself. It may be more difficult to listen with acceptance and empathy and be non-judgemental when interviewing the bully. However, this is essential, if you wish to find out what really happened in the relationship, and also to have any chance of encouraging the bully to look at their own behaviour. Sometimes it comes down to whose story you believe, and in these cases you need to be very sure that you have identified your own bias and put it to one side before reaching a decision.

Case study

Alice has been the head of a social service team for six years and had already had one period of maternity leave and returned successfully. Six weeks after her return from the birth of her second child, Alice was sent for by the department manager and told that serious accusations of bullying had been made against her by her staff team. Alice was devastated, none of the staff had ever given any indication that they disliked her style of management. She regarded herself as fair but firm. She had been at great pains to be sensitive to her return, especially since one of the team, had been acting head in her absence.

The department manager had received written allegations from six of the seven staff in the team. The longest list of allegations came from Fiona, the person who had been acting head and who was Alice's deputy.

The department manager investigated the allegations with the head of personnel and interviewed all the staff individually. All of the team said they had been asked by Fiona to put in a complaint to add to her own. When two people had replied that they had no complaints about Alice, Fiona had said 'Surely you can think of something you don't like about her management. Go away and think of something'. One remembered that someone had told them that Alice had once told someone off in such a way that she burst into tears, and so wrote that. In one letter Alice was accused of bullying another member of staff by criticising their performance at a time when Alice was actually absent on maternity leave.

The department manager and head of personnel decided that Fiona had orchestrated malicious allegations against Alice and had bullied the other staff.

ACTIVITY

- What made Alice particularly vulnerable to this attack?
- What might have motivated Fiona?
- If you had been a member of staff in this team approached by Fiona to support her complaint which of the following responses would you have made?
  - Refuse to support her and challenge Fiona about her behaviour.
  - Refuse to support her and do nothing.
  - Support her, write a letter but try to cover yourself by saying Alice has never bullied you but you had been told that she had bullied someone else.
  - Support Fiona, write a letter of complaint putting in every time Alice had commented on the work you'd done, your appraisals and how bullied and put down you felt.
- What might be the consequences for you of responses one and two, if Fiona became the head of the team?
- How might you feel if this happened?
- What might be the consequences for you of responses three and four if the complaint against Alice was disproved and Alice remained head of the team?
- How might you feel if this happened?
- If you were the departmental head what help and support might you offer to:
  - Alice
  - Fiona
  - the staff team?
- If you were the personnel officer what actions would you take after the investigation to try to ensure that this kind of false accusation did not happen again?

STRATEGIES FOR DEALING WITH RACIAL AND SEXUAL HARASSMENT

Racial and sexual harassment are unacceptable behaviours in the workplace and well documented as such. Most people know what is meant by racial and sexual harassment. In the case of sexual harassment, labelling it as a socially unacceptable behaviour has helped to address it. The strategies that can be used to address these two forms of harassment are similar to those used to address bullying:

◆ name the behaviour
◆ describe it
◆ say you find it offensive
◆ ask the perpetrator to stop it.

Men and women have different perspectives on what constitutes sexually harassing behaviour. At the extremes both sexes would agree that stalking, not taking no for an answer, unwanted groping and touching, persistent unwanted suggestive remarks, could fit under the label of sexual harassment. Other behaviours such as telling blue jokes, making personal remarks with sexual connotations, 'nude pin-up' calendars in the office, are likely to be interpreted differently by men and women. A woman might see a nude calendar as a deliberate display of pornography, intended to be offensive to all women in the office. A man might see it as a pleasant sight during a stressful day and in no way related to the women with whom he works. Similarly, some people think it is acceptable to make racist jokes because 'they don't really meant it' and 'some of my best friends are from Trinidad/Pakistan/ Croatia'. This kind of behaviour shows clearly the underlying racist or sexist prejudices of the speaker.

Case study

Maria began a new job in an advertising agency in a rambling Victorian building in the town centre. The photocopiers were in a basement room and used by all the staff. As the newest and most junior member of staff, Maria did most of the photocopying. She was eager to please and to make friends as she had just moved into the area. Many of the staff were about her age, in their twenties and thirties. One day in the basement, Neil came in and they began chatting about the town and where to go for a drink and a good night out. He was a good six inches taller than Maria and she noticed that he stood so close to her that she had put her head back to look up into his face. She instinctively stepped back, but Neil just followed her. This happened again in the basement. Not only was Maria getting a stiff neck, she also became more and more uncomfortable when Neil was around. She began to make excuses to leave the photocopying whenever he came in, but sometimes she was in the middle of a job and couldn't get away. Then he began to come into the kitchen when she was there.

ACTIVITY

◆ What could Maria do to deal with this situation?
◆ How would you deal with this situation?
◆ What do you think motivated Neil's behaviour?
◆ Are your answers to the last two questions linked?

Impact on victims

Some adult victims of bullying and harassment are able to use their experience, and learn and 'grow' as a result. This is especially true if they have received help and support to look at their own behaviour, coping styles and fears in order to understand why this has happened to them. If this is combined with learning new strategies, the victim is less likely to find themselves in such a powerless position again. Some victims already know that they are vulnerable to bullying, and the sense of powerlessness is of such long standing that it is very difficult for such people to break the pattern without outside help. Some victims have been trapped in this pattern since childhood. The majority of bullies are in positions of power over their victims, either organisationally, that is as a supervisor or manager, or psychologically, for example, they may have been in the organisation longer. In situations like this, there is often no good outcome for the victim of workplace bullying. Many victims who confront bullies or lodge formal complaints find that it is they, the victims, who have to leave the job. Senior management, even if they found the complaint valid and the victim vindicated, will often move the victim rather than the bully. Many victims accept this to save their sanity. Senior managers often do not support staff against a manager, especially if the bullying manager is seen as successful in meeting company targets. At present, the main hope for victims is that taking steps to address bullying, using the strategies outlined, may go some way towards restoring the confidence and self-esteem so damaged by the bully.

In the area of racial and sexual harassment in the workplace, it is different, and many perpetrators change their behaviours when challenged about it. It may be that if and when workplace bullying is defined and described, is generally accepted as socially unacceptable behaviour, and when such behaviour is no longer rewarded by senior management, then the outcomes for victims and victims who complain may improve. The evidence suggests that currently this is not the case. The overlooking of, or tacit support for, bullying behaviour by managers is often justified as a 'manager's right to manage'. Senior management also often see it as their duty to support supervisory staff in their dealings with subordinates, regardless of the behaviour involved.

Impact of strategies on bullies

Bullies in organisations may be challenged about their behaviour, informally or through formal procedures. However, if they are successful in supervisory or management positions, the chances are that they will not have to look at, or consider changing their behaviour. If it is made clear that the behaviour is unacceptable, the bully will stop that behaviour in that setting. However, they may resort to other forms of bullying, or the bullying may become more extreme. A bully when faced with a victim employing the strategies outlined, will often defend themselves with even more aggressive attacks on the victim. If these fail to work, the bully is likely to become confused. In a confrontation of this kind, the bully is not in control, therefore their strategies have failed. One response may be for the bully's behaviour to become more and more extreme and overt, and therefore no longer perceived as successful by the organisation. Other bullies will move on to new victims.

Support for bullies

In much of the work and guides on this subject, the bully is talked of in terms of being identified and encouraged to change their behaviour. It is recognised that for many bullies, the behaviour is deeply entrenched and is a successful coping strategy. For these people, behaviour change is very difficult. Bullying behaviour is often deeply embedded, and resistant to change, even if on the surface the bully wishes to be different. Bullies tend to change their behaviour only when that behaviour ceases to work for them and the consequences of continuing in the same way have become unbearable. Such people who wish to change need to be provided with support, training and the opportunity for counselling. The main success in changing a bully's behaviour comes from the internal motivation of the bully themselves. Most bullies are happy to talk about the situation as long as they feel heard and accepted. When dealing with a bully, therefore, it is important to try to empathise and to communicate on equal terms, rather than from a position of superiority. Showing an alleged bully anger or indignation over their behaviour will make the situation worse. It is better to allow the alleged bully to tell their story and to challenge by the use of reflection and summary, so that the bully hears their own account given back to them. It is crucial to try to confront the behaviour whilst at the same time accepting the person.

Organisational strategies for the promotion of anti-bullying and harassment policies and procedures

This section looks at the strategies that can be successfully adopted in the organisation and environments in which bullying and harassment take place; for example schools, the workplace and the community. There are some common features to effective interventions in all these settings:

◆ the involvement of the whole community or organisation in the strategy, with an emphasis of collective responsibility in both preventing bullying behaviour and responding to it when it happens

◆ a clear understanding of what constitutes bullying and harassing behaviour, and that these behaviours are socially unacceptable, and what to do about it

◆ consistent prevention and response strategies.

Approaches to bullying in schools

A great deal of work has been done in schools to develop a culture where bullying is not acceptable. It is widely accepted that when bullying does occur, it should be recognised and dealt with quickly. The incidence of bullying in schools had been reduced in some schools by the way the problem is approached. Social relationships are at the heart of bullying. The aim of addressing the social relationships within the school, is to influence the wider ethics and behaviours of the school and community. There are often direct links between school and community bullying when the behaviours and values of the community are imported into the school. Therefore the active involvement of parents in school anti-bullying policies is critical for their success.

In schools, there are three main strategies which will help individual victims, if the bullying is already well established:

◆ the acquisition of skills to enable them to become more assertive
◆ the knowledge that it is all right to seek help from peers and adults
◆ the ability to escape the bullying situation as quickly as possible.

These strategies for the individual can be strengthened by the involvement of the whole school community, and in particular the peer group and parents. The active involvement of the peer group can have an immediate effect, if the student group is taught simple ways to challenge the bullying behaviour. Telling the bully to leave the victim alone, standing beside the victim, walking them away from the bully and telling an adult, are effective strategies.

However, if the bullying relationship is already well established, it is unlikely that the victim will be able to bring about change on his/her own and will need a combination of inputs, actions and support. Similarly, bullying is an entrenched behaviour in the bully, so there needs to be regular monitoring to ensure that the behaviour has stopped. Whole-school approaches are therefore necessary.

Successful approaches in schools have two features in common. First, the whole community is involved in a consistent approach. Bullying is defined as socially unacceptable and the behaviours that constitute bullying are set out. Peers trained in basic skills and responses seem to be especially successful and reinforce the fact that bullying is socially unacceptable.

Second, the bully or bullies are not openly identified, thus avoiding the risk of a retreat into defensiveness and aggression by either the bullies or their parents. Two separate methods have been employed successfully in UK schools the 'no blame' approach and 'the method of shared concern' (Sharp and Cowie, 1998). When used in an anti-bullying project in Sheffield schools the 'shared concern' strategy was effective in 75% of cases. These two strategies have in common a problem-solving approach rather than a blaming approach to both alleged bullies and their parents. In the 'method of shared concern' an adult in the school works with the children involved both individually and in a group. The fact that bullying is happening is openly acknowledged, as is the fact that a particular pupil (or pupils) is a victim. The pupils are then asked to think of ways to help and support the victim and thereby to change the bullying behaviour. At no stage is any pupil named as a bully. These undertakings to change are followed up to see if they have been implemented and maintained.

Case study

Richard was a year four teacher in a primary school, in an inner-city residential area that had a high proportion of ethnic minority families. In recent years, houses had tended to be bought by Muslim families. When walking home after school one day, Richard saw a group of year five boys calling two of his class names. He heard 'go home Paki' and 'Paki bastard', and then saw the group begin to chase the two younger boys. He wasn't sure if any of the children had seen him. The next day Richard tried to provide an opportunity for his two pupils to talk to him, but they didn't. He wasn't sure if it would be helpful for him to raise it with them. Richard didn't usually go that way home so he had no idea if this was an everyday occurrence for them, or a one-off. Richard raised the matter in the weekly staff meeting and said that obviously the school policy against bullying and racism wasn't working.

Some of the staff disagreed with him and said that it had probably only been a game. Others were very surprised, especially Stella, the year five teacher, because year five had spent some 'circle time' on racism and bullying last term. In a class survey, most of the children had expressed a strong dislike of bullying and held anti-racist views.

The headmistress decided to look at the school's behaviour and bullying policies, to see if more could be done. However, she wasn't sure what the school could do about behaviour outside the school grounds, unless she called in the police.

ACTIVITY

What could you do if you were Richard? For example:

◆ How could you encourage the two pupils to talk to you?
◆ Would you consider talking to their parents?
◆ Would you do anything that involved the whole class?

What could you do if you were Stella the year five teacher? For example:

◆ Would it be important to identify the bullies?
◆ How could you encourage the bullies to talk to you?
◆ Would you consider talking to their parents?
◆ Would you do anything that involved the whole class?

What could you do if you were the headmistress with regard to:

◆ The children who had been at the receiving end of racist bullying?
◆ The bullies in year five?
◆ The safety of pupils travelling to and from school?
◆ The members of staff who did not seem to take this seriously?

Approaches to bullying and harassment in the workplace

Employees should feel secure in the workplace. Employees should be treated with dignity, respect and valued as people by employers. Good management will endeavour to avoid appointing potential bullies to the workforce, and will encourage open communications through the organisation. In organisations such as this, there will be an anti-bullying and anti-harassment environment, and policies and procedures to deal with this behaviour if it occurs. Staff will be aware of what constitutes these forms of anti-social behaviour and will know what to do about it when it happens.

ACTIVITY

If you were being bullied or subjected to sexual harassment at work to whom would you go for help? What policies and procedures are in place in your workplace? Are they used?

This kind of good management of the working environment is legally required by the 1974 Health and Safety at Work Act. It is also in the interests of employers to make harassment and bullying unacceptable, because bullying in the workplace is costly to organisations in the long term. A workplace culture of bullying results in lower productivity, higher rates of absenteeism, higher staff turnover – resulting in higher recruitment and training costs, and low staff morale. An organisation risks damage to its reputation and prosecution. An individual bully may be seen as effective, but if the effect of their behaviour is to diminish the effectiveness of other workers, then there is a net loss to the organisation.

Many organisations would claim to be against bullying and harassment in the workplace. At the same time, bullying and harassment is one of the major causes of stress at work. A survey for the BBC in 1995 found that one in eight employees had been bullied at work. It seems obvious that more could be done, or done more effectively. One use for the skills and knowledge gained from this book can be in addressing bullying and harassment in your workplace.

Many companies have policies and procedures that are unintelligible and therefore dusty from lack of use, and cynical staff who say laughingly, 'If you tried to use that, they'd just get rid of you'. Policies and procedures should be clear and simple and supported by firm action. Bullying and harassment thrives on secrecy. Naming and describing the behaviours that go under these headings is a step towards dealing with them. All allegations should be investigated promptly. Many company policies include lists of unacceptable behaviours, so there is often no excuse for ignorance. As in schools, although the behaviour is secret from those in authority, most employees, like most children, know the bullies in the workplace. This does not mean that victims find it easy to recognise and own up to what is happening to them.

Case study

Carol worked with long-term unemployed people who had emotional, psychological or physical difficulties. It was her job to assess her clients for appropriate help and then plan a programme with them over a one- to two-year period. Initial assessment and progress reports were required for each client. Carol and her colleagues had undertaken training in mental health problems, counselling skills and disability assessment. They prided themselves on being a client-focused efficient team. A new manager called Jean was appointed to the unit. Almost immediately Carol's reports were returned by Jean with red ink all over them and comments such as, 'Not up to the standard required', 'Not thorough enough – rewrite this'. The manager rewrote sentences that changed the whole meaning of the assessment of the client, without ever meeting the client. Carol asked for regular meetings with Jean, for guidance on how, as the new manager, she wanted the reports presented. The consistent reply was that Carol's work was not good enough, that Jean was having to spend weekends rewriting the reports to get them up to scratch. Carol was mortified . She checked and cross-checked the reports and wrote several versions before sending them to Jean, but they still came back as not good enough.

Then, Carol discovered that the other staff were also receiving the same responses. As a group, they asked the personnel officer to intervene, since individually they had got nowhere with Jean. The personnel officer read several of the criticised reports. He decided that Jean's changes and criticisms were largely trivial and a matter of personal style. Sometimes Jean's corrections were ungrammatical, and some changed the entire meaning of the report.

The personnel officer arranged a meeting with all the staff and the manager. At this meeting, the personnel officer outlined the problem. Jean's initial response was that the performance of all the staff in the unit was poor, and their complaint was just a way to cover that up. The personnel officer stated that he had read several of the reports in question and he considered that Jean had been excessive in her criticisms. It became obvious to him during the meeting that Jean knew nothing about the professional aspects of the unit's work and felt too threatened to admit this.

After the meeting the criticisms of the reports stopped. However, soon after, Jean increased the case load of each member of staff by 20% and often refused to authorise holiday requests, citing the high level of demand as the reason. After three months, one member of the unit went off sick with stress and one left for another job. Carol and her remaining two colleagues went back to the personnel officer for help.

ACTIVITY

If you were the personnel officer what actions would you take with regard to

◆ Carol and her colleagues
◆ Jean the manager
◆ The organisation's policies and procedures on bullying and harassment?

What can employers do?

As Sharp and Cowie (1998) wrote, 'Bullying is difficult to prove, easy to overlook and resistant to change'. So what can employers do? Given that bullying is common and deeply entrenched in the individual and cultural change is difficult to bring about, there are no quick fixes to dealing with workplace harassment and bullying.

Employers can take a two-strand approach to addressing and dealing with workplace harassment and bullying. They can put in place policies and procedures to address bullying and harassment when it occurs. They can ensure that it is dealt with quickly, fairly and in accordance with the policy whoever the alleged perpetrator. One of the key principles in addressing harassment and bullying is that the behaviour is defined by the reactions and perceptions of the recipient of the behaviour, not by the intentions of the perpetrator.

─◁ **ACTIVITY** ▷─────────────────────────

Do you think that defining bullying by the reactions of the victim is fair? Are there other ways in which such behaviour could be defined?

Employers can work to create an environment and culture in which bullying and harassing behaviour does not occur. This can be done through careful selection and recruitment, staff training and leading by example.

These are some of the strategies that can be used:

◆ training for managers, and staff in supervisory positions in: listening and responding skills, the management of change, conflict resolution and effective communication, and team building
◆ training in the recognition of bullying and harassment and strategies for dealing with it
◆ awareness raising of bullying and harassment and of the organisation's own policies and procedures, so that employees know what constitutes anti-social behaviour and what to do about it, both personally and in terms of the policy and procedures.

Approaches to bullying in the community

Most bullying is carried out by people with some sort of authority or power over others. In other words there is often some obvious power imbalance in the relationship at the outset, whether it be a supervisor over a subordinate or an older pupil over a new 'boy'. In the community, the reason for the power imbalances that exist in bullying relationships is less clear, and may well go back generations. The origins may be lost. All that may remain is the sense in both bullies and bullied that the one group or family is less worthy than the other and, therefore, it is alright to bully this group. This power imbalance may well be accepted by both sides, and may be connected to social or cultural norms. This relationship imbalance can be addressed by assisting the bullied group to recognise what is happening, and their own part in it, and by supporting and introducing strategies to change the balance of power. A problem-solving approach can be successful, with the aim running through the whole process of enabling and empowering the bullied group to see itself as capable of solving their problems by their own interventions, aided and assisted, when necessary, by professional support. The key first stage in this kind of approach is for the bullied group to recognise and accept some responsibility for the situation. The underlying approach of the empowerment of the victim and the redressing of the power balance is then the same as that for individuals.

BIBLIOGRAPHY

Adams, A. (1998 edition) *Bullying at work* , Virago Press.

Brown, H. *Stalking and other forms of harassment: an investigators guide,* Home Office.

Costigan, L. (1998) *Bullying and harassment in the workplace,* The Columba Press.

Field, T. (1996) *Bully in sight,* Success Unlimited.

Health and Safety Executive. *Help on work-related stress: a short guide for the employer,* Health and Safety Executive.

Herbert, C. (1995) *Bullying: a quick guide,* Daniels.

Home Office (1998) *Guide to the Crime and Disorder Act,* Home Office.

Ishmael, A. (1999) *Harassment and bullying – violence at work,* Industrial Society.

Metropolitan Police Service, *A streetwise guide to bullying,* New Scotland Yard.

Randall, P. (1996) *A community approach to bullying,* Trentham Books.

Randall, P. (1997) *Adult bullying – victims and perpetrators,* Routledge.

Sharp, S., and Cowie, H. (1998) *Counselling and supporting children in distress,* Sage.

Stephens, T. (1999) *Bullying and sexual harassment,* CIPD.

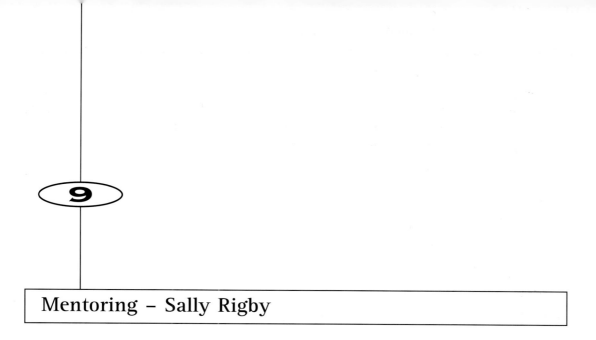

Mentoring – Sally Rigby

INTRODUCTION

You will find the ability to use counselling skills extremely beneficial if you become involved in mentoring. Whether as mentor (the person providing the mentoring) or mentee (the person receiving the mentoring), using counselling skills will enable you to act effectively and with clarity. This should result, hopefully, in a successful outcome for all parties.

This chapter is designed to provide you with a basic understanding of the concept of mentoring and will be divided into three sections. The first section will describe what mentoring is. It will cover: the functions of mentoring; the different styles of mentoring; the different situations, or contexts, in which mentoring can take place; and the benefits of mentoring to all participants.

The second section will examine the mentoring relationship. This will include: the different characteristics of a mentoring relationship; the range of possible commitments for those involved in a mentoring relationship; the range of activities which may take place in the mentoring relationship; what constitutes a good mentoring relationship; and the potential difficulties arising from the mentoring relationship.

Finally, the third section is designed to act as a stepping stone, from which you may decide to embark on a mentoring relationship – either as mentor or mentee. The qualities of a good mentor and the qualities of a good mentee will be covered in sufficient depth for you to recognise good practice and develop in a mentoring role.

Throughout the chapter some activities are included. They are designed to help you understand the concepts associated with mentoring, and their application.

WHAT IS MENTORING?

The Ancient Greeks introduced mentoring as a concept, although the contexts in which it is applied have changed. Rather than being an adviser, whose position evolves from friendship, a mentor is now used in a variety of circumstances, to facilitate development. Clutterbuck (1991) asserts that mentoring is an efficient form of developing talent, not only by the mentee, but also by the mentor. He suggests that a good mentoring programme should help people to recognise their abilities and limitations, help them to seize opportunities and come to terms with the reality of their career potential.

Mentoring is, in most circumstances, a one-to-one relationship and it is this one-to-one aspect of the relationship that allows the development of trust – particularly when issues under discussion go beyond the transfer of skill or knowledge. Group mentoring does take place in some contexts and can be just as effective in terms of encouraging personal and professional development, however one-to-one mentoring will be the focus of this chapter.

Functions of mentoring

Individual advancement

Mentoring, broadly speaking, has two main functions. The first is related to the advancement of the individual – usually in the workplace. This involves a number of different mentoring activities. Teaching is one such activity, during which time knowledge and experience is shared – for example the mentor may explain to the mentee about procedures and protocol. Coaching is another activity, involving, for example, the mentee being taught about how to set priorities, and develop interpersonal and core skills. The mentor may also give the mentee guidance on how to deal with problems relating to people, and encourage them to learn from experience.

Other activities may include the mentor arranging challenging assignments for the mentee, with a view to them putting into practice the skills they have developed. The mentor may also provide the mentee with exposure and visibility to those who might control their advancement, and generally act as a sponsor and champion for them.

Personal needs

The second function of mentoring relates to the personal needs of the mentee. Once again, there are a number of mentoring activities associated with this function. In some instances the mentee will go to their mentor if they have a problem in either their personal or professional life. A qualification in counselling skills will help the mentor deal with this, and also enable them to realise when the person should be referred on to someone else – for example a specialist counselling agency.

Another activity the mentor may be engaged in is providing advice and guidance. The mentee may, for example, approach the mentor for guidance and support in career planning. The mentor may also be approached to act as an independent arbiter if the mentee becomes involved in a situation that they cannot resolve.

Links with the organisation

In respect of both functions the mentor's prime concern should be with their mentee. They should not see their role as acting primarily on behalf of the organisation in which they work. It is important that management within the organisation recognises this and does not try to compromise the mentoring process.

Styles of mentoring

There are different styles of mentoring and the one in which the mentor is engaged will determine, in part, in which of the activities discussed he/she will be involved. Research into mentoring has divided the styles into four broad categories, or models.

Apprenticeship corporate

The apprenticeship corporate style of mentoring, as put forward by Maynard and Furlong (1994), relates to the advancement of the individual. This involves the mentee learning through emulating the example set by his/her mentor. This links with Parsloe and Wray's (2000) description of corporate mentoring. Corporate mentoring takes place in the workplace and the aim is to facilitate the development of the individual, in order to develop the organisation further. Parsloe and Wray (2000) describe the corporate mentor as someone who:

> acts as a guide, adviser, and counsellor at various stages in someone's career from induction through formal development to a senior management position and possibly into retirement.
>
> (Parsloe and Wray, 2000)

Competency qualification

The second style of mentoring put forward by Maynard and Furlong (1994) is called 'competency based'. This involves the mentor becoming a systematic trainer, coaching the mentee in specified competencies. This links with Parsloe and Wray's (2000) description of qualification mentoring. Qualification mentoring is very often a requirement of NVQs or other externally set courses. Parsloe and Wray (2000) describe the qualification mentor as someone who is:

> required by a professional association or government-sponsored agency to be appointed to guide a candidate through their programme of study, leading to a professional qualification or National Vocational Qualification (NVQ).
>
> (Parsloe and Wray, 2000)

Reflective

The third style of mentoring identified by Maynard and Furlong (1994) is termed 'reflective'. This involves the mentor encouraging the mentee to critically reflect on his/her performance and to discuss the outcome. The mentor becomes a 'co-enquirer' and can give the mentee feedback, both positive and negative, to enable them to examine the things that go wrong and move forward.

Community

The fourth, and final, style of mentoring is a relatively new, and important, development. Community mentoring, as outlined by Parsloe and Wray (2000) is mentoring that takes place in a variety of situations, where:

> the individual may be disadvantaged or in an actual or potentially distressful position.
>
> (Parsloe and Wray, 2000)

Community mentoring is very different from the other three styles, because the focus of the majority of programmes is to help those who have no qualifications and do not work. These community mentoring programmes developed as a direct result of the government's policy on social exclusion. The government has created the learning mentor post in the education system, with a view to helping those in deprived areas, raising standards and reducing truancy and exclusion.

Mentoring situations

Mentoring can take place in different situations or contexts. In a business or work setting mentoring can occur in a variety of ways. Sometimes people from one business will mentor someone from another. For example, a mentor from a large organisation may mentor someone from a small or medium-sized organisation.

Banks, or agencies such as 'business links', may provide an organisation with a mentor to help with the development of the business.

Chief executives and company directors often seek mentoring from outside their organisation. This is known as executive mentoring and is similar to other types of mentoring, although the mentor does need to have credibility in the business world, together with sufficient knowledge and experience of the sector.

Organisations may have internal mentoring schemes to support specific people within the organisation. These may include: people who have recently joined the organisation; those about to embark on a career change or redundancy; and graduate trainees.

Mentoring is often used for career development. Organisations may appoint someone to provide career and personal development support for their employees. Career mentoring can also take place in schools and colleges.

Benefits of mentoring

If undertaken appropriately, mentoring can be extremely beneficial for everyone involved. Both mentor and mentee can benefit in a number of ways, depending on the style of mentoring being undertaken. Some benefits are specific to a particular style, whereas some apply to all styles.

Apprenticeship/corporate

If the apprenticeship style is adopted the mentee will benefit in the following ways. They will learn the organisation's protocols and procedures quickly and this will enable them to settle into the job and, hopefully, be effective as soon as possible. Furthermore, this style of mentoring increases knowledge and understanding, which will reduce the stress associated with starting a new job.

The apprenticeship style also benefits the mentor. Self-esteem can improve, particularly when the mentoring relationship is deemed successful. It also gives the mentor the opportunity to learn from shared experience, as a mentee can very often provide a fresh perspective on issues. Also, mentoring enables the mentor to develop themselves, for example, in the use of communication skills.

Competency/qualification

If the competency style of mentoring is in place the benefits are as follows. The mentee's knowledge and understanding will increase. This should result in their performance improving in respect of the competencies being tested. They may also learn, from their mentor, new and effective ways of undertaking tasks.

The mentor will benefit from the competency style because they are given the opportunity to clarify, to themselves and the mentee, what they do. By doing this the mentor can evaluate current practice and, possibly, find different ways of doing things.

Reflective

The reflective style can be very beneficial to the participants. The mentee, through personal contact with their mentor, can discuss ideas relating to the job and their personal development. It also enables them to build, with their mentor, a solid relationship based on trust. The mentee's self-esteem may improve, particularly as they self-develop. Furthermore, having the opportunity to reflect on performance, identify ways to improve and discuss anything giving them cause for concern, can lead to a reduction in stress – which is a feature of many working environments.

The mentor can also benefit from this style. They too can develop themselves, particularly in terms of communication skills and problem solving. They may also learn to approach issues in different ways. Finally, as with the mentee, being able to build a relationship based on trust is most beneficial.

Community

The community mentoring style not only benefits the mentee and mentor, but also has an impact on wider society. The mentee, as with the other styles, will develop his/her self with this style of mentoring. They will also increase their self-esteem, as their life chances improve. Furthermore, they will develop their self-awareness and an acceptance of their strengths and weaknesses. All this will lead them to taking more responsibility for themselves and their actions.

Although community mentoring can be very challenging for a mentor, it can also be extremely beneficial. The mentor may develop both personally and professionally from working with such a diverse range of people. They will also be able to learn from the mentees' situations and share experiences with them.

There are a number of benefits for society from this type of mentoring style. If successful, the mentoring will help reduce social exclusion. In other words those people who, for whatever reasons, are excluded from the world of work and qualifications will be helped, in order that they can be included. Possible ways of doing this are as follows: removing barriers to learning, which may include, for example, previous experiences, learning difficulties and family situation; encouraging self-development; reducing truancy; raising standards; and raising skill levels.

Any programme aiming to reduce social exclusion, therefore, might include: identifying those who need the most help and working with them and their schools (if relevant) on a programme designed to encourage development.

ACTIVITY

Your employer is thinking about scrapping the organisation's mentoring scheme, because he doesn't think it is valuable. He asks your opinion and you say that it can be a worthwhile investment. He then asks you to prepare a presentation, to give to senior managers at their next meeting, outlining the benefits of having a mentoring scheme. Either on your own, or with a partner, prepare the presentation and present it to the rest of your group. Your presentation should not last more than 15 minutes.

MENTORING RELATIONSHIP

Whatever style of mentoring is adopted, it is widely accepted that most mentoring involves the pairing of a more skilled or experienced person with someone who is not so skilled or experienced – with a view to developing the less skilled person in particular agreed-upon ways. This pairing can involve a peer or some other appropriate person, a manager or trainer, for example. Hankey (1999), in her review of a staff development project, points out that peer mentoring provides a useful framework for reflective practice. Other appropriate people might be used in those contexts where training is required, for example the competency model.

Mentoring relationship characteristics

However, it is important to note that, irrespective of who undertakes the mentoring, or the context or adopted style, the most successful type of mentoring relationship (in terms of learning) is one in which the process is two-way. Parsloe (1995) further adds that unless the balance of personal qualities is right, effective mentoring will not be possible. Establishing the right balance, however, is not easy, because the mentoring relationship is complex and varied.

Garvey (1994) put forward a model of the dimensions contained within such relationships. He described the elements as points on a continuum:

open ... closed
public ... private
formal ... informal
active ... passive
stable ... unstable

(Garvey, 1994)

If a relationship is **open** then the participants will feel free to discuss any topic, whereas if it is **closed** there are only specific agenda items and certain issues are not mentioned.

A **public** relationship involves other people being aware of the relationship, and some topics discussed may also be discussed with another party, subject to the agreement of the participants. However, a **private** relationship is one of which either no-one, or only a few people, are aware.

Within a **formal** relationship there are agreed appointment times and venues. The content is not necessarily formal, rather the organisation of the meetings is grounded in rules of good conduct. An **informal** relationship is managed on a more casual basis, and works particularly well when the participants work in close proximity – enabling them to 'pop in' and see one another. As in the case of a formal relationship, this refers to the structure of the meeting and not the content.

An **active** relationship involves both participants taking some sort of action following the mentoring discussions. For example, the mentor intervening on behalf of the mentor, or the mentee undertaking a change in behaviour. A **passive** relationship, on the other hand, produces very little action from either side. There may even be a lapse in contact between the parties. It is possible to have a mentoring relationship where one party is passive and one active – which more often than not will result in it being ineffective.

A **stable** relationship involves both parties feeling secure, and there being a consistent and regular approach to meetings. Both parties are committed to the relationship and trust one another – an important aspect of any effective mentoring relationship. An **unstable** relationship is the opposite, both insecure and inconsistent. This element can produce some negative outcomes – no trust and little commitment.

Garvey (1994) points out that, because each mentoring relationship is unique, these elements can be found in a variety of different combinations. He further adds:

Time plays a crucial dynamic role in the mentoring process for, as time progresses, the relationship may alter and different dimensions may emerge or come to the fore as a result.

(Garvey, 1994)

> **ACTIVITY**
>
> Think of three different relationships you have with, for example: colleagues, managers, supervisors. Classify each relationship in terms of the characteristics put forward by Garvey. Are they all different? Are some of them similar? Think about the similarities and differences between each set of relationships. How can you account for this?

Mentoring relationship commitments

There are a number of potential commitments for those involved in a mentoring relationship and these should be considered by all participants – before agreeing to become involved in a mentoring scheme.

Time

Both mentor and mentee will need to allocate time to the relationship. Time for meetings is required, usually between one and two hours per meeting – sometimes longer. It is necessary, at the outset, to decide who will be responsible for making the necessary arrangements for a mentoring session. These arrangements may include booking a venue that is free from interruption and conducive to free and open discourse; obtaining permission from relevant people – for example the line manager; arranging cover, if required; and deciding who will produce any action notes.

It is important for any actions resulting from the meeting to be undertaken, and time is needed for this. This may involve the mentor or mentee doing some research; investigating ways of doing things; or changing a behaviour pattern. Time is also needed to prepare for meetings. This may necessitate the mentor and mentee looking back and reviewing past action notes to see whether or not the actions were completed; the mentor undertaking research into the quality of the mentee's performance; and preparing topics for discussion. Finally, time should be allowed by both participants to reflect overall on what has happened in the intervening period between the mentoring sessions – taking into account performance, action points, research and preparation.

Boundaries

An issue in many relationships, not just mentoring, is that of boundaries. Both mentor and mentee need to be clear about what the boundaries are. An example of this is the issue of a person being both manager and mentor to someone. As a mentor, a person's priority should be the development of the mentee. However, as a manager the basic responsibility is to the work. If discipline and monitoring is the responsibility of a manager this can inhibit the development of a trusting relationship, which is an integral feature of an effective mentoring relationship.

There can also be boundary issues if a mentor and mentee are friends and have other mutual friends. The mentor must not discuss any aspect of the mentoring relationship and its outcomes with the friends. Also, the mentor and mentee, if they are friends, need to be careful to stick to issues within their mentoring remit and not drift into conversations more associated with their relationship as friends.

Finally, the mentor must be clear about where the mentoring relationship should end and when to refer the mentee on to someone else, should the need arise. For example, the mentee may require specific career advice that the mentor cannot give and isn't able to access via research.

Confidentiality

For a mentoring relationship to be effective, all parties – particularly the mentor – should treat discussions as confidential. This will help establish trust between the mentor and mentee. There may be occasions when someone else needs to be informed about an issue. This is fine providing both parties are aware that this will happen and have agreed what information will be disclosed.

If confidentiality is breached, and trust lost, it can severely damage the mentoring relationship, sometimes irreversibly. Trust is something that is established gradually, and once lost it is very difficult to regain.

Financial

There are financial costs associated with mentoring, which are usually met by the mentee's organisation. These include travel costs, if the meetings are held away from the office or if the mentor is from another organisation, for example executive mentoring. The organisation will also finance any cover required during the mentee's absence. In the case of executive mentoring, or the mentoring of a small organisation by someone from a large organisation, the mentor may be paid an hourly rate – the amount of which will be determined by the skills and expertise the mentor has.

Contractual

Clear contracting is important for a successful mentoring relationship. Mentors must agree with their sponsors what their role entails and what they will not undertake. For example, it should not be the role of the mentor to discipline their mentee, rather they should be looking at ways the mentee can develop.

Once the mentor has agreed their role with the sponsor, it is necessary to enter into a contractual relationship with the mentee. This should involve discussing the format of the sessions, their duration and any costs involved.

ACTIVITY

Discuss with members of your group any difficulties that may arise from the possible commitments involved in a mentoring relationship. Brainstorm ways of dealing with them.

Mentoring relationship activities

There are a range of activities which can take place within a mentoring relationship and these can be explained as follows.

Teaching

Mentors teach their mentees by demonstrating procedures or lessons. They also provide the link between theory and practice and will assess and give feedback on performance. A good teacher can make all the difference to someone's success, as our past experience will verify.

Advocacy

Often the mentor will act as an advocate for the mentee. This may entail representing the mentee at higher levels; for example suggesting their expertise is used for a particular project. It may involve writing a reference or, in the case of a community mentor, working with senior management and teaching staff in a school to provide a programme of learning for the mentee.

Support

The mentor can provide different types of support for their mentee. They can support them by being willing to listen, being warm and caring, and making themselves available in times of need or during potentially distressing situations. They can also support job applications and promote career development. They can offer support and encouragement when the mentee is undertaking fresh challenges, or in their everyday work.

Informing

The mentor, particularly in the early stages of a relationship, will inform the mentee of the protocols and procedures employed by the company. It is important that this is undertaken because it will facilitate a quicker settling in period and take away some of the stress involved (as mentioned previously).

Advising

If mentors provide specialist advice they must be clear about what they are doing, because the mentoring role is not one of adviser. The mentee must explain to the mentor that they are stepping out of the mentor role and becoming an adviser. The mentee can then deal with the advice accordingly.

Features of a good mentoring relationship

A suitable pairing

A successful mentoring relationship does not happen by chance; it involves detailed consideration of a number of issues. Paramount is finding a suitable pairing. To do this consideration must be given to individual needs, which will be determined by a number of interacting factors, such as the mentor and mentee's role in the company, their experience, knowledge and ability to take on board new ideas.

Training

Training is also important. Research by Daresh and Playko (1992) found that, even if mentors have all the characteristics deemed desirable for the post, to be effective a mentor needs training. This training should particularly include interpersonal skills, as the need to have strong interpersonal skills is very important. Little (1995) suggests that both the mentor and the mentee should have training which, at the very least, should comprise an initial meeting, at which a basic description of the role is discussed and a guide for mentoring given to both the mentor and mentee.

Equal participation

Another feature of an effective mentoring relationship is equal participation. Both mentor and mentee should commit themselves to the relationship and be prepared to participate fully. This is not just attending meetings, but also doing the necessary preparation beforehand and undertaking any agreed actions. The process should be a two-way communication.

Trust and empathy

Finally, effective relationships are characterised by mutual trust and empathy. Both the mentor and mentee should feel able to discuss any issues without fear of reprisal or being made to feel foolish. The mentor, in particular, should be able to empathise with the mentee's situation and support them accordingly.

ACTIVITY

Imagine you are going to be allocated a mentor. List the characteristics, knowledge and experience you would need, for it to be a suitable pairing. Give reasons for each point on the list. Compare your list with another member of your group and note any similarities and differences.

Potential difficulties with the mentoring relationship

There are a number of difficulties that can arise with the mentoring relationship. These can be broadly categorised into 'institutional' or 'interpersonal'.

Institutional

Coleman (1997), when reporting on the mentoring of newly qualified teachers, points out that senior management needs to recognise the time commitment involved in mentoring. They also need to ensure that the practice of mentoring is consistent across the whole organisation. Little (1995) found inconsistency existed even when mentoring was an integral part of organisational procedures.

A further institutional difficulty is linked to training. Kram and Bragar (1991) argue that it is better not to introduce a mentoring programme, than to implement one that costs very little and prepares or informs participants inadequately.

Gay (1994) echoes this, when pointing out that three of the most common problems in planned mentoring programmes are: assuming anyone has the ability to mentor; not enough suitably qualified mentors; participants who are not sufficiently prepared. He adds that it is easy for people to believe they will make a good mentor because they have been asked to be one – and that their job is to act as a role model. However:

> mentoring is about the development of autonomous individuals; it is not about cloning.
>
> (Gay, 1994)

Gay and Stephenson (1998) also point out that in instances where the role of mentor is included in the role of 'supervisor of practice', for example student nursing, then this:

> may be at odds with their responsibility to be the assessor of performance.
>
> (Gay and Stephenson, 1998)

Interpersonal

As previously mentioned, there is a potential difficulty in relation to the compatibility of the two roles of mentor and manager. As Jowett and Stead argue:

> Conceptually, they are distinct: a mentor's priority is the development of the learner, while a manager's basic responsibility is to the work ... Nevertheless, discipline and monitoring remain substantive responsibilities of managers and, at the same time, a central element of the mentor/learner relationship is trust.
>
> (Jowett and Stead, 1994)

It is possible, therefore, to conceive of potential role conflict for a mentor.

Other difficulties presenting themselves to mentors, are highlighted by Garvey (1995), in his research into a health service mentor scheme. Of those surveyed 45% found pressure of time a serious problem, 18% found dislocation (moving job) a serious problem, 36% found achieving a focus for the relationship a mild problem.

This can be compared with the mentees, who experienced the problems differently. Of these, 20% found time pressure a mild problem, 27% found dislocation a serious problem, 27% found achieving a focus for the relationship a serious problem, 20% found misunderstandings or resentment of other people outside the relationship a mild problem – something mentors did not highlight.

Garvey (1995) responds to these difficulties by stressing the importance of developing a culture which incorporates mentoring into senior management activity. He believes that this will reduce the pressure of time – which does not facilitate learning.

Other interpersonal difficulties relate directly to the relationship between the mentor and mentee. Coleman (1997) points to the potential problems that can arise when the mentor is a senior member of staff, who is unapproachable.

Berkeley (1995) examines the suitability of mentors generally, within the mentoring relationship, and concludes that

An inappropriate mentor, unable or unwilling to satisfy the expectations and needs ... is infinitely worse than no mentor at all.

(Berkeley, 1995)

ACTIVITY

Think about the organisation in which you work. Describe a possible difficult situation that you might encounter when acting as a mentor. Describe the things you can do to manage this situation.

MENTORING PROCESS

This section will examine the mentoring process in respect of the qualities required to make a good mentor or mentee. Some of these qualities are generic and apply across all styles of mentoring. Some, however, are more pertinent to specific styles: apprenticeship/corporate, competency/qualification, reflective and community.

A good mentor

Essential characteristics

A good mentor should aim to help the mentee recognise their abilities and limitations. It is also important for the mentor to encourage the mentee to seize opportunities and make a realistic appraisal of their career potential. Berkeley (1994) modifies an NHS model of mentoring to identify certain 'essential characteristics' possessed by successful mentors, although they do not apply to all mentoring styles. The characteristics are as follows.

The mentor should be a model, who the mentee can look up to, value and admire; and may also wish to emulate. They should also be an envisager, giving a picture of what it is like to work in the company and be enthusiastic about the opportunities or possibilities. It is also important for them to be an energizer, who is enthusiatic about working for the organisation. Another characteristic is that of being a teacher–coach, who can help in the development of interpersonal skills and in developing the most effective working methods.

The mentor should also invest a lot of time in the mentee and be able to spot potential and capabilities. They should offer support, be willing to listen and be there in times of need. It is also important for them to challenge the opinions and beliefs of the mentee and confront any myths or misconceptions. This should enable the mentee to reflect on decisions and develop a maturity in their outlook. This is linked to the characteristic of the mentor being an ideas bouncer, who discusses any issues, difficulties and goals, allowing ideas to be bounced off them. They should also help the mentee develop these new ideas and create ways of using them that will benefit the organisation.

Other characteristics include the mentor being a feedback giver, who gives both positive and negative feedback, thus enabling the mentee to examine both successes and failures.

The mentor also should encourage the mentee to take an active interest in new developments and help them understand organisational policies and strategic plans. Finally, the mentor should encourage the mentee to meet the required standards, either those that are externally set or internally set ones.

Underpinning skills

Non–judgemental

Underpinning these characteristics are a number of skills. The mentor should be non–judgemental in their approach. The mentee may have different values, attitudes and beliefs from the mentor, which may stem from, for example, the culture they have been bought up in, or their age, or their gender. It is important for the mentor not to let these differences affect their relationship with the mentee, as this will create a barrier between them and the mentoring process will not be so effective.

In respect of the community mentor this is particularly important, as is evident in the government's newly created post of learning mentor. One of the key skills required is

> The ability to engage constructively with, and relate to, a wide range of young people and families/carers with different ethnic and social backgrounds.

> (Parsloe and Wray, 2000)

Good motivator

The mentor also needs to be a good motivator. To be a good motivator the mentor must first understand that not all people are motivated by the same things. Some people are motivated by external rewards; such as pay, promotion, praise and status symbols. Some people, however, are motivated by internal factors, such as a sense of duty, self-satisfaction or a sense of responsibility. The mentor would not be so effective, therefore, if they highlighted the potential monetary reward for the mentee if that wasn't important to them.

Good negotiator

Good negotiating skills are needed by the mentor, not only when dealing with the mentee, but also when championing the mentee to other, often more superior, people in the organisation. These skills involve being diplomatic, so that the mentee will accept what is said without being affronted or hurt; being assertive so that the mentor can put across their point of view without being aggressive; being able to identify what the mentee's needs are, through listening and asking questions, and communicating how the mentor can help meet them.

Good teacher

The mentor, particularly in the apprenticeship/corporate style, or competency/qualification style, should be a good teacher. This involves them being able to advise and instruct the mentee without interfering. They should also be able to recognise when to interrupt the mentee and when to let them continue.

Perceptive

The mentor should also be perceptive. They need to be able to identify changes in the mentee's behaviour, or be aware when situations have the potential to become problematic. The mentor should also be able to analyse their relationship with the mentee, identify the issues and situations arising, and take appropriate action to keep things on track. The learning mentor, for example, is expected to have the:

> Ability to identify potential barriers to learning and jointly engage in strategies to overcome these barriers.

> (Parsloe and Wray, 2000)

Establish a good and professional relationship

Finally, the mentor needs to have the skills to establish a good and professional relationship. This can be achieved by being sympathetic, accessible and knowledgeable about the mentee and their area of interest. Good interpersonal skills are required, including listening and questioning, which are an integral part of this and are discussed fully in section two of this book. Other interpersonal skills are the ability to relate to and really get to know the mentee, encouraging confidence and establishing rapport. It is also important for the mentor to be open, so that the mentee feels more comfortable – which also helps to promote the establishment of trust.

ACTIVITY

The choice of mentor is a very important one, needing a lot of consideration. Imagine you are looking for a mentor. What qualities would you look for? Write a list of these qualities. Compare your list with that of another member of the group.

Are any of the qualities you want similar to those wanted by the other group member? Are any of the qualities you want different? What reasons can you think of to account for these similarities and differences?

ACTIVITY

Now imagine that you are going to start mentoring someone. What qualities do you have that will help you? Write a list of these qualities. Compare your list with that of another member of the group. Do you have any qualities that are similar to the other group member? Do you have any different qualities? What reasons can you think of to account for these similarities and differences?

A good mentee

Most discussions on mentoring focus on the mentor and the knowledge and skills they need to facilitate an effective mentoring relationship. However, as previously mentioned, mentoring is a two-way process and both the mentor and mentee need to feel that they are gaining something from the relationship.

It is important, therefore, for the mentee to possess certain qualities – that will enhance the relationship and help move it forward.

Open to learning

The mentee shouldn't embark on a mentoring programme unless they are willing to take on board new ideas and try new ways of working, however strange they might first appear. They should be prepared to have their beliefs and attitudes, in respect of their work, challenged and be able to justify their approach.

Reflective

The mentee should be able to reflect on their performance, both on their own and with the help of the mentor. This reflection should involve looking at what went well, and what didn't go so well. Then the mentee should be able to think about why some things went better than others – what was it about the mentee's behaviour that led to some things being successful? The mentee should then be able to use the strategies employed when successful to improve areas that weren't.

Ability to listen

A good mentee should listen to, and observe, their mentor. The skills developed in the second section of this book should provide the tools with which to do this. A useful tip is to remember that far more is learnt by listening than talking.

Motivated

For a mentoring programme to be effective both mentor and mentee should be motivated. Not only should the mentor understand what motivates the mentee, as previously discussed, the mentee should know their own motivation.

ACTIVITY

Spend 15 minutes thinking what motivates you in the different aspects of your life: home, work, friends, leisure. Are you motivated by the same things in all parts of your life? Or do some things motivate you in some situations and not others? Ask a friend, or member of your family what motivates them. Compare the things that motivate them with the things that motivate you. Note any similarities and differences.

Fulfilling responsibilities

It is imperative that the mentee is willing, and able, to fulfil their responsibilities, if the mentoring relationship is to be effective. It is very disheartening for the mentor if the mentee doesn't commit themselves fully to the relationship and undertake all that is required of them.

These responsibilities include:

Meetings

The mentee should always turn up for any pre-arranged meetings. If, due to any unforeseen circumstances, it is not possible to attend, the mentor should be informed. As much notice as possible should be given to the mentor and a new date arranged as soon as possible.

Preparation

The mentee should be willing to prepare fully before each meeting. This can entail reading through past notes, preparing an agenda or reflecting on what has been achieved over the intervening period.

Undertaking actions

It is usual for both mentor and mentee to leave the meeting with some actions to complete before the next meeting. The mentee should always undertake these, otherwise the mentoring process will be compromised. Occasionally, often through no fault of their own, the mentee may not be able to complete an action. If this happens, the mentor should be informed of the reasons why and, if appropriate, a new deadline set.

ACTIVITY

Think about your current work or home situation. If you were a mentee what do you consider might prevent you from being able to fulfil your responsibilities? What could you do about this? Discuss your difficulties with a member of the group. See if you can help each other come up with any other ways of dealing with your difficulties. Repeat this exercise as if you were a mentor. Are the difficulties the same? How would you account for the similarities and/or differences?

CONCLUSION

This chapter has focused on the theory behind mentoring, identifying what mentoring is, the nature of the mentoring relationship and the qualities required to make a good mentor and mentee.

You should now be in the position to take the knowledge you have acquired in this chapter, together with that from throughout the book, and embark on a mentoring relationship – as either mentor or mentee.

The main thing to remember is that each mentoring relationship is unique and could develop in a number of ways. This development is, in part, determined by the style of mentoring being adopted. If an apprenticeship or corporate style is adopted then the relationship focuses very much on the workplace and doing the job as effectively as possible. If it is competency or qualification based, the focus is on standards and achievement. The reflective style, however, is much more to do with the development of the individual in terms of interpersonal skills and personal relationships. Finally, the community style is specifically about helping those in the community, who are, for whatever reason, at a disadvantage.

The other important determinant in the development of the mentoring relationship is the nature of the pairing. If the pairing is right both mentor and mentee will feel as if they are gaining from the relationship.

BIBLIOGRAPHY

Berkeley, J.P. (1994) 'Young people mentoring: an employment perspective' in *Education and Training*, vol 36, no 5, pp 27–31.

Clutterbuck, D. (1991) *Everyone needs a mentor* 2nd ed., London: Institute of Personnel Management.

Coleman, M. (1997) 'Managing induction and mentoring' in Bush, T., and Middlewood, D. (eds.), *Managing people in education*, London: Paul Chapman Publishing.

Daresh, J., and Playko, M. (1992) 'Mentoring for headteachers: a review of major issues' in *School Organisation*, vol 12, no 2, pp 145–152.

Garvey, B. (1994) 'A dose of mentoring' in *Education and Training*, vol 36, no 4, pp 18–26.

Garvey, B. (1995) 'Healthy signs for mentoring' in *Education and Training*, vol 37, no 5, pp 12–19.

Gay, B. (1994) 'What is mentoring?' in *Education and Training*, vol 36, no 5, pp 4–7.

Gay, B., and Stephenson, J. (1998) 'The mentoring dilemma: guidance and/or direction?' in *Mentoring and Tutoring*, vol 6, nos 1–2, pp 43–54.

Hankey, J. (1999) 'A staff development project: peer mentoring, self assessment and reflective practice' in *NASD Journal*, vol 40, pp 35–40.

Jowett, V., and Stead, R. (1994) 'Mentoring students in higher education' in *Education and Training*, vol 36, no 5, pp 20–26.

Kram, K.E., and Bragar, M.C. (1991) 'Career development through mentoring: a strategic approach for the 1990s' in *Mentoring International*, vol 5, nos 1–2.

Little, B. (1995) 'Mentoring in higher education: a synoptic overview' in *Mentoring and Tutoring*, vol 3, no 2, pp 19–20.

Maynard, T., and Furlong, J. (1994) 'Teachers' expertise and models of mentoring' McIntyre, D., Hagger, H., and Wilkin, M. (eds.) *Perspectives on school-based teacher education*, London: Kogan Page.

Parsloe, E. (1995) *Coaching mentoring and assessing*, London: Kogan Page.

Parsloe, E., and Wray, M. (2000) *Coaching and mentoring*, London: Kogan Page.

Index

UNIVERSITY OF WOLVERHAMPTON
LEARNING & INFORMATION SERVICES